Religion
in Education: 1

The Religion in Education Series

a programme for professional development

in religious education and in church school education

is edited by

The Revd Dr William K. Kay

and

The Revd Professor Leslie J. Francis

from

The Centre for Theology and Education

Trinity College

Carmarthen

The development of the series has been supported by grants from St Gabriel's Trust, Hockerill Educational Foundation, All Saints Educational Trust and St Luke's College Foundation. The collaborative nature of the project has been supported by a co-ordinating committee, including staff from the Church Colleges, Anglican Dioceses and The National Society: Ruth Ackroyd (University College Chester), the Revd Marian Carter (College of St Mark and St John, Plymouth), Dr Mark Chater (Bishop Grosseteste University College, Lincoln), the Revd Professor Leslie J. Francis (Trinity College, Carmarthen), the Revd Dr John D. Gay (Culham College Institute, Abingdon), Dr Fred Hughes (Cheltenham and Gloucester College of HE), Dr Sheila Hunter (University College of St Martin's, Lancaster), the Revd Dr William K. Kay (Trinity College, Carmarthen), Dr Anna King (King Alfred's College, Winchester), David W. Lankshear (Secretary, The National Society, London), Ruth Mantin (Chichester Institute of HE), Carrie Mercier (College of Ripon and York St John, and National Society RE Centre, York), the Revd Canon Alan Nugent (Diocesan Director of Education, Durham), the Revd David Peacock (Roehampton Institute, London), Dr Christine Pilkington (Christ Church, Canterbury), Gaynor Pollard (University College Chester), the Revd Canon Robin Protheroe (Diocesan Director of Education, Bristol), the Revd Alex M. Smith (Hope University College, Liverpool).

Religion
in Education: 1

Church Schools: history and philosophy
Belief and Practice
Philosophy of Religious Education
Method in Religious Education

edited by
William K. Kay
and
Leslie J. Francis

First published in 1997

Gracewing
Fowler Wright Books
2 Southern Avenue
Leominster
Herefordshire HR6 OQF

UK ISBN 0 85244 425 7

Typesetting by Anne Rees

Printed by Cromwell Press
Broughton Gifford, Wiltshire, SN12 8PH

Contents

Foreword

This book is designed to meet the needs of a growing number of people in Britain who are embarking on higher degrees in religion and education. In an era of rapid social change and when the working population needs constantly to be 're-skilled', distance learning provides the most painless method of progress. Learning materials come to your own home. You may work at your own pace. You can work in your own way. All you lack is the immediate stimulus of a lecturer or teacher and other students off whom you can bounce your ideas. So, to try to compensate for the lack of a teacher, most distance learning institutions provide a *tutor*, someone who is available to give technical and academic help and, where the need arises, a shoulder to cry on. To compensate for the lack of fellow students, there are various strategies: some colleges will run residential courses, others will aim for summer schools or lead lectures. Moreover, the activities that are built into this text (see Introduction) have, in many instances, the secondary purposes of prompting you out into the world of people and away from the world of books. Contained within these pages, then, are ideas which should make you a better teacher, lecturer, diocesan adviser, parent, governor or cleric. Here is knowledge waiting to be applied, and here are applications waiting to be turned into knowledge.

Within the changing social nexus of British society, the church and church schools continue to make an important contribution. One of the driving forces that brought about the production of these materials was the realisation that the church colleges in Britain need to do more to help both the church schools and those who teach religious education. This book is the outcome of an imaginative collaboration between representatives of the Anglican colleges in England and Wales and the church college trusts. In this connection, thanks should go to John Gay of Culham College Institute and to Ruth Ackroyd of University College Chester for their patient work in putting together the team and the funding that were necessary for all these materials to be written.

The work of editing these volumes has been undertaken within the Centre for Theology and Education at Trinity College, Carmarthen, a research centre stimulated by the Principal and Governors of the College specifically to facilitate developments of this nature.

Finally the editors record their gratitude to Diane Drayson, Anne Rees and Tony Rees for their help in shaping the manuscript.

William K. Kay
Leslie J. Francis
Easter, 1997

Introduction

Overview

This book, the first in a planned set of three, contains four modules, each of which is broken down into three units. Each unit, however, is written by a separate author and is to some extent independent of the others. Although we anticipate you would choose a pathway through this material that would lead you to work through all the units in a particular module consecutively, other options would also make sense. In other words, the materials given here are designed to be as flexible as possible within the constraints of a modern British degree at master's level.

So far as possible, these distance learning materials are free-standing - they should not require you to obtain vast numbers of extra books. Nevertheless, it has proved impossible to do without reference books altogether but, to help you, and in the realisation that not all students will be able to obtain all books, we almost always include summaries of the texts to which you are pointed, so that you have at least an outline of what these texts say.

In addition, these materials have been written with a view to the Readers edited by Francis and his collaborators and published by Gracewing. Each of these Readers contains about thirty original papers that have been carefully selected and then reprinted from a wide range of journals across the world. The Readers therefore function like a miniature library and will save you many hours of tracking down important but out-of-the way literature. The Readers are:

- L.J. Francis and A. Thatcher (eds) (1990), *Christian Perspectives for Education*, Leominster, Gracewing.
- L.J. Francis and D.W. Lankshear (eds) (1993), *Christian Perspectives on Church Schools*, Leominster, Gracewing.
- J. Astley and L.J. Francis (eds) (1994), *Critical Perspectives on Christian Education*, Leominster, Gracewing.
- J. Astley, L.J. Francis and C. Crowder (eds) (1996), *Theological Perspectives on Christian Formation*, Leominster, Gracewing.

At the end of each unit, you will find a reference to the most helpful sections of the Readers and a full bibliography of other books either referred to by the author of the unit or to which you might want to refer in pursuing a particular topic in greater detail.

The next sections provide an overview of the modules in the order in which they appear before moving on to the details of activities and assessment.

Church Schools: history and philosophy

Unit A introduces the historical development of the dual system (church schools and non-church schools together in one state-supported whole). William Kay traces the origins of the present situation back to the last century and shows how and why the state financially supported church schools before finally entering the educational arena itself. Though political passions have cooled with the passing of time, the furore created by the spending of public money on church schools and the equal furore created by the attempt to provide from the public purse entirely secular schools resulted in what is often glibly called a typically 'British' compromise. Another way of viewing the result is to see it as an inevitable and brilliant result of democracy in action. Be that as it may, whatever one's personal judgement on what was accomplished, the consequences have lived on into the present century. Church schools live side-by-side with county schools and religion has a place within the curriculum of both. Without an historical perspective it is impossible to understand and value the present arrangements.

Unit B shows how church schools can operate within a plural society, that is, a society in which opposing religious and secular views are held to be equally valid. A church school can aim to prevent racial intolerance, promote respect for all its pupils regardless of their beliefs and help pupils gain a positive self-image. The unit focuses very much on the school itself, with its staff, pupils and parents and would be of practical benefit to those involved in any aspect of the life of a school.

Unit C explains and presents ways of constructing a theology of education. Adrian Thatcher's intention is to enable the reader to work out what a Christian theology essentially is and then to show how it might be applied to real educational issues. He demonstrates how theology can inform, illuminate and critique education and, at the same time, how theology is not a matter of learning a few rules of dogmatic thumb but is essentially a *process*. Armed with theological concepts and a (Christian) theological approach the practitioner is better empowered to deal with new situations and to evaluate old ones.

Belief and Practice

Unit A of this module introduces you to beliefs and practices by asking you to reflect on your own beliefs and practices. This is a unit designed to make you think about your own opinions and the way you have acquired them. It encourages you to consider what sort of learner you are and how you have learnt. But it encourages you to reflect critically, and not simply to reminisce.

The purpose of this is to give you an insight into the whole process of the acquisition of belief since successive units in the module move on from the individual to a wider perspective, encompassing both the institution of Anglican schools and also the beliefs and practices of Anglicanism in Britain.

Unit B explores the way beliefs might be expressed within the context of a school and the role that these beliefs might have in the mission statement and policy documents adopted by the school. The unit looks at the role beliefs, especially theological beliefs, have in shaping relationships between pupils, school worship, religious education, staff relationships and discipline policies. It invites you to see whether you can draw lines of implication between the beliefs which you think should influence a mission statement and the life of a school, both as it is actually lived and as its documentation describes it.

Unit C gives an overview of the beliefs and practices of the Anglican Church. It does this partly by an historical perspective going back to the Reformation so as to show the characteristic sources of Anglican theology and partly by examining the role of the liturgy, which expresses these beliefs in a way that draws together disparate theological viewpoints. It then considers how these beliefs and practices are relevant to, and important to, church schools and it concludes by looking at the relationship between a parish priest and a school within his or her parish.

Philosophy of Religious Education

Unit A of this module introduces you to the philosophy of religious education and it does so by showing you what the legal requirements of religious education are. We could have begun by considering all the theories and philosophical ideas that have influenced religious education in the 20th century, but we decided that you ought to see how religious education looks from a legal perspective since this allows your philosophical understandings to be rooted in practicality.

Unit B explores the relationship between religious education and other aspects of school life. Especially in primary schools, religious education takes place in the context of the whole school and the whole curriculum. To understand a philosophy in isolation would be unhelpful for serving teachers and those engaged in the support of education through administration and advisory services.

Unit C tackles the approaches that have influenced religious education since the 1960s. This unit delves back into philosophical movements that have swept Europe since the Enlightenment and focuses on three approaches that have been adopted since the 1960s. The first of these, the *confessional* approach, operated entirely within a faith-based framework. It was largely replaced by the *phenomenological* approach which tried to be more neutral and objective, though, as you will see, questions are and have been raised about how successful this attempt was. More recently the *experiential* approach has underlined religious experience, the inwardness of religion, as an important component in its delivery within the classroom. Each approach has its strengths and weaknesses and we invite you to reflect on these at the end of the unit.

Method in Religious Education

Unit A of this module follows on from unit C of the module *Philosophy of Religious Education*. It looks in detail, and by reference to actual practice within the classroom, at the approaches to religious education that unit C considered theoretically and philosophically. Yet, the current unit is written so that, as far as possible, it makes sense on its own and without extensive prior reading. Unit A would most effectively be completed by either teaching lessons using different approaches or observing lessons using different approaches. But, if this is an impossibility, the materials presented here, provided that they are imaginatively studied, will enable the student to form a judgement about the strengths and weaknesses of each approach.

Unit B introduces the contribution that can be made by religious education to the creative arts and the contribution the creative arts can make to religious education. Dance, drama, pictorial and representational arts, music and information technology are all considered. The unit explores the emotional content of religious education, or the way religious education speaks to the emotions, and also encourages contemplative stillness. It casts a light on creativity in the classroom which should be matched with the more formal and philosophical light thrown by the approaches considered in the previous unit.

Unit C gives an overview of a range of research methods. It allows the student to grasp the principles behind the methods and to make an assessment of the sorts of educational problems that would be best served by one method rather than another. The methods range from qualitative, which make little use of mathematical and statistical techniques, to quantitative methods which, in essence, require measurement and numerical precision. The final, and longest part of the unit, deals with action research since this is the type which allows policy changes to be implemented during the research process. Examples of action research within the field of religious education are the particular focus of the final activity.

Activities and assessment

Your assessment will be based on a piece of work carried out by you at the end of the module. The activities that punctuate these materials are not intended to be assessable, though in some cases your tutors may base an assessment around them. But your tutor will tell you *in advance* what your assessable assignment will be. Do not, however, treat the activities as an optional extra. They are designed to consolidate and deepen the learning process, to make you benefit more fully from the information and the processes laid before you.

Each activity is followed by a 'Comment' in which the unit's author has given an opinion on the kinds of things you might have thought or written in response to the stimulus you were given. The comment should be taken as just that, a comment, and not a definitive answer to the activity's stimulus.

All modules are broken into three units, A, B and C. All the activities are labelled by a letter and a number and indicated by double parallel lines in the margins. Activity A1 is the first in unit A, activity B3 is the third in unit B, and so on. The units themselves are broken into sections, each prefixed by the unit's identifying letter. A3 is the third section of unit A, B2 is the second section of unit B, and so on. This means that it is easy to refer to any part of a module in an assignment: *all you need is the module's name and a letter and a number*. For example, 'Developing the pupils' self-image' is found at B4 in the module *Church Schools: history and philosophy*. 'Religious education' is discussed at B4 in the module *Belief and Practice*.

Contributors

The twelve units in this book have been written by the following contributors.

- *Dr Mark Chater* is Senior Lecturer in Religious Studies at Bishop Grosseteste University College and Course Leader of Religion in Contemporary Society.
- *The Revd Professor Leslie J. Francis* is D.J. James Professor of Pastoral Theology at Trinity College, Carmarthen, and University of Wales, Lampeter.
- *Dr Sheila Hunter* is Senior Lecturer in Religious Studies at the University College of St Martin's, Lancaster, and Director of the Centre for Adult Learning and Ministry (CALM).
- *The Revd Dr William K. Kay* is Senior Research Fellow at the Centre for Theology and Education, Trinity College, Carmarthen.
- *Mr David W. Lankshear* is Deputy Secretary and Schools Officer of the National Society and Schools Officer of the General Synod Board of Education.

- *Ms Gaynor Pollard* is Senior Lecturer in Theology and Religious Studies at University College, Chester, and Religious Education Adviser for Chester Diocese.
- *The Revd Alex M. Smith* is Senior Lecturer in Theology and Religious Studies at Liverpool Hope University College.
- *Professor Adrian Thatcher* is Professor of Applied Theology at the University College of St Mark and St John, Plymouth.

Activity symbols

This book is designed to be read interactively: there will be things you are asked to do while reading it. Sometimes you are asked simply to read a text, or re-read information given in the activity section, and then to think about it and write down what you think. At others the assumption is that you will work with a group of children or with a friend. The symbols shown below are placed in the text's wide margin to alert you to the activity you will be asked to undertake.

Read

Reflect

Write

Teach or observe a lesson

Work with a group

Discuss with a friend

Church Schools: history and philosophy

Church Schools: history and philosophy

Unit A

Historical development of church schools

Dr William K. Kay

Trinity College

Carmarthen

Contents

Introduction

Aims

After working through this unit you should be able to:

- describe how the dual system developed;
- describe the differences between aided and controlled schools;
- understand why the dual system developed.

Overview

Our intention in this unit is to show you how the dual system developed historically. This will require a visit to the nineteenth century and a look at some of the factors and controversies which shaped the present century. Yet, without understanding these factors, and the resolution which was found to them, it is impossible to understand how the present situation arose. Had the educational system of Britain been designed by someone starting from a blank sheet of paper, no doubt a completely different result would have been reached. But, by its nature, history is complex and involves many layers and strands. Each successive epoch transforms the cultural and legal achievements of previous epochs.

The dual system is one which includes schools of two different types within one integrated system. Imagine a town which is built around a church. The houses near the church have been built for a long time and were originally constructed by the church's congregation for the family of the choristers and the clergy. During the town's development, many new houses are built and fitted into the gaps between the church houses. Then, as the years pass, the town council wants to bring gas and electrical connections to all the houses and the congregation which attended the church has grown smaller so that it does not need all its houses. So the old church houses and the new council houses are integrated into a single town, each having the same facilities, but now some of the clergy live in the council houses and some of the townspeople who have nothing to do with the church live in the old church houses.

The dual system of education in England and Wales is a little like this. It includes schools of different types amalgamated together into a single system. The church and the town council want the whole town to be united and so they agree that the new houses shall have certain features of the old houses and, at the same time, that some of the old houses shall be modernised.

The analogy is not a perfect one but it illustrates the way the education system in England and Wales has grown up from haphazard beginnings going back to the last century.

This unit will examine the place of church schools in the dual system of education in England and Wales. It will briefly explore the involvement of the church in education from the earliest times but will concentrate on the nineteenth and twentieth centuries, particularly the period from 1870 onwards.

In a wider, and more speculative, sense you should also be able to appreciate how the dual system might develop in future. What are the options open to future governments? How might a weakening or a strengthening of the church have an impact on the education system as a whole? Is it possible, on the basis of historical precedent, for the system to be enlarged into a system including other kinds of schools, new kinds of houses, within the same town?

Finally, you should note that unit 1 of the module *Philosophy of Religious Education* contains detailed reference to the legal basis for religious education which complements and supplements much of the material given here.

A1 Historical development: setting the scene

Cruickshank (1963), the Durham Report (1970) and Murphy (1971) all briefly mention the importance and pervasiveness of the church's role in education in the middle ages. Actually, we may go further back than that to the ministry of Christ as depicted in the Gospels and the history of the church in the centuries before the fall of the Roman Empire. Priests needed to be educated in order to catechise new converts and to correct heresy. After Rome fell in 410, and European civilisation faltered, monastic libraries and translators kept learning and literacy alive. The career of the Venerable Bede (673-735) illustrates the process: he entered monastic life at the age of seven by becoming a choirboy at Wearmouth on the north-eastern coast of England. There, and at Jarrow where he was transferred in about 681, he received an education which allowed him to work in several languages and to calculate well enough to make a contribution to the debate about the correct Sunday on which to celebrate Easter. Among his enduring works (written in Latin) is his *History of the English Church*.

The impetus given to the church by the Reformation also applied to its educational role. Luther wrote a 30 page tract entitled *To the Councilmen of All Cities in Germany that they Establish Christian Schools* (1524) in which he argued that the public purse should fund new schools with the double purpose of laying the foundation for learned civic officials fit for public life and clergy competent in the biblical languages of Greek and Hebrew for the newly

Reformed church. The subsequent excellence of the German educational system can at least in part be traced to this initiative.

But in Britain there were similar effects. Although some of the best known 'public' schools, like Winchester (founded in 1382) and Eton (founded in 1440), predate the Reformation, others, like St Paul's (founded in 1509), Shrewsbury (1552), Westminster (1560), Merchant Taylors (1561), Rugby (1567), Harrow (1571) and Charterhouse (1611), were directly influenced by it. All of them had strong links with the Anglican church and required attendance at worship as part of what they offered to their pupils. The same may be said of many of the endowed grammar schools, some of which were connected with cathedrals and chantries, and which were found 'in nearly every town of any size' from the thirteenth century onwards (Boyd, 1964, p 156). Such schools, like the grammar school at Stratford-upon-Avon where Shakespeare learnt his 'small Latin and less Greek', were popular among the sons of merchants and those who could afford to pay.

For the gentry private tutors were an option (Heal and Holmes, 1994), a choice especially attractive to Catholics who were not then forced to take part in Protestant worship.

In the centuries following the Reformation, Protestantism in Britain fragmented energetically into several denominational groups which were unestablished, that is, separate from the Church of England and the machinery of government within the House of Lords. The Presbyterians and Congregationalists belonged to the first cluster of denominations in the sixteenth century. They were quickly followed by Baptists and Quakers in the seventeenth century. The eighteenth century saw the arrival of Methodists and Unitarians. The nineteenth century saw further proliferation and Methodists split into New Connexion (1797), Primitive Methodists (1811), Bible Christians (1815), United Methodist Free Churches (1857) and others. The Plymouth Brethren were formed after 1825, the Seventh Day Adventists after 1844 and the Salvation Army in 1865. Yet the division among Protestants, despite the pain it caused, expressed a religious vitality that resulted in numerical growth.

Among Roman Catholics numerical growth was a consequence of immigration from Ireland. The poverty of Ireland made England a popular destination. Between 1800 and 1851 the Roman Catholic population in England and Wales increased from 120,000 to 900,000 (Bédarida, 1979, p 90).

Undoubtedly the best data on the state of religious preferences and strengths in England and Wales, however, come from a religious census in 1851. It was found that between 35-47% of the population attended a place of worship on Sunday, and about half of these were in an Anglican context and the other half 'sat under' a Nonconformist minister (Harvie, 1984, p 449)[1]. About 4% of all recorded attendances were at a Roman Catholic place of worship. The density of church (or chapel) attendance varied considerably area by area. For instance, in Wales attendance was between 50-59% and in the west country between 40-50%. In the big cities, especially in Birmingham and London, attendance ran at 20-29% (Bédarida, 1979, p 91). This inequality of distribution was to have an influence on the subsequent course of political events. More immediately significant, though, was the relative strength of the Anglican and Nonconformist camps. As we shall see, the Anglican congregations and the bishops tended to be politically conservative while the growing Nonconformist cause tended to be politically liberal. An upsurge in the strength of Nonconformity was likely to push parliamentary legislation in the direction of large-scale change.

We are particularly interested in the period after 1790. Whatever the relative strengths of religious groups within England and Wales, social changes were anyway likely to occur in the nineteenth century. The eighteenth century had seen the Methodist revival in England, the American War of Independence and the French Revolution. When the nineteenth century began, British society was ripe for change. In France the removal of the aristocracy by means of the guillotine and in America the setting forth of the democratic ideal in the American Constitution (1787) had shown that the old monarchies ruling by 'divine right' were disposable. From 1800 onwards education of the masses was viewed 'as a prophylactic against revolution' and a means of change without bloodshed (Harvie, 1984, p 448).

The pressure for social change (which inevitably included educational change), then, could be attributed to changes in the religious composition of Britain and to the circulation of radical political ideas. But there was one more factor which was crucial. The population of England and Wales doubled between 1811 and 1861, p in 1811 it reached just over 10 million, but by 1861 it reached just over 20 million and continued climbing steadily through the next decades (Gregg, 1973). The cities of London, Birmingham, Manchester, Leeds and Liverpool expanded enormously and it was partly their clamour for representation in Parliament that led to the extension of franchise in the Reform Acts of 1832 and 1867.

---

[1] There is debate about the interpretation of the figures given in the census. The information asked ministers to give an account of all attendance on Sunday, 30th March 1851, but it did not take account of multiple attendance (i.e. people who attended church more than once on the same day). Moreover, it was not able to deal with people who would have wanted to go to church but were unable to attend because of illness or age. However, one way of reading the figures suggests that 47% of the population over the age of ten years attended church on the Sunday in question. See Inglis (1960), Pickering (1967) and Gill (1993). We use the term 'Nonconformist' as excluding Roman Catholics.

Activity A1

Write half a page of notes drawing together the reasons why the church (making no distinction between separate denominations) was interested in education.

You will need to look back here at the historical information we have already presented. Think also of the broad educational implications of Christian theology.

Comment on activity A1

Christ himself was a teacher and the church felt itself bound to continue his teaching activity. From the beginning, then, the church was a teaching community. As doctrinal controversies raged in the first three centuries, the church realised the importance of a trained priesthood and, even more than that, some form of instruction for its congregations. Congregational training took the form of a catechism, which was a simple and set form of question and answer that had to be learnt by heart but which conveyed doctrine. Where there was catechism, there was memory and learning.

But, after the Reformation, when there was an enormous emphasis on scripture, there was also a realisation of the importance of mass literacy. There was a renewed desire to wrestle with the text of scripture both in the original languages of the bible and in contemporary translations. Where there was an emphasis on scripture, there was reading, writing and commentary, in short, there was education. And, because education could be seen as a preparation for the next life as well as for this life, a high priority was placed on it. Luther's views, however, were very practical. A Christian society ought to be governed by officials who were properly educated and who understood the role of the church. Christian schools could make this provision.

Beginnings

Robert Raikes (1735-1811), a journalist and philanthropist, was disturbed by the uncontrolled and idle behaviour of Gloucester children on Sundays and so in 1780 hired women to teach them scripture. These 'Sunday schools' proved so popular that they began to open on other days than Sunday and to teach reading and other elementary subjects. Very quickly the concept of the Sunday school spread to the larger cities of England and was taken up by a variety of denominational groups. By 1795 there were over 250,000 children enrolled in this way, and the figure rose to over 900,000 by 1835. Cruickshank characterises this work as 'essentially a rescue operation to get children off the streets and to inculcate in them some sense of decency and order' (Cruickshank, 1963, p 2). Whatever its motivation, however, the spread of the Sunday school system was partly due to the novel method of instruction which was developed for its use and partly to its willingness to include reading (and later writing) and arithmetic in its curriculum.

Joseph Lancaster, a Quaker, and Andrew Bell, an Anglican, adopted a monitorial system which allowed one teacher to instruct the more capable older pupils in the school. These pupils were then able to pass on what they had been taught to the younger pupils. In this way a single paid school teacher could be responsible for a much larger number of pupils than he or she could teach at any one time. Basic, though unimaginative, education could be provided in this way.

In 1808 the British and Foreign School Society (associated with Lancaster) was founded in its embryonic form with the aim of 'the education of the labouring and manufacturing classes of society of every religious persuasion'[2]. Reading was taught by using scripture extracts, but no catechism or peculiar religious tenets were taught and every child was expected to attend the place of worship to which its parents belonged (Murphy, 1971, p 4). The inter-denominational and evangelical basis of the society was still evident in 1838 when it estimated training equal numbers of Anglicans, Wesleyans, Congregationalists and Baptists as teachers each year (Murphy, 1971, p 5).

The success of the British and Foreign School Society prompted a specifically Anglican response in the founding of the National Society for Promoting the Education of the Poor in the Principles of the Established Church (associated with Bell) in 1811. But, although there was a rivalry between Nonconformists and Anglicans in the support of their respective societies, not all Anglican schools were affiliated to the National Society, as it came to be called, and nor did all Anglican schools which were affiliated receive support. Both societies received children from a variety of church backgrounds, though the National Society strictly insisted that all its teachers should be Anglican, that the Authorized Version of the bible and church liturgy and catechism should be taught and that church attendance on Sundays should be within the Anglican communion (Murphy, 1971, p 5).

The insistence upon the Authorized Version of the bible, whatever arrangements might have been reached about church attendance, had the effect of barring Roman Catholic children from National Society schools. Roman Catholic priests absolutely forbade their flocks from attendance at any school where the Authorized Version was in use. In practice this attitude also

---

[2] The Society was originally called the Royal Lancasterian Society.

prevented Catholic attendance at British and Foreign School Society schools. If Roman Catholics were to be educated, they would need to form their own system.

The two societies, despite the unwillingness of Roman Catholics to attend their schools, and despite the rivalry between them, were both marked by tolerance. Curtis (1961, p 221) points out that, certainly up to 1818, the National Society was quite willing for non-Anglican children to learn 'the doctrines and forms to which their families are attached' and a similar point is made by Murphy (1971, p 5).

None of the schools organised by the British and Foreign School Society or the National Society was free. Parents were required to make a contribution to running costs. But there were some children whose parents were too poor even to find the small fees which the other schools charged. From 1818 onwards John Pounds, a Portsmouth shoemaker, set up Ragged schools for the vagabonds and urchins of the urban poor. These schools offered food and clothing, as well as rudimentary education designed to prevent a return to life on the streets. By 1852 there were 132 of these schools in London and they catered for 26,000 children[3]. Many of these schools went hand in hand with the evangelistic efforts of the London City Mission. Eventually, as we shall see, the Ragged schools were incorporated within the Board school system.

A2 Political change and state support for education

The two societies worked hard to increase their systems in the years which followed. The National Society, which kept careful statistics, grew from 52 schools in 1812 to 3,670 schools in 1830. In 1807 Whitebread introduced a Bill in the Commons for the establishment of parochial schools. The Bill was rejected in the Lords. After Whitebread's death Brougham took up the cause and persuaded Parliament to appoint a Select Committee which reported on 'the Education of the Lower Orders' in 1818. The report revealed a growing demand for education and inadequate resources (Curtis, 1961, p 220). Speaking on a Bill he introduced in 1820 Brougham was able to calculate that about 200,000 children were educated in the National Society and British and Foreign School Society schools, which appears to have been just under a third of the total number of children receiving education, though, when all the children in school were added together, only about one fifteenth (7%) of the total population were receiving education (Curtis, 1961, p 221).

---

[3] Victorian education at its worst is portrayed by Dickens. Dotheboys Hall run by Wackford Squeers in *Nicholas Nickleby* shows the maltreatment of children similar to those who would have attended Ragged schools. *Oliver Twist* presents a similar world. Dickens certainly visited The Field Lane Ragged School after a report in *The Times* in February 1843. See also Curtis (1961, p 234) and Smith (1931, p 169).

In 1828 the repeal of the Test and Corporation Acts removed discrimination against Nonconformists. A year later the Catholic Emancipation Act allowed Roman Catholics to stand for Parliament. Vidler (1974, p 45) points out that these reforms killed the ideal of a single basis for church and state. Christian pluralism, together with the political complexity generated by the representation of multiple social viewpoints within a single Parliament, was about to arrive.

It arrived in stages. In 1832 the Reform Act extended franchise from about 435,000 to 652,000 and 'gave greater political importance to the industrial centres of the North and the Midlands, but left the counties under aristocratic control' (Gardiner and Wenborn, 1995, p 639). The middle classes were mollified by their new voting rights, but the excluded working class continued to feel aggrieved. One particular matter gave concern. Until 1868 a 'church rate' was levied for the upkeep of the parish church and graveyard. The Nonconformist working class bitterly resented this payment which, in urban parishes, became increasingly difficult for the churchwardens to collect.

The general election of 1832 produced a new House of Commons keen for reform. Of the 658 MPs, 473 were Whigs opposed to the high Toryism of the Duke of Wellington (Blake, 1985, p 369). Mr Roebuck, acting on utilitarian principles[4], proposed a compulsory universal and national system of education for all pupils aged between six and twelve years of age. Both political groupings opposed the measure. Economic theory suggested that government should not interfere with voluntary efforts, that is, the efforts of the churches and, in any event, the Factory Act (1833), which prohibited the employment of children under the age of nine in the textile mills, had not yet been passed. Roebuck withdrew his motion but, on a suggestion from Brougham, and before a House of Commons in which only 76 MPs were present, £20,000 was voted 'for the erection of school houses for the education of the poorer classes in Great Britain' (Smith, 1931, p 139). The conditions determining the use of the annual grant were set out in a Treasury Minute and laid down that the money only be given for buildings after local subscriptions had raised half the estimated cost. The National Society or the British and Foreign School Society must support the application and be satisfied that the school would be permanently maintained.

The first government money voted for education was specifically intended to enhance and support the voluntary efforts of Anglicans and Nonconformists. The dual system, when it eventually came into being, may be said to have been necessary because, from 1833 to 1870 when the infrastructure of much of modern Britain was put in place, the government believed itself to be right to

---

[4] Utilitarianism associated with Jeremy Bentham and later with John Stuart Mill proposed that an action was right or wrong insofar as it facilitated 'the greatest happiness for the greatest number'. Utilitarianism provided an ethical system which dispensed with either the notion of duty or the sanction of God.

spend as little public money as possible while at the same time encouraging religious and charitable enterprises. Had the government listened to Roebuck's proposal it is unlikely that the schools of the National Society and British and Foreign School Society would have survived in any numbers into the twentieth century. Once the government decided to take a different course, it was more or less honour bound to continue to support church schools.

Activity A2

Compare voluntary effort and state expenditure as ways of funding educational enterprises. What are the advantages and disadvantages of each? How do these considerations apply to education in the first part of the nineteenth century?

These questions are general and require general answers. You should aim to deal here with ideas and concepts and not with the fine-tuning of grants and dates.

Comment on activity A2

This is a question which goes to the heart of much political philosophy. It is a question that lies behind the struggles in the first part of the nineteenth century. In favour of state expenditure is the way a fair system of raising money by taxation can be used for the general and public good. If the rich pay more than the poor and both benefit equally from this expenditure, then state expenditure appears to be fair. On the other hand, the collection of money by taxation is itself costly. Moreover, the expenditure of public money needs to be monitored and controlled, and this also is expensive. Thus part of the money which is collected by taxation only funds a bureaucratic mechanism. On the other side of the balance sheet decisions about the way public money should be spent are complicated and may be unjust if a government overrides the wishes of many of its people. In other words a democratically elected government could still spend money on projects which did not command the support of the majority of people.

Furthermore, money raised by taxation detracts from the money available for voluntary projects. Once education was supported by public money, voluntary subscriptions were bound to be reduced. If voluntary funds are reduced, then the possibility of local, flexible and creative initiatives may be stifled by a lack of resources.

Victorian England was unhappy about increasing the role of the state. The state might reduce civil liberties. Yet, Victorian England came to see that the resources of voluntary groups, even voluntary groups as well organised as the churches, were unable to meet the educational needs of a growing population.

State involvement in education 1833-1843

During this period the religious complexion of Britain was influenced by the Oxford Movement. The Anglican church, in many respects easy-going and tolerant, was infused by spiritual fervour that came to have a distinctly Catholic bias. The Whig government's administrative reform of the Church in Ireland generated Oxford-led disquiet and hostility among clergy who held differing theological views, whether broad church, high church or evangelical. But gradually the Oxford Movement began to stress 'apostolic succession' and other distinctively Catholic doctrines, and to underline the importance of ritual. Evangelical clergy were affronted and most bishops withdrew their support. With regard to education, the Oxford Movement, whose beginnings can be dated from 1833, stiffened the exclusiveness of the National Society and made co-operation with Nonconformists difficult.

The annual grant continued to be given. However, because of the way it was distributed through the two main societies and because of the requirement that it be given to supplement existing voluntary subscriptions, by 1839 about 80% of the money went to the National Society (Murphy, 1971, p 17). In addition, though an attempt was made to set up training schools for teachers, the money voted for the purpose was not immediately spent because agreement in Parliament and between the churches could not be reached. As a result the government put in place a mechanism, which did not require annual parliamentary approval, for the distribution of public money to education.

The distribution of the annual grant was taken out of the hands of the Treasury and given to a special committee of the Privy Council, a body with a long constitutional history that had once advised the monarch. The new committee came to be called the Committee of Council on Education whose task was 'to superintend the application of any sums voted by parliament for the purpose of promoting education' (Murphy, 1971, p 21). The Committee of Council, by the Whig government's decision, were all laymen and included the Home Secretary and the Chancellor of the Exchequer. By this means it was recognised that the composition of the Committee would change as the government changed, but continuity was ensured by appointing a permanent non-political secretary to be the chief administrator. The man chosen for this job was Dr Kay, later to become Sir James Kay-Shuttleworth.

In 1840 Kay negotiated a satisfactory conclusion, a 'Concordat', to a 'bitter struggle' (Cruickshank, 1963, p 3) over inspection of church schools. Schools in receipt of public money were to be inspected in both secular and religious subjects, but Archbishops had a right to nominate members of the Inspectorate.

A year later the School Sites Act was passed. This allowed land owners to make donations of land for the provision of church schools and showed how the government of the time wanted to encourage charitable and voluntary schooling.

Education was growing in political importance. Kay had already established a teacher training college at Battersea that, in 1843, was handed over to the National Society and which stimulated the church to build further colleges so that, by 1845, there were altogether twenty-two Church of England training colleges. The real question that seemed to face the government was whether the education system at elementary level could be expanded without alienating either the Nonconformists or the factory owners who depended on child labour.

Graham's Factory Bill of 1843 tested the new Conservative government's ingenuity and resolve. Graham proposed that children who worked in factories should receive an education in schools built with money loaned to the factory owners by the government. The maintenance of these schools was to be through the poor rate (a form of local taxation), but their management was to be in the hands of Anglican clergy. Before the second reading of the Bill the Nonconformists showed their intransigence and disapproval of the scheme. They objected to having to pay poor rates for an education that would be managed by Anglican clergy. Despite sensible concessions to meet Nonconformist objections, the Bill failed to win necessary support. Graham withdrew his Bill. According to Cruickshank (1963, p 4) Nonconformist scepticism about state-sponsored education can be dated from this time. Nonconformists, in large numbers, began to campaign for an entirely voluntary principle in education. All education should be free of state interference and therefore of public money. Voluntaryism was born.

Thus there was an impasse. The churches opposed an entirely secular system of education, but could not agree among themselves that public money raised locally should be given to one denomination rather than another. The Voluntaryist principle insisted that the churches should turn their backs on public money, and this was a principle which appealed both to some Anglicans and some Nonconformists. The governments of the day were unwilling to take children away from the workplace or to spend large sums of taxpayers' money on a public service. In short, the churches did not have the resources for the education of the nation and the government did not have the political will or economic philosophy to make education a matter of compelling priority.

State finance of education 1843-1870

Although no major education act was passed during these years, educational spending increased. For a start, the Methodist Conference decided to enter the field in 1843 and received its first grant in 1847. The same year the Catholic Poor School Committee was formed and, after some delay, was able to receive government grants; by 1850 there were about 500 Roman Catholic schools (Cruickshank, 1963, p 9). Writing in 1868 Kay-Shuttleworth was able to argue that the Committee of Council had drawn 'into co-operation with the Government' a 'vast denominational system' which included all religious groups apart from 'Congregational Dissenters' (Murphy, 1971, p 37). Government policy was to work with and through the churches wherever possible. Expenditure rose from £100,000 per year in 1847 to £500,000 per year in 1857. By 1859 it had risen to £836,920 (Curtis, 1961, p 254). This increase did not simply reflect additional building because, by 1857, the government had begun to contribute towards teachers' salaries, equipment and maintenance costs (Cruickshank, 1963, p 10).

Teacher training was also improved by the introduction of the pupil-teacher system, though this had cost implications because the young teachers were paid £10 in their first year and slightly more each year thereafter and the headteachers who taught them received an additional £5 a year for this work. At the end of their five year apprenticeship pupil-teachers sat a Queen's Scholarship examination and those who passed went on to training colleges.

At the same time there was an increase in the number of schools in the two main societies. From 1812, when it had comprised only 52 schools, the National Society had grown to 564 schools in 1815, to 3,670 in 1830 and to 17,015 schools in 1851. In 1812 it had catered for approximately 8,620 children (some of these through Sunday school) but in 1851 it counted 956,000 on its books. The expansion of the British and Foreign School Society was not quite as dramatic, but still impressive. Its statistics were not kept as carefully as the National Society's but the 1851 return gave it 1,500 schools with 225,000 pupils (Curtis, 1961, p 208; Francis, 1993, p 152). By 1861, in the Newcastle Commission's report, it was estimated that of a child population of 2.5 million, 1.5 million were in inspected schools, that is, schools in receipt of public money (Cruickshank, 1963, p 11).

The Voluntaryists also built up their system, though they cost the government nothing. The Congregational Union had opened 364 schools and a training college by 1851 (Smith, 1931, p 196). Some Anglicans also adopted this position (Francis, 1993, p 153).

Roman Catholics were in a special position. On the one hand, they were firmly committed to education and, on the other hand, they lacked the moneyed middle class which was able to give financial support to educational causes. The Roman hierarchy found itself willing to accept public money, but not on the state's terms. Cardinal Manning himself was to ask 'Gladstone for rate aid payable by the decision of the government, not at the discretion of a local board' (Murphy, 1971, p 61).

Although the government steadily increased its contributions to the education of pupils at inspected schools during these formative years, one important proviso must be remembered. The government did not pay the *full* cost of educating each child. It is estimated that in 1861 the government only paid *about a third* of the cost of educating each child at church schools. The remainder was more or less equally divided between school fees and church contributions (Murphy, 1971, p 40). Moreover, the cost of education, growing though it was, remained tiny when compared with the cost of the Crimean War which amounted to more than £78 million (Curtis, 1961, p 249).

State influence in education 1843-1870

As government expenditure on education increased, government control was also tightened. The Voluntaryists saw this clearly and thought education too closely intertwined with religion to be left to inspection by government officials until, in 1867, the Voluntaryist cause collapsed. Despite unremitting effort for more than 25 years, most Voluntaryists came to appreciate that their schools were too expensive to operate and could not be opened fast enough to cope with the growing population. When the 1870 Education Act came before parliament, most Voluntaryists supported state funding for education; by this time 'secularists and Voluntaryists had a good deal in common' (Cruickshank, 1963, p 12).

Most clergy throughout the period welcomed state aid provided that religious sensitivities were observed. In the 1850s the Committee of Council insisted that trust deeds for new schools insert a clause to allow children of other creeds to 'secure entire exemption from religious teaching' (Cruickshank, 1963, p 10). The National Society, fortified by the Tractarians of the Oxford Movement, resisted this demand for an absolute right to a conscience clause. But when the government insisted on it, and the Nonconformists, especially in single-school areas, felt it was justified, the High Church party was bound in the end to be defeated.

Indirectly, too, the government came to influence the secular curriculum. In a series of developments, the abrasive utilitarian Robert Lowe, an able administrator and Vice-President of the Council (Briggs, 1965, p 240-271), brought in a set of financial regulations ordering that government grants only be paid to school managers if children passed national criteria-referenced examinations. The system was heartily disliked. It stunted the curriculum and degraded the teaching profession, but between 1863 and 1869 over 1,000 more schools opened (Cruickshank, 1963, p 11).

A3 Prelude to the 1870 Education Act

The 1867 Reform Act increased the range of people allowed to vote. Fifty-three parliamentary seats were made available for redistribution to the large urban centres and franchise qualifications were amended to allow all rate paying householders and some rent payers to vote. Altogether the electorate amounted to about a third of all adult males, and no women (Gardiner and Wenborn, 1995).

When there was a general election in 1868, the Liberals, under Mr Gladstone, swept to power with a majority of 100 seats. They came with a mandate to improve and extend the provision of education[5]. But they faced a series of problems and dilemmas. Within their own party they included both the newer Radicals (perhaps equivalent to the 'hard left' of today), Nonconformists, broad church Anglicans, free thinkers (who were often atheists) and aristocratic Whigs (perhaps equivalent to millionaire socialists of today). Gladstone himself had moved from the evangelicalism of his youth (Jenkins, 1995, p 27) to a broader but still committed Anglicanism.

Two powerful pressure groups had been organised, and both of them found spokesmen in Parliament. The *National Education League*, based in Birmingham, campaigned for universal, free and non-sectarian state education. The National Education League contained Nonconformist clergy as well as atheists and agnostics. There was confusion in the minds of some of its members about whether they were in favour of non-sectarian or secular education. The Nonconformist clergy, of course, wanted 'the exclusion of catechisms, creeds or tenets peculiar to any particular sect' (Cruickshank, 1963, p 16). But they agreed that simple bible reading without comment might be allowed if local rate payers so decided (Murphy, 1971, p 51).

In opposition to the National Education League the *National Education Union* was formed, also in 1869. It members included many Anglicans, but also Methodists and Roman Catholics and some of the now disbanded Voluntaryist group. The Union wanted to abolish school fees for paupers and vagrants, though not for everyone else, and it reluctantly conceded the right to

[5] Some Tories understood that extension of the franchise would only lead to good government if it led to an extension of education.

a 'conscience clause'. Money from rates and taxes should be paid to lighten the load placed on the denominations and thereby secure their schools for the future.

The need for state intervention in education became obvious as a result of a government survey early in 1870. Despite the vigorous work of the churches over nearly 50 years, there were great gaps in the country where children received very little teaching. Fewer than a third of the total number of children in England and Wales between the ages of six and twelve were in regular attendance at inspected schools. In Birmingham, Leeds, Liverpool and Manchester fewer than one fifth of children received a proper education (Cruickshank, 1963, p 17).

There was, therefore, an uneven distribution of existing schools. Any solution to the problem of national education would have to take account of this fact.

A second problem arose from the funding of schools. There were approximately 18,000 church schools in existence at that time and, though these schools were receiving money from central government funds, they were relatively cheap to run because much of their financial support came from voluntary contributions. In 1870, before the Education Act was passed, there were 4.3 million children of school age in England and Wales of whom 2.0 million were outside any educational provision. The church provided 1.3 million places in state-aided schools and there were a further 1.0 million places in purely voluntary schools (some of them 'dame schools') that fell well below the standards delivered by inspection (Jenkins, 1995, p 322). Clearly the churches made a very substantial contribution to the nation's educational requirements. If the government were to fulfil its pledges and provide an adequate primary education for every child, it would need roughly to double the number of school places in England and Wales.

A third problem stemmed from the management of schools. While the majority of church schools were Anglican, there were significant numbers of Wesleyan, Congregationalist, Roman Catholic and British and Foreign School Society (general Nonconformist) schools. In many respects the Church of England and the Nonconformist churches were in competition and members belonging to one group did not want their children taught in the tenets of the other. For example, Nonconformist parents did not want their children to learn the Thirty-Nine Articles or the Catechism, especially as the Church of England appeared to be vulnerable to the influence of the Tractarians. The problem was particularly acute in single school areas. This meant that some of the people who most vigorously opposed the extension of one kind of church school belonged to another kind of church.

A fourth problem stemmed from the raising and expenditure of public money. Money raised by general taxation and spent by central government was difficult to contest. But money raised by local rates and spent by local councils was quite a different matter. Local passions were easily inflamed. Rate-aided schools were likely to be the target of bitter wrangles.

A fifth problem stemmed from the broad range of political views held by members of Gladstone's government. How could a parliamentary majority be guaranteed?

What was to be done?

Activity A3

Ask yourself how the problem could be solved. How could the education system be expanded in a way which satisfied everyone?

Spend half an hour considering the options facing Mr Gladstone's Liberal government. Read back on the earlier part of this unit to remind yourself of the options.

Comment on activity A3

You may have thought of the two broad alternatives: a completely state-run system or a completely church-run system, the proposals of the National Education League or the proposals of the National Education Union.

You may have thought of the difficulties each of these broad alternatives faced. A state-run system would alienate the church schools which, in many instances, had been built up on the expectation that centrally provided government money would continue more or less indefinitely; on government advice trust deeds had pointed in this direction. Moreover, if the state starved the church schools of cash and then built parallel secular schools, this would be an extremely expensive option.

On the other hand, a church-run system, especially if government money continued to be given, would not have gained the support of *all* the churches because, for example, the children of a Baptist living in an area where the only school was Anglican would have had to learn the Thirty-Nine Articles. It would have been impossible to build church schools to suit every shade of theological opinion.

Perhaps you have thought that rate aid and central government funding could be used in distinct ways. Could the rates support non-denominational or secular schools and central government funds support denominational schools? This idea was proposed before the 1870 Education Act, but it came to nothing. There would probably have been tensions and competition between central and local government spending if such a scheme had been adopted. People would have accepted good denominational schools to avoid paying higher rates.

Could state schools and church schools run side by side? They could, but what sort of religious teaching was to take place in each? Some sort of fair arrangement had to be reached if the churches were to continue to receive public money. If the state offered only a secular curriculum, church people would complain; after all they helped to fund these schools with their taxes or rates. If the churches, in their denominational schools, insisted on teaching religious doctrine to people who did not want it, there would be complaints about the misuse of public money.

Eventually, as we shall see, it was agreed that basic, non-denominational teaching of the bible should be offered in all schools which received public money and that the rights of minorities should be protected by a timetabled application of the conscience clause to allow children to be withdrawn at the time when they knew religious education was being given.

Parliamentary debate and the 1870 Education Act

Forster presented a Bill on behalf of the government. He rejected the National Education League's plan on the grounds that it was going to be too expensive and that it would 'deprive the nation of those who really cared for education' (Curtis, 1961, p 275). In a memorandum to the Cabinet Forster suggested that for a limited period of time (6 months as it turned out) the churches be given extra incentives to erect schools in each district where they were needed. These new church schools should be open to non-denominational inspection and must operate a conscience clause for those who did not wish to receive religious teaching. If, after a period of time, the churches failed to provide the necessary new schools, local School Boards should be elected by town councils[6] or, in rural areas, vestries with the mandate to provide schools from rate aid. Each Board would be free to decide the kind of religious instruction to be provided subject to a conscience clause in every school (Curtis, 1961, p 276).

After reflection members of the National Education League decided to oppose the Bill. They disliked:

- the time given for the establishment of more church schools;

---

[6] This was changed during the course of debate so that voting to the Boards was made by those whose names were on the burgess roll of the borough and rate payers in rural areas (Curtis, 1961, p 278).

- the meaninglessness of the 'conscience clause' in rural areas where labourers could not make written application for its implementation;
- the likelihood of bitter wrangling within School Boards over the kind of religious instruction to be permitted;
- the likelihood that in some areas denominational teaching would be given and paid for by rate aid.

The discussion was complicated because not all members of the League took exactly the same view: some wanted non-denominational teaching and others wanted completely secular schools. A reading of the debate which followed in the House of Commons shows that members of Parliament tended to adopt extreme views or to attribute extreme views to those with whom they disagreed.

After running into criticism from its own party, the cabinet agreed to the adoption of Cowper-Temple's famous amendment. During the debate Cowper-Temple pointed out that his proposal 'combined an important principle of the Union with an important principle of the League'[7]. The clause (Section 14.2) stated that the following principle should apply in every grant-aided school.

> No religious catechisms or religious formulary, which is distinctive of any particular denomination shall be taught in the school.

Further, the conscience clause was coupled with an insistence that religious instruction should be timetabled either to the beginning or the end of the day so that withdrawal of the children whose parents showed religious scruples, should be less disruptive.

The House of Commons sat for three successive nights and eventually, with the help of the conservative opposition, the amended Bill was passed. Its provisions contained a raft of compromises, though considering the strength of the various parties in the debate and the vehemence with which they expressed their positions, this was inevitable. The outcome was that the dual system, where church schools and Board schools functioned together to provide national education, came into being (Murphy, 1971, p 62).

Board schools could provide religious teaching (though it had to be non-denominational) if they wished and this was funded by local rates. These schools were to be situated where there were gaps in existing educational provision. There was no intention to replace denominational schools by Board schools. Denominational schools were not to receive rate aid since bad relations between the churches would cause political friction at local level. Instead denominational schools were to receive additional central government

---

[7] V*erbatim Report of the Debate in Parliament during the Progress of the Elementary Education Bill*, p 222.

aid so that they competed on a roughly equal footing with the new schools. All schools in receipt of public money were to be open for inspection and to operate the conscience clause.

The aftermath of the 1870 Education Act

The six months of grace given to the churches produced a huge number of extra applications for building grants; 1,633 applications were made by Roman Catholics and 2,885 by the Church of England (Curtis, 1961, p 281). But once this period terminated, public money of any kind for building abruptly stopped. The increased government money for running church schools was off-set by the loss of public money for denominational religious instruction. The timetabled conscience clause and the removal of inspection of religious teaching favoured the church schools very little. Religion was now compartmentalised within the school rather than an integral part of the curriculum.

On the other side, the Board schools, offering non-denominational religious instruction, could now be funded by rate aid[8]; the decision whether or not to provide religious education rested with the individual School Board. Most followed the lead given by the large London Board which permitted the reading of the bible and 'such explanations and instructions' as were suited to the capacities of the children (Curtis, 1961, p 279). Indeed, a report published in 1888 showed that, of the 2,225 School Boards, only 7 in England dispensed entirely with religious teaching; in Wales there were 50 Boards which did so (Murphy, 1971, p 69).

The British and Foreign School Society report of 1871 declared that 'if British Schools are merged in the schools of the nation, it will not be because their distinctive features have been lost but because those features have become general if not universal'[9]. Ten years later the British and Foreign School Society 'rejoiced' in the recognition and adoption of their schools by the School Boards.

In contrast, by the end of the century the Church of England was still able to offer 60% of all available school places. Between 1870 and 1893 the National Society spent over £7 million on erecting 5,838 schools with accommodation for 1.3 million children (Curtis, 1961, p 282). Yet, the churches were finding it increasingly difficult to cope with the cost of education. Some of their

---

[8] Where the upper limit of a 3 penny rate providing money for the school was considered insufficient, Board schools could receive a grant from the exchequer. The theory was that Board and Voluntary schools should be funded equally except that where Voluntary schools received voluntary donations from churches, Board schools received rate aid. Remaining costs, for both kinds of school, were divided between the exchequer and the fees charged to parents (Murphy, 1971, p 56).

[9] This information is taken from a British and Foreign School Society leaflet. The Society concentrated on teacher training at the end of the nineteenth century and its colleges continued into the 1970s. Its last, the West London Institute of Higher Education, was eventually transferred to Brunel University in 1995.

teachers, having been trained at colleges run at the National Society's expense, transferred to Board schools. In addition, the cost of education per child rose steadily. By 1880 Board schools were spending 30% more per child than the Church of England (Cruickshank, 1963, p 49), and their schools tended to be more lavishly designed and more modern. The churches had no hope of keeping pace with the School Boards and by 1900 exhaustion had begun to set in. Although in 1900 there were over 14,000 church schools with a population of nearly 2.5 million, they were beginning to close at the rate of 60 per year, especially in urban areas, and some were transferring to the control of Boards which, in rural areas, were often anyway largely under the influence of the church. The only real hope of rescue seemed to lie with the local rating system, even though acceptance of its money would necessarily lead to some loss of church control.

A4 The 1902 Education Act and beyond

The 1902 Education Act provided rate aid for voluntary schools, though its purposes were much more wide-ranging and varied[10]. It created local education authorities to superintend education, both elementary and secondary, both denominational and non-denominational, in the areas covered by county or country borough councils[11]. The 2,500 School Boards, which had been responsible for small geographical areas, were absorbed into the 300 new local education authorities (Curtis, 1961, p 315). One consequence of this was that the squabbling that marred some School Boards could be largely avoided. Denominational schools would receive government grants *and rate aid* and their managing bodies would still contain a majority of church appointees. Managers were allowed to ignore a school's trust deed by appointing teachers (usually Nonconformist staff) without reference to their religious beliefs. In return for the right to give denominational instruction and to ensure the appointment of suitable teachers, the voluntary body was obliged to keep school buildings in good repair.

Denominational schools or colleges receiving local authority aid could not compel a pupil to receive religious instruction on the school premises or elsewhere and the niche chosen for religion need not in future be confined to the beginning or end of the day. The content of the religious instruction offered should follow the lines laid down by the Cowper-Temple amendment

[10] The Act spoke of 'provided' and 'non-provided schools'. 'Provided schools' were the old Board schools and any which were maintained wholly from public funds. In the 1944 Act these schools were called 'county schools' though Murphy often calls them 'council schools' for the sake of terminological consistency. The 'non-provided schools' were the voluntary schools.

[11] In fact not all local authorities had responsibility for higher education; the so-called Part 3 authorities only dealt with elementary education (Curtis, 1961, p 315).

32 years before. Nevertheless additional denominational religious instruction might be given at the request of parents. As a whole, however, in accordance with the Kenyon-Slaney amendment, religious instruction in denominational schools was removed from the control of local clergy and vested in the managers, clerical and lay together. The purpose of this amendment was to curtail the influence of High Churchmen (the descendants of Tractarians)[12].

There was enormous bad feeling about aspects of the 1902 Education Act. The arguments of extremists, from today's perspective, look wild and foolish. For instance, Nonconformist rhetoric condemned the Education Act for allowing 'Rome on the rates' even though the greatest beneficiaries of the financial changes were Anglican. Equally, the view expressed by an Anglican clergyman that the Kenyon-Slaney amendment amounted to 'the greatest betrayal since the crucifixion' is similarly emotive and inaccurate (Murphy, 1971, p 92f).

In course of time the 1902 Education Act was seen to have achieved a settlement that ought not to be disturbed. This was especially so once the now powerful Trade Union Congress dropped its specifically secularist agenda. Despite its repeated calls for a free and secular education system from primary school to university in the years between 1906 and 1913, the unwillingness of Roman Catholic working class voters to agree, and the threat that the working class vote might be divided on education, led the Trade Union Congress to tackle less contentious issues.

Subsequently nationally-led educational reform languished. The attempts by Fisher after the 1914-18 war came to nothing because of financial stringencies, and the attempts by Ramsey Macdonald's minority Labour government of 1929-31 failed because of opposition in the Lords and among many Roman Catholics. Yet there was one innovation, carried out at a local level from 1924 onwards, which was to have lasting results. Cambridgeshire worked out an *agreed syllabus* of religious instruction in consultation with the religious denominations, and this device was quickly adopted by another seven counties. Where an agreed syllabus was in use, Anglicans were much more willing to transfer their schools to local authority control.

In 1936 the 'National' government (Conservative and Liberal combined) made important financial adjustments by offering significant help to voluntary schools. By the 1936 Education Act (England) the government set up *special agreement* schools which were an attempt to enable the churches to begin the expansion of secondary education; all of these schools, therefore, were then secondary schools. The government intended to raise the school leaving age to fifteen in September 1939 and local authorities were empowered to make

---

[12] This proposal had the effect of favouring Roman Catholic distinctiveness because their lay representatives were unlikely to defy the instructions of their clergy (Murphy, 1971, p 92).

grants to voluntary schools of 50-75% of the associated building costs. Many Anglican authorities felt unable to accept this limited financial assistance and so surrendered many of their schools to the local authorities but, on the day when the school leaving age was due to be raised, the 1939-45 war began and school leaving remained where it had been; education was relegated to a lower place in the national consciousness.

Activity A4

Using the figures in the text draw up a table with dates showing:

* the number of church schools of different types;
* the number of pupils at different types of school;
* the cost of education.

Comment on activity A4

Your table should show how the numbers in each category constantly go up.

A5 Preparation for the 1944 Education Act

In the pre-war period ecumenical ties between churches had developed (Hastings, 1986). At the beginning of the war senior officials of the Board of Education had drawn up a provisional scheme for reform that was circulated to educational institutions and selected individuals (Cruickshank, 1963, p 145). At the same time, in 1941, R.A. Butler came into the cabinet and was placed by Churchill in charge of education. It was Churchill's expectation that Butler would spend most of his time supervising the evacuation of children and do his best to keep education ticking over. Butler, a patient and enigmatic man with both Anglican and Nonconformist churchmen among his ancestors, saw his task in grander terms and cautiously laid plans for educational reconstruction.

There were several factors in Butler's favour. First, the officials at the Board of Education (as it then was) were favourable to reform and had issued a green paper in 1941 outlining their proposals for expanding and integrating the educational system. Second, William Temple became Archbishop of Canterbury in 1942. He was committed to interdenominational work and the British Council of Churches owed its existence largely to his efforts. He was also committed to education and had been President of the Workers' Educational Association (1908-24). His theology was infused with the flexibility of philosophical idealism but in his popular paperback *Christianity and the Social Order* (Temple, 1942) he had worked out how Christianity should apply both to education and other social agencies like the banking system. He saw Christianity as being able to fulfil the double function of fostering individual development and of creating bonds of union with fellow-citizens. Christian teaching and religious instruction should be carried out in schools so as to bring the whole life of the school-community together (Souper and Kay, 1982, p 6; see also Lankshear and Lankshear, 1993).

Moreover, Temple was sufficiently realistic to understand that, when Butler pointed out to him the poor condition of many church schools and their need for repair or improvement, huge expenditure would be necessary, expenditure that weakened the bargaining position of those churchmen who resented any partnership with the state (Cruickshank, 1963, p 151).

In December 1940 religious leaders (including Anglicans, Roman Catholics and Nonconformists) wrote to *The Times* calling for an overhaul of the British education system. In February 1941 the Archbishops of Canterbury, York and Wales issued a public statement advocating five points which were as follows:

- that a Christian education be given to children in all schools;
- that religious instruction should become a full 'optional subject' in training colleges;
- that existing restriction on the time of day when religious instruction could be given should be abolished;
- that religious teaching be inspected by the Inspectorate;
- that all schools start the day with an act of worship.

Then the war itself had the effect of drawing people together. Patriotism encouraged national unity; strikes and industrial disputes did not take place. The government itself was a coalition; normal party politics were suspended. After about 1943 when it became clear that Britain would not be invaded, people's minds turned to the future. As was made clear in the later Parliamentary debates, members of both Commons and Lords recognised that the nations against which Britain was fighting were dictatorships which had suppressed the churches. As Lord Teviot (Hansard, 128, 1054). put it:

> Let us think what has happened in the world. The nations who have struck down religion have become the curse of the world. They have brought great tragedy upon us.

There was considerable public support for religion in schools. A Gallup poll carried out in 1944 demonstrated that 56% of the population agreed that 'religious education should be given a more defined place in the life and work of schools'. Butler in the White Paper, *Educational Reconstruction* (1943), had written 'there has been a very general wish, not confined to representatives of the churches, that religious education should be given a more defined place in the life and work of schools' and Murphy (1971, p 115) points out that 'scarcely any managers' had availed themselves of the right they had gained in 1870 to dispense with religious instruction.

Consolidation of the dual system

The painstaking preparations and negotiations of Butler led to the acceptance of his legislation both inside Parliament and among all the main Christian groups. In essence:

- the dual system was strengthened;
- church schools within the dual system could choose either controlled or aided status (explained later);
- religious education, including collective worship, was made a legal requirement for the first time;
- religious education was made up of two components, collective worship and classroom instruction;
- schools provided by the churches became known as voluntary schools;
- schools not provided by the churches became known as county schools;
- in all schools (except the aided category), classroom instruction in religious education was given according to an agreed syllabus.

Certainly, as a result of the 1944 Education Act, church schools were even more firmly established by public finance than before. At the same time, the almost universal practice in county schools of religious instruction and religious worship was made obligatory. Moreover many church schools and all county schools worked to the same 'agreed syllabuses' of religious education. The funding of church schools was more complicated and varied than that of county schools, but the education provided in secular subjects was identical and, in religious subjects, was similar and sometimes identical. There is a sense, then, in which the 1944 Education Act is a final consolidation of the dual system because it clearly makes church schools and county schools operate within one educational framework. The duality of the system brings the church and state into what should theoretically be a close partnership.

One innovation provided by the 1944 Education Act was in the creation of two separate statuses for church schools: they could either choose to be *controlled* or *aided*. Controlled schools were controlled by the state. Aided schools were aided by the state.

Church schools could make an application to belong to the controlled or aided category. All but two Roman Catholic schools opted for the aided category, but the Church of England schools were much more varied in their choices.

In controlled schools the managers or governors[13] were not responsible for any expenses in maintaining the school, neither the salaries of staff nor the costs of buildings or equipment. In aided schools the managers or governors were responsible for capital expenditure on alterations required by the local authority and for expenditure on external repairs (Dent, 1944, p 23).

Although managers and governors were responsible for particular areas of expenditure in aided schools, they did not have to raise all the necessary money themselves. Until 1959, they had to find 50% of the money needed; between 1959 and 1967 they had to find 25%; and since 1967 they have had to find 15%. The rest was provided from public funds.

Differences between aided and controlled schools are expressed in the composition of the governing body of each. According to the 1944 Education Act, in aided or special agreement schools two-thirds of governors were 'foundation governors', appointed by the voluntary body owning the school. In controlled schools only one third of governors were appointed by the voluntary body. Therefore in aided Church of England schools there is a built-in majority of church appointees on the governing body; in controlled Church of England schools, this is not the case. In effect the advantage to the church in having greater influence over what happens in a school is off-set by the extra funds which have to be provided from voluntary sources.

Differences between aided and controlled schools are expressed in the denominational instruction they may offer. The differences are complicated, but the principle is simple. In aided schools religious education may be entirely denominational, in controlled schools religious education in the classroom is subject to the agreed syllabus though with the option of special denominational religious education if that is requested by parents. In order to provide denominational religious education 'reserved' teachers may be appointed for this purpose. All teachers are appointed by the local education authority and may only be dismissed by the local education authority, but governors in controlled and special agreement schools have a voice in the appointment of 'reserved' teachers and may lay down special conditions for their appointment.

In aided schools, however, the teacher(s) appointed to give denominational religious instruction may be dismissed by the governors without the consent of the local education authority. Again, though the detail is complicated, the principle is straightforward: the entire purpose of controlled or aided status might be undermined by unsuitable denominational teaching but as much

---

[13] Between 1944 and 1980 primary schools were managed and secondary schools were governed. Governors had more extensive powers than managers. After 1980 all schools were governed.

protection as possible against wrongful dismissal is given to teachers who carry out this function.

Both controlled and aided schools may offer denominational school worship. Aided schools offer denominational religious education, though if the parents of children attending aided schools wish their children to receive instruction according to the agreed syllabus, the school must make this provision if the children cannot conveniently attend a school where that syllabus is in use.

Aided schools and special agreement schools normally use a syllabus recommended by the diocese for all the schools of these types within its area. Schools which wish to use the religious education syllabus of another diocese or denomination[14], or indeed the agreed syllabus, are at liberty to do so. The matter is in the hands of the governors of individual schools.

In both kinds of school the appointment of teachers lay with the governing body. In both kinds of school the right of withdrawal given by the conscience clause continued to apply.

The choice between the two types of status was made differently by Anglican and Roman Catholic schools. In general the Anglicans were much more inclined to opt for controlled status. Roman Catholics opted entirely for aided status: they saw their schools as being designed to provide a Catholic education for Catholic children[15].

Francis (1993, p 160-162) points to nine assumptions or outcomes embodied in the 1944 Act. These are:

- collective worship in all schools, county and voluntary, became obligatory;
- religious education became compulsory in all county and voluntary schools;
- churches had a key role in preparing agreed syllabuses for country schools;
- the parental right to withdraw children from collective worship or from religious instruction was safeguarded;
- churches felt secure in their continued involvement in teacher training;
- churches were able to opt for controlled status for their schools and this allowed denominational worship to be provided in single-school areas;
- churches were able to opt for aided status for their schools and this allowed denominational religious instruction to be provided in single-school areas;
- churches, through their aided schools, were enabled to develop a distinctive system of denominational education to serve the needs of religious communities rather than neighbourhoods;
- parents were given the right to free transport for a reasonable distance to enable their children to attend the denominational school of their choice.

---

[14] For example a Church of England school might wish to use the syllabus prepared by a Roman Catholic diocese.
[15] As part of an administrative error two small Catholic schools chose controlled status. All the rest chose aided status (Murphy, 1971, p 118).

A6 To the present

The National Society continues to work actively in the field of education. There are now 1,907 Anglican aided primary schools catering for 331,504 pupils in England and Wales and 2,786 Anglican controlled primary schools catering for 414,825 pupils[16]. This means that a quarter of the nation's primary schools belong to the Anglican Church and that these schools educate a sixth of all primary pupils in England and Wales. These are significant proportions which signal the importance of the voluntary sector in the dual system.

At the secondary level the Church of England's stake has never been large. In 1995 there were 204 Church of England secondary schools of which 82 were aided, 71 controlled, 11 special agreement and 40 grant-maintained. In Wales there were 2 Church in Wales controlled secondary schools and 3 aided.

The Roman Catholic contribution to education in England and Wales is even more substantial. There are 1,806 Roman Catholic aided primary schools catering for 424,362 pupils and 380 aided, special agreement and grant-maintained secondary schools catering for 299,409 pupils[17].

There are also 30 Methodist primary schools and 18 Jewish aided primary schools. When all the aided schools are added together, the total number in England and Wales reaches 4,131 and the total number of controlled schools in England and Wales is 2,990[18].

There has been a general weakening of the church's place in society over a long period of time. As we have seen, at its lowest estimate, 35% of the population of Britain attended church in 1851. The *UK Christian Handbook 1996/97 Edition* (Brierley, Wraight and Longley, 1995) carries figures showing that church membership in England and Wales has declined from 18.5% of the total population in 1975 to 13.9% of the total population in 1994. The projection for 2010 gives the church a membership of 10.8% of the total population. In whatever way the figures are interpreted, they unarguably demonstrate a creeping decline that is inevitably associated with a loss of the church's self-confidence[19]. Nevertheless, the churches' schools and colleges continue to offer a service to the current generation. There are philosophical, theological and educational questions about the kind of education church institutions should offer, but questions relating to the continuance of the church's position in the educational arena appear to have been resolved. What has not been resolved, however, is the exact status of church schools.

---

[16] Figures provided by the DfEE and the Welsh Office for January 1995. We have referred to the schools as 'Anglican' to cover Church in Wales schools along with Church of England schools.

[17] Figures provided by the DfEE and the Welsh Office for January 1995.

[18] Figures provided by the DfEE and the Welsh Office for January 1995.

[19] In 1983 the preface of *Crockford's Clerical Directory* spoke of 'a crisis of confidence in the hearts of many ordained ministers who work hard but are not sure what they should be doing' (p xxiii)

Current Labour Party policy suggests that in future voluntary controlled schools will have to make a choice about their status[20]. They may become either voluntary aided schools or take on the new status of *foundation schools*. Such schools will be governed by a body whose balance is in favour of parents, though it will also contain local education authority representatives. Staff will be appointed by governors. Aided schools will be slightly changed. Though religious appointees will make up the majority on governing bodies, parents and local authority representation will be increased. Admissions policies will be set by the governors after consultation with the local authority and parents and appeals will be heard by a new independent body. The appointment of staff will continue to be made by governors in consultation with the local authority.

Finance will also be handled slightly differently. Foundation schools will control 90% of their budgets (instead of the present 85%). Aided schools will also control 90% of their budgets (instead of the present 85%) and will continue to have to provide 15% of any capital projects.

It is not clear whether the increased representation and power of parents will alter the way church schools operate. Certainly the distinctiveness of controlled schools in largely Muslim areas, for example, is likely to be altered, but it is still uncertain whether Christian worship or denominational religious education will remain a living option.

Activity A5

Looking back over the period since 1870 do you think education was improved or worsened by religious commitment? What choices do you think lie ahead for church schools? You may need to look at documentation published after the publication date of this module. Check on government policies and political declarations of intent.

Obviously these questions invite you to speculate, but your speculations should now be informed by a knowledge of the course of historical development over more than a century.

Comment on activity A5

On the one hand, religious commitment leads to the building of schools, the training of teachers, voluntary finance and political concern for educational matters. On the other hand, religious commitment can lead to intolerance, misleading slogans and a weakening of the very religious position which the commitment is intended to advance. If Nonconformists and Anglicans had

---

[20] See *Church Times* 30th June, 1995 and amplified in Appendix 3 of *Diversity and Excellence: a new partnership for schools* (London, The Labour Party, 1995).

worked together rather than against each other during the latter part of the nineteenth century, their schools would have been in a much stronger position.

The principle that public money entails public regulation has been well established. Where public and private money are spent together on the same project, a regulatory compromise must be reached. As the church diminishes in size, it has less money available and must make a choice about spreading its resources thinly over a range of institutions across a wide geographical area or funding a narrower choice of prestige enterprises. If the idea of 'foundation schools' becomes a reality, then parents in schools containing a large proportion of non-Christian families may begin to insist that church schools are used for overtly non-Christian purposes. For example a catchment area containing 90% Muslims might wish to use the religious possibilities of a foundation school for Islamic teaching and worship and, assuming the local education authority accepted this, Church of England controlled schools would be metamorphosed into Muslim 'controlled' schools.

Readers

You will find helpful sections 5.1 and 5.2 of L.J. Francis and D.W. Lankshear (eds) (1993), *Christian Perspectives on Church Schools*, Leominster, Gracewing.

Bibliography

Bédarida, F. (1979), *A Social History of England 1851-1975*, London, Methuen.

Blake, R. (1985), *The Conservative Party from Peel to Thatcher*, London, Fontana Paperbacks.

Boyd, W. (1964), *The History of Western Education*, London, Adam and Charles Black.

Brierley, P., Wraight, H. and Longley, D. (eds) (1995), *UK Christian Handbook 1996/1997 Edition*, London, Christian Research.

Briggs, A. (1965), *Victorian People*, Harmondsworth, Penguin.

Cruickshank, M. (1963), *The Church and State in English Education*, London, Macmillan and Co.

Curtis, S.J. (1961), *History of Education in Great Britain*, London, University Tutorial Press.

Dent, H.C. (1944), *The Education Act 1944*, London, University of London Press.

Durham Report (1970), *The Fourth R*, London, The National Society and SPCK.

Francis, L.J. (1993), Church and state, in L.J. Francis and D.W. Lankshear (eds), *Christian Perspectives on Church Schools*, Leominster, Gracewing, pp 151-162.

Gardiner, J. and Wenborn, N. (eds) (1995), *The History Today Companion to British History*, London, Collins and Brown.

Gill, R. (1993), *The Myth of the Empty Church*, London, SPCK.

Gregg, P. (1973), *A Social and Economic History of Great Britain* (seventh edition), London, Harrap.

Harvie, C. (1984), Revolution and the rule of law, in K.O. Morgan (ed.), *The Oxford Illustrated History of Britain*, London, Guild Publishing, pp 419-462.

Hastings, A. (1986), *A History of English Christianity 1920-1985*, London, Collins.

Heal, F. and Holmes, C. (1994), *The Gentry in England and Wales 1500-1700*, Basingstoke, The Macmillan Press.

Inglis, K.S. (1960), Patterns of religious worship in 1851, *Journal of Ecclesiastical History*, 11, 74-86.

Jenkins, R. (1995), *Gladstone*, London, Macmillan.

Jones, G.E. (1997), *The Education of a Nation*, Cardiff, University of Wales Press.

Labour Party (1995), *Diversity and Excellence: a new partnership for schools*, London, The Labour Party.

Lankshear, D.W. and Lankshear J.F. (1993), Negotiating the Education Act: lessons to learn from Butler and Temple, *Crosscurrent*, 40, 4-5.

Murphy, J. (1971), *Church, State and Schools in Britain, 1800-1970*, London, Routledge and Kegan Paul.

Pickering, W.S.F. (1967), The 1851 religious census: a useless experiment? *The British Journal of Sociology*, 18, 382-407.

Smith, F. (1931), *A History of English Elementary Education 1760-1902*, London, University of London Press.

Souper, P.C. and Kay, W.K. (1982), *The School Assembly Debate: 1942-1982*, Southampton, University of Southampton.

Temple, W. (1942), *Christianity and the Social Order*, Harmondsworth, Penguin.

Vidler, A.R. (1974), *The Church in an Age of Revolution: 1789 to the present day*, Harmondsworth, Penguin.

Church Schools: history and philosophy

Unit B

Church school ethos and the plural society

David W. Lankshear

The National Society

London

Contents

Introduction

Aims

After working through this unit you should be able to:

- identify the issues raised for the ethos of a church school by its setting in a plural society;
- develop policy and action within your school context that reflects an appropriate response to these issues.

The main resource needed for this unit is a church school. If you do not have access to a church school, contact your tutor who will help you find one and support your application to it for copies of its public documentation.

Overview

At the end of this unit you should be able to:

- identify key policies and practices in a church school that create its ethos;
- identify factors in British society which lead to it being identified as plural;
- identify factors in the context of the community served by your school that would lead to it being identified as plural;
- identify key areas in the ethos of your school where review is necessary;
- consider appropriate action as a result of the foregoing review.

In the course of this unit you will be asked to undertake a study of two booklets published by The National Society, *The Multi-Faith Church School* (1992) and *Respect For All* (1996), in the context of other reading on the subject and apply the results both to a stereotyped (and therefore mythical) Anglican school and to your own school context.

The study will be structured by focusing on a number of different issues and allocating to each an activity. The activities, with the exception of activity one, are planned to take about five hours. Activity one is intended to take longer and the theme of activity six provides the potential for an assessed piece of work based on the unit.

In order to proceed with your study you will need to read the following description and documentation from St Gary's CE (Aided) Primary School. It should be emphasised that none of the material from St Gary's is being commended as good practice. It has been written only for the purposes of this study, and to stimulate thought. You should also obtain or create an equivalent set of information about the school on which you are basing your study. All the policies should be in existence. Many of them will be in the school brochure of *Information for Parents*.

B1 Introduction to St Gary's

St Gary's CE (Aided) Primary School is a one form entry school in the market town of Over Singing. The school address:

> St Gary's CE Aided Primary School, Bel Canto Road, Over Singing, Bachshire, K23 WA.

In Over Singing there are two other primary schools, both county schools. St Gary's used to be in the town centre but moved into new premises as part of a new housing development in the town in the 1960s. It continues to provide a church school alternative for the whole town, which is a single ecclesiastical parish. The school has an attached unit for partially hearing children. The school roll of 259 (including the partially hearing unit) includes six Traveller children, three Chinese children and four Asian children. The Asian families are both Hindu.

Within the town there are two Anglican churches, one Roman Catholic Church, one Methodist Chapel, one Baptist Church and two House Churches. The nearest non-Christian places of worship are in Verdichester which is twenty miles from Over Singing. The property immediately surrounding the school is a 1960s council housing development. Within the town of Over Singing two thirds of properties are owner occupied. The town has a range of small family businesses, but the main employer is the European assembly and distribution base of a Japanese musical instrument manufacturer. A significant number of workers also commute to Verdichester. Unemployment is below the regional and national average. Five children on the roll of the school itself and four children in the partially hearing unit are in receipt of free school meals.

St Gary's staff

St Gary's School is supported by a well qualified staff comprising:

- the headteacher is Mr G.F. Handel BEd, aged 45, an Anglican Evangelical;
- the deputy head is Mrs I.V. Purcell, aged 53, of no active faith;
- the teacher in charge of maths and science is Mr R.V. Shankar MA, aged 37, a Hindu;

- the teacher in charge of history and religious education is Miss E. Taverner MEd, aged 27, a charismatic Anglican;
- the teacher in charge of english is Ms B. Britten BA, aged 52, a liberal Anglican;
- the teacher in charge of games and physical education is Miss E. Bax BEd, aged 28, of no active faith;
- the teacher in charge of technology and geography is Ms R. Williams, aged 31, a lapsed Catholic;
- the teacher in charge of arts and music is Miss J. Smith, aged 26, of no active faith;
- the teacher in charge of the partially hearing unit is Mr I. Stravinsky, aged 42, an atheist.

B2 Extracts from the school brochure

Mission statement

St Gary's provides a stimulating learning environment within which every child is valued and encouraged to achieve the best of which they are capable. The school is a lively Christian community with worship at its heart.

Information for parents

The introductory letter in the *School Information for Parents* brochure is given on the next page. The letter goes on to make the following two points.

- The support of parents is requested in ensuring that all children wear school uniform whenever they attend school or a function organised by the school.
- The headteacher is available to see parents on Tuesday afternoons between 3 and 4 pm and by appointment at other times.

The *School Information for Parents* brochure provides information about the admission policy (including how the policy is implemented), the discipline policy (including school rules and the sanctions employed) and the worship policy (including details about frequency, leadership and style).

Admission policy

If the number of applicants exceeds the number of places available the governors will give priority to:

St Gary's CE Aided Primary School
Bel Canto Road
Over Singing
Bachshire
K23 WA

Dear Parents,

Welcome to St Gary's. We hope that your children will be very happy at our school. You will find that Anglican worship is at the heart of everything that we do at St Gary's. We believe that it is very important that all children experience worship within the traditions of the established church as part of their education.

In the classroom we are committed to offering children exciting opportunities to learn the subjects laid down in the National Curriculum. We provide this within a context where children know that they are expected to do their best at all times.

Although our limited space means that we sometimes have to operate our admissions policy, details of which come later in this booklet, everyone is welcome at St Gary's.

The school has a well qualified staff led by the head teacher, who is happy to meet parents at any time.

Yours sincerely

Revd William Sullivan
Chairman of Governors

- the children of parents who are involved in the work and worship of the Anglican parish of St Gary's, Over Singing;
- the children of parents who are involved in the work and worship of other Anglican parishes in the Deanery of Over Singing and Under Breathing for whom this is the nearest church primary school;
- the children of parents who attend a Christian church in Over Singing which is in membership of Christians Together in Bachshire;
- the children of parents resident in the ecclesiastical parish of Over Singing, whose parents wish them to come to a church school.

Within these categories the governors will give priority to those children whose parents can demonstrate particular social, medical or educational reasons why their children should attend this school. In the event of equality of applications the governors will allocate places to those with the shortest distance to travel to the school. The admissions to the partially hearing unit are a matter for the Local Education Authority.

Implementation of admission policy

In most years some children are admitted to the school from the fourth category of the policy. Only rarely does a child in the first three categories fail to obtain a place. As a result of the pressure for places many children living on the estate surrounding St Gary's attend the county primary school in the opposite sector of the town. The non-Christian children and those whose parents are Travellers have obtained admission to the school by applying mid-year for Key Stage two places when some vacancies arise as a result of children being moved to private education at the age of eight. The failure of the school to admit all the children from the council estate is sometimes suggested as the cause of the high levels of vandalism experienced by the school and the fighting between the older children from the different primary schools in the town that sometimes erupts after school hours.

Discipline policy

The school expects that children will demonstrate the highest standards of courtesy and consideration for others throughout the school.

Rules

The school expects the following rules to be observed at all times.

- Running is only permitted on the playground and school field.

- Adults are to be respected at all times.
- Instructions given by teachers must be obeyed.
- No-one should steal or damage property belonging to someone else.
- Fighting or name calling will not be tolerated.
- Everyone should do their best at all times.

Punishment

If pupils misbehave the following sanctions will be applied.

- An informal warning will be issued by the responsible teacher.
- Any child receiving three informal warnings during a session will receive a formal warning and will lose the privileges normally available to members of the class.
- Any child receiving three formal warnings in a day will be sent to the headteacher.
- If a child is sent to the headteacher three times in a week his or her parents will be asked to attend the school to discuss their child's behaviour
- If there are incidents of gross breaches of school rules the child's parents will be asked to attend the school to discuss the matter.
- If it has been necessary for a child's behaviour to be discussed with their parents three times in a term the child will be excluded from school for one day.

Worship policy

Worship is the heart of St Gary's School. While use will be made of material designed to enable children to worship, which may include material written by the children themselves, the basis of worship in St Gary's is provided by the *Book of Common Prayer* and those parts of the *Alternative Service Book 1980* approved for use by the Parochial Church Council of Over Singing.

Frequency

There shall be two whole school acts of worship each week, usually on Monday and Friday mornings at 9.15. Where it is not possible to hold a whole school act of worship on a Monday or Friday as a result of school holidays or other good reason, the headteacher will inform the staff and announce the other days on which the whole school will worship together.

Usually there will be two Key Stage acts of worship each week. These will happen on Tuesdays and Thursdays at 9.15 unless paragraph one above applies. The Key Stage two act of worship will take place in the school hall. The Key Stage one act of worship will take place in Mrs Purcell's room.

On Wednesday, if there is no eucharist and paragraph one does not apply, class teachers will lead an act of worship for their class in their own room.

Leadership

The whole school acts of worship will be led by the headteacher or the deputy. The Key Stage acts of worship will be organised by the class teachers of the relevant Key Stage. The rector will preside at the eucharists. Visitors will only be invited to lead acts of worship for the whole school with the approval of the rector.

Music and other material

The music for worship will be chosen by the headteacher and the deputy in consultation with the teacher in charge of music. The selection will be made from *Come and Praise* and *One Hundred Hymns for Today*, this latter being one of the hymn books being used by the parish church.

B3 The context of the school

In the preceding pages a range of information has been presented for St Gary's. This has been created only for the purposes of this unit and should not be assumed to be commended as an example of good practice.

In *Inspection Handbook: for section 23 inspections in schools of the Church of England and Church in Wales*, Brown and Lankshear (1997) write:

> When the law refers to the spiritual, moral, social and cultural development of pupils this will be included in the ethos of a church school. This broader heading enables such issues as the contribution of school buildings, school staffing policies, links with local community and a wide range of school policies to be included in the inspection report where these are significant.

Brown and Lankshear (1997) recognise that the ethos of a church school will always be difficult to define. The following are some of the aspects of school life which will contribute to the ethos of a church school:

- the manner in which the school's mission statement and/or policies draw attention to the Anglican and/or Christian foundation of the school;
- the relationships between staff, between pupils, and between staff and pupils;
- the standards of behaviour, the policies on discipline and the values inherent in classroom organisation and relationships;
- the links the school has with the local community, particularly the religious communities near to the school and from which pupils may come;

- how effective the pastoral system is and whether it is effective from the pupils' point of view;
- whether the building is well cared for, is tidy and clean and whether the standard of display is adequate;
- the provision made for pupils with special educational needs and abilities;
- whether it is clear from the ambience of the school that it is a church school; whether there are Christian symbols in evidence;
- whether the school notice board and headed paper indicate the Christian foundation of the school;
- how the above contribute to the spiritual and moral development of all the pupils regardless of faith or denomination.

In addition to the above there will be specific areas of the school to be judged with regard to spiritual and moral development. For example, the school should offer pupils the opportunity to:

- reflect on the importance of a system of personal belief;
- recognise the place a Christian faith has in the lives of people;
- develop a sense of wonder, awe, curiosity and mystery;
- understand the difference between right and wrong and the consequences of their actions for themselves and for others;
- be creative, questioning and imaginative within a broad Christian framework which recognises the importance of experience, personal values and respect for the beliefs of others.

It is clearly not possible to respond to all the challenges offered by Brown and Lankshear (1997) on behalf of St Gary's. You would need to know much more about it. You can, however, begin to identify areas where an inspector following this framework would begin to ask questions.

Activity B1

Write six points which as an inspector you would want to raise at St Gary's as a result of studying their documentation.

You were asked to assemble an equivalent set of documentation for your own school. You should now read these through with the same framework which you have just applied to the St Gary's documentation. If you were inspecting your school what six points would you be asking?

Comment on activity B1

In your reflections on the document's for St Gary's, first, you may feel that the school mission statement and the introductory letter do not carry the same message about the expectations that the school has of its pupils.

Second, you may feel that it is significant that the introductory letter does not mention religious education (which is not a National Curriculum subject).

Third, you may have spotted the discontinuity of message between the introductory letter's statement that the headteacher is happy to meet parents at any time and the subsequent information that he is only available between 3 and 4 on Tuesday afternoons and by appointment. This latter statement may be realistic, but the message is confused.

Fourth, the notes on the implementation of the admissions policy identify a number of problems. What action would you expect the school to be taking to address them?

Fifth, you may have considered that the school rules pose some interesting questions. Take, for example the statement: 'adults are to be respected at all times'. Does this imply that it is permissible to fail to respect children? How does this accord with the approach adopted in *Respect for All*? A second example is the rule 'Instructions given by teachers must be obeyed'. This leaves other staff apparently without similar support.

Sixth, there is a table of punishments based on the 'Three strikes and you are out' principle, but there is nothing about rewards. How does the school encourage good behaviour and reward achievement?

You will have spotted many more issues that an inspector would wish to follow up during the inspection process.

B4 The multi-faith church school

At the beginning of your work on this section you should read *The Multi-faith Church School* (Brown, 1992). Having read the booklet you should re-read the documentation for St Gary's and for your own school.

The Multi-faith Church School begins by considering the tension between the stability implied by guardianship of Christian tradition and the change implied by the concept of religious pilgrimage. The framework for this tension is found in the National Curriculum. Brown considers that the tension may be particularly strong where the Christian faith is emphasised in religious education and worship to the exclusion of other faiths. He argues that true Christian witness is shown by demonstrating concern for those of other faiths.

In other words, he emphasises the caring nature of the church school and the rich, broad and balanced curriculum it can offer to all its pupils. He tackles the theological issues raised by inter-religious contact and, while recognising that some Christians wish to ignore or convert those of non-Christian faiths, presses the case for seeing Christ both as confident in his Jewish identity and as challenged by the religious clamour of his day. Brown believes this mixture between confidence and adaptability is what is called for today and what should be found in church schools.

Turning to the practical matter of admissions policies (which are in the hands of governors) Brown contends that such policies are, in effect, theological statements about the nature of Christianity, but he admits that the issue is complex and that no single answer to the problem of exclusiveness raised by admissions policies can be given because local circumstances vary.

On the selection of learning and teaching materials, the 'vitality and energy that is part of Christian commitment' need not 'inhibit teaching with integrity about other faiths' and such teaching can challenge superficial and unreflective secularism. All this may be worked out within the institutional realities of controlled and aided schools. While the controlled school may claim to be a microcosm of society, an aided school may offer something more specialist; while the controlled school is an inclusive religious school, the aided school may be exclusively religious, and this represents the paradox of the United Kingdom - a set of exclusive religious groups gathered within the greater inclusiveness of the democratic state.

Activity B2

You should now be able to respond to the following questions:

- To what extent is St Gary's a multi-faith church school?
- To what extent is your school a multi-faith church school?
- In St Gary's there are Hindu staff and children. To what extent does the worship policy address the needs of these people? To what extent does it address the needs of other children in the school? In what ways would you expect it to?
- To what extent does the worship policy document of your school address the needs of all the children and staff?

Comment on activity B2

St Gary's contains an interesting mix of pupils and of staff. A particular issue for the school will be the presence of Traveller children. Their cultural experience will be different from the very Christian intake that the school's admissions policy seems to imply.

While St Gary's is multi-cultural it is not clear that every class will be, for the numbers representing non-Christian cultures are quite small. Indeed the notes on the admissions policy imply that at Key Stage one the school may be much less obviously multi-cultural than at Key Stage two. The school will need to look for support and guidance in this area to the diocese, possibly through the Diocesan Syllabus for religious education. Multi-cultural education is not achieved solely through religious education, however, and the school will want to ensure that the contribution of different cultures to the whole of the curriculum is valued.

A particular issue of concern for St Gary's may be the control exercised by the headteacher and the rector on school worship. Do their personal understandings of the issues meet the needs of the pupils?

B5 The prevention of racial incidents

For this section you should read *Respect For All* (Griffith and Lankshear, 1996). *Respect for All* suggests that it is the responsibility of every church school to develop policies and practices which will contribute to the development of a society in which all its members are respected and valued. It argues that schools should conduct a policy audit to this end and provides guidelines for how this can be undertaken.

After considering recent tragic deaths caused by racial hatred, it argues on the basis of three key biblical texts that church schools must reject racism in all its forms. The three texts are Genesis 1.27 (which shows that all human beings are made in the image of God), John 13.34 (where Jesus commands Christians to love each other as he has loved them) and Romans 13.8 (where the rule to love our neighbours as ourselves is set in the wider theological context of Christian doctrine).

The rejection of racism is best achieved by an active equal opportunities policy, and an equal opportunities policy is most effective if it engages with the school's existing policies and documents. All the documents issued by the school (for example, the pupil handbook, the job descriptions, the curriculum statements, and so on) should be checked to see what they say on equal opportunities and, once the new policy has been written, they should refer to it and be harmonious with it. The policy itself should define racial harassment and set out in advance how racial incidents might be handled. Beyond this, however, the policy should identify how, for example, tuition in community languages might be provided, and what the educational consequences of bilingualism are. The recognition and support of a community language is a way of affirming the value of cultural diversity.

Activity B3

How would the conduct of a school audit as described in *Respect For All* impact on St Gary's?

- What documents from those provided in this unit would need to be revised in the light of the principles outlined in *Respect For All*?
- What documents or sections of documents would be affirmed? Having considered the potential impact of this publication on St Gary's you should now consider the impact on your own school.
- What documents from those provided in this unit would need to be revised in the light of the principles outlined in *Respect For All*?
- What documents or sections of documents would be affirmed?
- From your personal experience, knowledge and further reading, to what extent do you think that *Respect For All* represents an adequate response to the challenges that it identifies?

Comment on activity B3

You have not been provided with an Equal Opportunities Policy document for St Gary's. It would be reasonable to suggest that the development of such a document would be a result of the school audit. Writing the policy, however, is not sufficient in itself. There may be much work to be done to ensure that all adults in the school implement the spirit of the policy in their work.

B6 Developing the pupils' self-image

Each pupil's self-image is affected by many experiences in the home, amongst peers, with significant adults including teachers, through experiences of success and failure and through reflection. This section will invite you to reflect on those aspects of school life which make a contribution to the pupil's self-image.

In *Mission, Management and Appraisal*, Louden and Urwin (1992, p 41) posed the following questions.

- A school's brochure states that the relationships between all members of the school community are modelled on the ideal of the Christian family. What would you look for as a parent of a prospective pupil, as a prospective employee, and as a visitor?

- Is there a distinctive 'house style' in the way that people are welcomed, enquiries answered and complaints handled?
- What aspects of pupil conduct and achievement are valued at your school? How is this shown, for example with badges, prizes, mentions in assembly, features in a newsletter, etc.?
- How is the personal worth of all in the community recognised and encouraged? How is this made explicit in the school's policy on equal opportunities?
- Is there 'safety' in the school community for those who are different in faith, opinion, interest or appearance?
- How often is there an agenda item concerning ethos or relationships at a meeting of the school staff, governors or parents?

In *A Shared Vision*, Lankshear (1992, p 64) writes:

> A school discipline policy should always be designed to provide a basis of self discipline. If it becomes too dependent on the staff enforcing the acceptable standards, then it does not carry the seeds of further growth to maturity. It only has within it the seeds of increased dependency. This implies that there must always be trust. It is only by being trusted that we learn to be trusted. Within a school where every human being is accorded that respect shown to unique human beings loved by God, this should come naturally, and where there are failures, as there will be, these can be dealt with, not as disasters, but as experience from which learning can grow.

Writing in *Respect for All*, Griffith and Lankshear (1996, p 27) reproduce a policy document from Townsend C of E (Aided) School, in Hertfordshire. This school policy document is unusual in that it was actually drawn up by the pupils themselves.

Respect for All

At Townsend, we believe that every person is equally important and that no-one has a right to harass, insult or cause offence to any other person for any reason. We particularly reject the way that some people abuse others:

- because they are richer or poorer, older or younger;
- because they are small or tall, thin or fat;
- because of the colour of their skin;
- because they are male or because they are female;
- because they are a teacher or a pupil;
- because of their religion;
- because of handicap or personal problems;
- because of their looks or what they wear;
- because of their likes or dislikes;
- because they are popular or unpopular;
- because of their ability or lack of ability;
- because of nationality or accent.

We are individuals with differences, but we are all members of Townsend and can learn from each other.

The school mission statement should contain within it the basis for all school policies. Often such statements talk about respect. In the extract from *A Shared Vision* quoted above Lankshear points out that respect and love challenge attitudes towards failure.

Why the emphasis on failure in a section on self-image? This is because it seems to be comparatively simple to discuss the development of a positive self-image and self confidence among pupils when things are going well. When things are going badly it is all too easy to handle matters in such a way that long term damage is done to a pupil's self-image and self respect. An example here may help to illustrate the point.

> A young friend of ours had a poor experience of primary school. She did not learn quickly and on transfer to secondary school was placed in the remedial stream. Suddenly things started to go better. By the time GCSE loomed she was in the top class although still struggling with mathematics. Her good results at GCSE confirmed her ambition to be a nurse. Mathematics at level 'C' was required and duly achieved at the second shot with a little help from a coach. 'A' levels loomed as did the choice of courses for nursing. The issue became to take the degree course or not? You would think that the success at secondary school would have out weighed the failure at primary and given her the confidence to tackle the degree that her teachers recommended. This was not the case. She was still convinced that she could not do it because she had learned that she was not good at learning! Three years later she passed her diploma with flying colours. Now having worked for a year on the wards she has gathered the confidence to tackle the degree.

Activity B4

In practical ways how can a school promote the self-respect of all its pupils? Comment on any theological implications of the notion of self-respect which might be relevant to the work of church schools.

Comment on activity B4

Schools can promote the self-respect of pupils in two basic ways: by giving them an opportunity to enjoy success and by valuing them for who they are regardless of their age, appearance, race, background or other external characteristics.

The success pupils can gain through academic work need not be as a result of competition. It is not necessary to do better than other pupils to be successful. It is simply necessary to master a skill or a difficult task, for example learning to work a new computer program or to understand a maths problem or to spell a long word. The experience of success in this way is linked with learning itself and, once learning becomes pleasurable, pupils will acquire a thirst for knowledge which provides much of the motivation for academic progress. Any pupils capable of learning should therefore be able to experience success.

Pupils should also be valued by teachers and staff. This will mean showing care for all pupils in small ways, for example remembering their birthdays and being sensitive to personal circumstances and personal preferences. Valuing pupils as individuals rather than as members of teams has to be attempted without, at the same time, encouraging selfish individualism. In all these matters a balance has to be struck between valuing the individual and valuing the community. Whatever else church schools do, they should not engage in destructive and public criticism of pupils in a manner that is designed to humiliate.

The theological implications of valuing the individual flow very naturally from much of the teaching of the New Testament. Jesus emphasised to the disciples how important they were as individuals and how important children were to him (Matthew 10.29, 30; Matthew 19.13).

B7 Developing mutual respect

The previous section focused on the individual. In this section the focus is on the relationships between individuals. Much of the material quoted in the previous section has relevance to this area as well and should be reviewed.

The document *Guidance on the Inspection of Nursery and Primary Schools* (OFSTED, 1995) requires that in reporting on the spiritual, moral, social and cultural development of pupils the inspectors should base their judgements on, amongst other areas, the extent to which the school:

> encourages pupils to relate positively to others, take responsibility, participate fully in the community and develop an understanding of citizenship.

Such a statement challenges each school to determine the basis on which in can undertake such work. In *Moral Education*, Ainsworth and Brown (1995, p 11) approach this problem. They wrote:

> *How can a school arrive at values upon which it will be based?*
>
> The answer to the question may well depend upon the type of school and the distinctive contribution of church schools will be considered later. All schools would probably accept the belief that the needs of pupils in regard to moral

education will be different at different ages. Pupils will move from the acceptance of parental opinion, through the realisation that in everything they do there are at least two people (or groups) involved - themselves and the other person they affect - until in adolescence they develop an awareness of themselves in relation to the community and the wider nation of society. So pupils' needs differ. This could be rather tritely characterised as moving from Dependence through Independence to Interdependence.

It is a moot philosophical point as to how young people *acquire* values but schools should provide a clear statement of what is (or is not) acceptable in order to foster moral understanding. This is controversial because it has become unfashionable to talk about 'duty'. It is often depicted as a right wing return to the Victorian era with overtones of Dickensian morality but in fact much of moral awareness is related to an awareness of one's 'duty' - to oneself, one's peers, one's school. It is a worthwhile concept to develop and is closely connected to one's own awareness of one's responsibility to others: in effect the whole of one's relationships.

Values *may* be acquired and developed through pupils 'making up their own minds' but this can never be a neutral exercise and the syndrome graphically displayed in *Lord of the Flies* of anarchy, oppression and amorality may be only just round the corner. Of course young adults (and sadly, older ones) too have to learn to live with the consequences of their actions, particularly their moral failings.

Younger people often need a framework which can be kicked against, even broken, as they begin to explore the boundaries of their own morality. They need something to react against, otherwise the frustrations of a particular morality become so acute that anarchy will reign! The exploration of boundaries is in itself a moral exploration - we often think of personal boundaries but social or national boundaries also provide us with moral dilemmas upon which we need to reflect.

At this stage we can choose two examples both of which will be relevant to what follows:

(a) *Behaviour expectations*: This is not to be confused with disciplinary procedures. Behaviour expectations are quite simply a code of behaviour that is seen to be acceptable within the school community. The emphasis is on expectation, for pupils will be *expected* to behave in a certain way. There may be an overt religious or social reason why certain forms of behaviour are expected but in any case if pupils are not made aware that they are expected to act in a certain way one can hardly either blame them for falling short or praise them for achievement.

(b) *Quality of relationships*: Perhaps more than any other aspect of life the nature of human beings' relationships with each other determines joy, misery, despair, happiness, violence and peace. So the quality of relationships in a school, between pupils, between staff and probably most seminally between staff and pupils is crucial and necessarily linked to behaviour expectations as the part of *everyone* in the school. Again this is not to be confused with a code of discipline. Relationships are about how people respond to each other but staff-pupil relationships will be the key to the quality of relationships in a school.

Relationships in school start with the staff, not just the teaching staff but the whole staff of the school, including those helpers who give their time voluntarily. How do they relate to one another? Do they demonstrate mutual respect? Could the staff room be described as a 'safe place'? The staff of a school do not have to spend their entire social life together, although they may enjoy each other's company, but they do have to demonstrate the reality of mutual respect and love that Jesus taught was the mark of Christians. In doing this they set an example to the pupils that they can then be encouraged to emulate.

Activity B5

Identify and write down up to three instances where:

- there are examples in the material from St Gary's which militate against the principle of mutual respect amongst the staff;
- there is evidence of ways in which St Gary's shows an understanding of the need to develop mutual respect and understanding among pupils;
- there are examples in the material from your own school which demonstrate the principle of mutual respect amongst the staff;
- there is evidence from your own school of an understanding of the need to develop mutual respect among pupils.

Comment on activity B5

First, it is arguable that the school worship policy fails to recognise the religious needs of Mrs Purcell, Mr Shankar, Miss Bax, Ms Williams, Miss Smith and Mr Stravinsky, all of whom are unlikely to be entirely happy with Christian worship. Against this, however, is the fact that each of these people applied to teach in an aided school and so, presumably, were aware of the kind of stress that might be given to Christian worship.

Second, there is little in the school discipline policy regarding respect for pupils. This is especially noticeable since it is clear that the school wants to encourage respect for adults. One of the rules says 'adults are to be respected at all times'.

Third, there is no reference to team games which might encourage understanding among pupils. Nor is there any mention in the school admission policy of allowing brothers or sisters of pupils already at the school to attend. In other words, there is no priority given to keeping families together, even if those families are not Christians or church-attenders.

B8 Applying the approach

In *The Multi-faith Church School*, Brown (1992, p 27) raised the issue of preparing pupils to meet people from other faiths later in life. Read *Respect for All* (Griffith and Lankshear, 1996) in the light of this question. It was not the intention of the authors to provide a complete response to Brown's question. How far did they succeed? What other aspects of a school's work need to be included to provide a full answer?

In *The Multi-faith Church School*, Brown (1992) presents twenty-three questions for governors of church schools. With which of these questions would the governors of your church school have the most difficulty? Which are the most relevant to your situation? How would you prepare for a governors' meeting during which they were to be discussed?

Note that governors may have a more direct experience of living and working in a multi-faith community than some of the staff, who may reside at a distance from the school. In some areas, however, particularly if there is no day-to-day experience of a multi-faith community, governors may not have had the opportunity to think through the implications of educating children to live and work in a multi-faith setting. The teachers in such schools may have reflected on this during the course of their initial teacher training or during inset activities. For many church schools, perhaps in rural areas, considerable preparatory work may need to be done before Brown's questions can be answered fully.

Activity B6

Provide the theological and philosophical arguments that you would use to support the case for a review of your school's policies that relate to the education of children to take their place in a plural society.

Comment on activity B6

The theological case for reviewing your school's policies will depend on exactly how you construct your theological position. There are various starting points for building a theology and the simplest and most fundamental starts by using the texts of the bible. These are the foundation documents of the church and give us a rich resource from which to derive our position. You could begin with the doctrine of God, and especially the Trinitarian nature of God, and, from this, draw out a set of priorities with regard to social and family relationships. Or you could begin with a doctrine of personhood, and draw out a set of priorities with regard to the balance between body and spirit that is the mark of a healthy and fulfilled human being. Alternatively, you could begin by making a study of what the bible teaches about children showing how Jesus thought of them and how they are treated in the Epistles. Adrian Thatcher's unit, unit C of the module *Church Schools: history and philosophy*, gives you a wealth of examples and ideas about how a theology can be put together.

Philosophically, you can also begin from various positions. You might want to start from the concept of justice and ask what is the fairest and most equitable way of using public resources for the benefit of the whole community. You might consider that it is right to give more to the poor or to the disadvantaged, rather than to give the same amount to everyone irrespective of whether everyone needs the same. This kind of argument is similar to that which has occurred over the payment of child benefit to parents with children of school age. Is it fair to give millionaires child benefit? The answer, you may think, is yes and no. Yes, it is fair because it is right that the state should treat everyone equally. No, it is not fair because it is right to help people on the basis of need. This is the nub of the argument.

Again, you might wish to begin your discussion on the basis of children's rights and entitlements. Are children's rights being observed, you may ask, by the current policies of your school? But, once you begin to dwell on rights and to apply them to the lives of children, it immediately becomes apparent that rights and responsibilities are two sides of the same coin. If children have rights, then schools have responsibilities and sometimes the balance between the rights of the child has to be struck against the rights of the teacher to be saved from an ever increasing workload. For, just as it is wrong to exploit children, it is also wrong to exploit teachers.

Alternatively, you might wish to begin your philosophical discussion from a review of the ideals of a democratic society. There is a sense in which the cultural and political mission and purpose of a school is to prepare children to live in a democratic society, and that only by considering how and why such a society works will individual freedoms be protected and preserved. Against this larger perspective the policies of the school must be reviewed to ensure the continuance of the society in which the school is embedded. Education is thus seen as the main way society renews itself generation by generation.

Finally, you may not have begun with any of these philosophical positions, but that does not mean that your justifications are incorrect.

Readers

You will find helpful chapters 2, 3 and 10 of L.J. Francis and D.W. Lankshear (eds) (1993), *Christian Perspectives on Church Schools*, Leominster, Gracewing.

Bibliography

Ainsworth, J. and Brown, A. (1995), *Moral Education*, London, The National Society.

Brown, A. (1992), *The Multi-faith Church School*, London, The National Society.

Brown, A. and Lankshear, D.W. (1997), *Inspection Handbook: for section 23 inspections in schools of the Church of England and Church in Wales*, London, The National Society.

Duncan, G.S. and Lankshear, D.W. (1995), *Church Schools*, London, The National Society.

Goulding, W. (1954), *Lord of the Flies*, London, Faber.

Griffith, D. and Lankshear, D.W. (1996), *Respect For All*, London, The National Society.

Lankshear, D.W. (1992), *A Shared Vision: education in church schools*, London, The National Society.

Louden, L.M.R. and Urwin D.S. (1992), *Mission, Management and Appraisal*, London, The National Society.

OFSTED (1995), *Guidance on the Inspection of Nursery and Primary Schools*, London, HMSO.

Church Schools: history and philosophy

Unit C

Theology of education and church schools

Professor Adrian Thatcher

University College of St Mark and St John

Plymouth

Contents

Introduction

Aims

After working through this unit you should be able to:

- understand why the dual system developed;
- affirm the practical relevance of a theological understanding of your work in education;
- examine issues in education and schooling from a theological perspective;
- be a wiser practitioner of faith in the context of your teaching and educational responsibilities.

Overview

While other units in this module contain some theological content, this unit is unusual in that it is the only one which is written from a conscious theological point of view. Since church schools stand in believing traditions of Christianity, it is essential that the work of education is addressed from the perspective of those believing traditions themselves. The single aim of this unit is *to help you to experience what it is like to think about your work in education and/or church schools from a specifically theological point of view.*

This aim is easy to state but quite hard to put into practice. Some students will have no background in theology. Even if you do, it is unlikely that your theology course encouraged you to think about your everyday life and work. So in order to set up a recognisable Christian theological perspective upon education it will be necessary to do some preliminary work. So the unit is divided into two parts. In the first part (sections C1, C2 and C3) you will be invited:

- to think about what Christian theology is;
- to consider some beliefs that are essential to Christian theology;
- to note a couple of approaches to the theology of education;
- to be wary of the impact which the surrounding culture and society has on religious and theological thought.

The second part (sections C4, C5 and C6) takes you directly into issues which are topical in schools at present. The issues which have been chosen are:

- religious education;
- spiritual and moral development;
- collective worship.

The point of this unit is not merely to familiarise you with a range of material about these issues, but to re-vision each of them from a believing, theological point of view.

C1 What theology is

We must begin somewhere. Theology provides vital knowledge and practice for Christians. It is capable of influencing everything they do. But what is it?

It is not always helpful to look at the derivation of a word to find out its meaning. That is because meanings change, and people use words in different ways. But with 'theology' the situation is different. Here, '-ology' means 'the study of', as in sociology, biology, and so on, while *Theos* is Greek for God, so theology is the study of God.

Activity C1

Every subject on the curriculum has something about it which is very basic, in fact so basic that without it that subject would be impossible to teach. Think for a moment whether it would be possible to teach any of the following subjects, and if not, why not. Then write down your reason.

- Mathematics without numbers?
- English without language?
- History without time?
- Geography without space?
- Music without sound?
- Science without cause and effect?
- Art without form?
- Biology without organisms?
- Sociology without societies?

Comment on activity C1

I think it would be impossible to teach any of these subjects as they are described. The reason for this is that there is something basic about the content of *any* subject and about the method for studying it, which is so essential that without them, the subject collapses. *What* is studied, and *how* it is studied is utterly basic to the subject. Now if this is true of all subjects, it will also be true of theology. God is utterly basic to theology, so that without God theology cannot happen. God is as basic to the study of theology as number is basic to mathematics.

How is God to be studied? That is a far more difficult question. All that will be said at this stage is that the reality of God will be assumed. God is no doubtful object whose existence or alleged activity is to be bracketed-out because of prior view of what constitutes an objective, scholarly approach. In other words, *faith* in God is built in to the 'how?' of studying God. One does not necessarily need faith in order to study theology. It is, however, the study of God which communities of faith undertake.

What Christian theology is

The theology we are interested in is Christian theology. Christians share some beliefs about God with other religions, for example that God is Creator, is One, and so on. But there are also some Christian beliefs about God which are as basic to Christianity as organisms are basic to biology. They are mentioned now because we will need to refer to several of them again when we come to consider education in the light of them.

We begin with the belief 'in one God, the Father, the almighty, maker of heaven and earth'. This belief is fundamental to Christianity, and the Nicene creed puts it before everything else it says about Jesus Christ and the Holy Spirit. The world and everything in it is dependent for its origin and its continued existence on God. The belief that God is 'maker of heaven and earth' is common to theistic faiths. However, Christians obviously hold beliefs about God which are not shared with members of other faiths, and these will be the ones which are basic to the identity of the Christian God. Some of these are as follows.

First, God has become revealed in Jesus Christ, so that if we want to know who God is or what God does, we have to look to him. According to some of the earliest confessions of faith Jesus is *vere deus, vere homo,* he is truly and completely God, and truly and completely human. St John says that Jesus Christ, God the Word, 'became flesh; he made his home among us, and we saw his glory, such glory as befits the Father's only Son, full of grace and truth' (John 1.14).

Second, the Holy Spirit is also God. 'Spirit' means 'breath' or 'wind'. This is a fine biblical and metaphorical name for God. Most vertebrates cannot live without breath. It is a pre-condition of life. Wind can be heard but not seen, although its powerful effects are seen and felt. As we shall see below, God the Spirit cannot be confined to churches, to Christendom, or to the inner lives of Christians. God the Spirit brings about her 'fruits' or 'harvest' in men and women everywhere. These are 'love, joy, peace, patience, kindness, goodness, fidelity, gentleness, and self-control' (Galatians 5.22). She shares with all humanity the love the Father brought into the world through the Son, and which the Son returns to the Father.

Third, Father, Son and Spirit are a trinity of Persons who are one God. God is a communion of divine Persons-in-relationship. The identity of each of the Persons in God is shaped by his/her relation to the other two. God is a communion of different but co-equal Persons who in their mutual love for each other are perfectly one. Our baptism was in the name of Father, Son and Spirit, and the invitation to the Christian life is a summons to share in the trinitarian life of God.

Fourth, human beings are sinful creatures. They are caught up in the state of selfishness, incompleteness and distorted relationships which affect us individually and socially. This belief, like belief in a creator, is not entirely unique to Christianity, and the idea that people are 'fallen' or alienated from each other, from nature, from their true selves, and so on, is widely held outside religion. What is unique to Christianity is God's way of dealing with it. Jesus inaugurates a kingdom or reign which may be described as an out-working of justice-love. He inaugurates a new life which is not bound by 'sin and death', but is life instead in Christ and the Spirit (e.g. Romans 8.1-12).

Fifth, Jesus Christ is present at the eucharist. Some Christians, for example Quakers and Salvationists, do not observe the eucharist. Most Christians, however, do have a service of mass, eucharist, holy communion, breaking of bread, ordinance of the Lord's Supper, etc. Notoriously that most sacred act of Christian worship has generated much hostile disagreement among Christians. All that is being introduced here is the fact that the eucharist is central to the worshipping practice of most Christians. No particular theology of it is being offered. If we allow ourselves to ponder those characteristics that make up a Christian identity, the very centrality of the eucharist makes it very hard to omit.

Activity C2

In this section of the unit we have asked what theology is, and then what *Christian* theology is. It was suggested that we could understand *Christian* theology by building in some beliefs which Christians hold in common but which are *not* held by people of other faiths. Please look back over the list of Christian beliefs mentioned in this section. You are asked to do two things. First, say whether the list is adequate and contains all that is essential to Christian theology. You can do this by asking yourself what has been left out which you might have wished to see included. The second part of the activity is to see if you can think of any dangers in drawing up such a list.

Comment on activity C2

The list contains no mention of any theory of the atonement (how God became one with the world through Jesus). It does not mention the church or the second coming of Christ, and it has no theory about the inspiration of the bible. The creeds of the church concentrate on the doctrine of God, and that is what has been done in the list.

There are at least two dangers of having a list of distinct beliefs. One is obvious enough: it seems to create a distinction between essential and less essential beliefs. The other is that if we begin with what is uniquely Christian we may overlook what Christianity holds in common with some of the non-Christian religions. Since many students on this course may not have studied theology, or may have done a degree in religious studies, it was thought best to begin by drawing attention to 'core beliefs' held by Christians.

C2 Theology of education

Theology of education is the attempt to think about education from a theological point of view. It is, however, more than just 'thinking', because theology has a peculiar kind of influence on the 'people of God' which it serves. In an attempt to relate theology to life, many theologians have spoken of 'doing' theology. They have wanted to indicate that beliefs show themselves in practice, and to overcome the gap between believing and doing. Sometimes this is called 'applied' or 'practical' theology.

There are two main ways of approaching the theology of education. One is the formal or definitional approach. The other is the informal or issues-based approach. In the 1970s the first approach was favoured. In the 1990s the second is generally adopted. We shall examine both briefly.

The formal approach

The formal approach to theology of education was an attempt to anchor Christian thought about education firmly in mainstream study of both theology and education. Education had become arranged in universities and colleges in sub-disciplines. Students studied a main subject together with the theory and practice of education. The term 'theory' was not despised then. Education was studied through the sub-disciplines of psychology, sociology, philosophy, and history. Those of us who were arguing for and trying to work out a theology of education in those days were fired up by two possibilities. We noted that education had no language or tradition of its own. It existed as a discipline in the university by virtue of what other more established disciplines contributed to it. These disciplines were pressed into service because they contributed to the understanding and practice of education. They claimed to be relevant. We wanted to introduce theology of education alongside the philosophy, psychology and sociology of education. We thought theology was relevant. We believed theology provided a genuine 'world-view' and real knowledge, equally worthy of consideration alongside other world-views and knowledge-claims (some of which were very contentious). Theology of education, so we thought, could justify itself on educational grounds.

Two of the most important essays demonstrating many of the difficulties which Christians working in education faced then were written by Professor John Hull and Professor Leslie Francis. In 1989 when Leslie Francis and I were editing the volume *Christian Perspectives for Education*, we placed these two essays first[1], because we wanted to acknowledge their importance but also because they demonstrated what theology of education is. We were conscious then that the study of education was changing very rapidly, that education theory was becoming disparaged, and that courses like 'the philosophy of education' were either being closed down or slashed and rehashed as components of something else called 'professional education'. Nonetheless we persevered with the subtitle 'a reader in the theology of education' because the term 'theology of education' provided a way of signalling that there were huge issues in education that cried out for a Christian theological approach.

It must be admitted that theology of education was never taken very seriously, even by Christians. There were several reasons for this, and twenty years on we can learn from them. Here are three.

Perhaps the main reason was that educators were generally unwilling to allow the theologian on to the playing-field. Education is a secular discipline, and religious understandings of education were generally unwelcome. There were very few university courses in the subject.

A second reason had to do with the unattractiveness of theology. Very few theologians, then as now, were prepared to make connections between theology and education. Theology was regarded as a highly traditional subject, concentrating on biblical languages, biblical studies and the history of the

---

[1] Leslie J. Francis and Adrian Thatcher (eds), *Christian Perspectives for Education: a reader in the theology of education* (Leominster, Gracewing, 1990), chapter 1. The two essays are 'What is theology of education?' by John Hull, and 'The logic of education, theology, and the church school' by Leslie J. Francis.

church and its doctrine. There were few attempts to 'apply' theology to particular contexts. Ethics and the practice of ministry may have been exceptions. What was intended as a bridge across the chasm between theology and education was never built. We could say the bridge-building project never got past the drawing-board stage. An analysis of the potential traffic-flow across it showed that very few travellers thought the journey worthwhile.

A third reason had to do with the apparent abstract character of what was envisaged. Theology of education remained largely theoretical. Theory is essential to every branch of academic study. The Greek word *theoria* means 'beholding', 'reflecting', but the danger of an excessive concentration on practical issues is that students and teachers do not learn how to stand back and 'behold' what they do. Nonetheless, there was and is a sense in which it is simply tiresome to ask questions like 'What is theology?' 'What is education? 'What is the theology of education?' 'What is 'the relationship between theology and education?' This approach owed too much to philosophy of education which, in the 1970s, was probably too preoccupied with arriving at neat definitions and clarifying concepts.

The informal approach

The informal approach to theology of education writes off attempts to define it as a formal sub-discipline of either theology or education. In any case, education is no longer structured in such a way as to permit such an approach. The informal approach takes its cue from the difficulties and problems which Christian people encounter in their day to day work in education. As a matter of method, that means that the experience of Christians themselves, as they go about their professional tasks in education, is the starting point for theology of education.

Having said that the experience of Christian educators provides the starting point for theology of education, it is necessary to say that it is *only* the starting point. This discussion takes us into the 'sources' or 'resources' of theology. Most writers include among the sources of theology, scripture, tradition, reason, and so on[2]. The *task* of Christian theology then becomes the task of showing how the resources of faith may illuminate, or clarify, or transform, the experience of being a Christian educator. Other theologies, for example the theology of liberation, feminist theology, sexual theology, put experience first among their sources.

---

[2] Peter C. Hodgson, *Winds of the Spirit : a constructive Christian theology* (London, SCM Press, 1994), p 27. Hodgson includes 'religious experience' as a source. While 'experience' is a very broad term which has to be qualified in some way, it is arguable that it should be qualified differently, e.g. experience of oppression, injustice, pain, or love, joy, wonder, etc.

Here are some of the issues in education which Christians may encounter and where Christian theology may be able to provide illumination.

- *The spiritual development of children*: The spiritual development of children has become one of the most hotly-disputed areas of the government's recent reforms. Yet spirituality is a religious and theological topic. Religious traditions know a great deal about it. Much of the writing about spiritual development wilfully ignores the contribution that theology is able to make. That is why we will soon have reason to take issue with government guidelines on spiritual development.

- *The moral development of children*: Many people believe that Britain is in a state of moral crisis; that children do not know the difference between right and wrong; that they are not taught what the difference is in schools. There is pervasive talk of 'values' within a broader context of almost complete inability to say what they are or how we arrive at them. The influential report, *Spiritual and Moral Development: a discussion paper* (National Curriculum Council, 1993), managed to omit both love and justice entirely from its (perfunctory) treatment of moral development. How might, say, the Sermon on the Mount (Matthew 5 to 7) transform this moral vacuum into a new vision of how our relationships with each other ought to be conducted?

- *Religious education*: Religious education is part of the Basic Curriculum in England and Wales, yet there is disagreement about the extent to which, if at all, the truth-claims which the Christian religion makes about God, the world and ourselves are even defensible, still less believable. What if religious education professionals, their associations, advisers, and ensuing generations of lecturers were to have neglected a source, i.e. Christian theology, which turns out to be the most crucial one of all?

- *Religious pluralism*: Britain, it is often confidently stated, is now a multi-religious, multi-cultural and multi-ethnic society. It is 'pluralistic'. But how do we cope with pluralism? If there were theological resources available to us in addition to the resources provided by a purely secular understanding of the problems and tensions involved in living in a pluralistic society, and these resources actually provided insight into and understanding of those tensions, would we not have a duty to deploy them? Well, there are such resources, and they ought to be made available.

- *Collective worship*: Worship in schools must be 'wholly or mainly of a broadly Christian character'[3]. But is not worship addressed to God? Is that what actually happens in schools? A government circular pronounces the distinction between 'corporate' and 'collective' worship[4]. Is collective worship really worship?

---

[3] *Education Reform Act* (1988), section 7.
[4] Department For Education, *Circular 1/94, Religious Education and Collective Worship* (London, Department for Education, 1994), paragraph 57, p 21.

- *The curriculum*: The term 'God' has no use for scientists since science understands the world on its own terms. We might say it prefers 'natural' explanations to 'supernatural' ones. Yet Christians think the world is a creation, dependent on God for its very existence, and that it has been redeemed by Christ. At the very least, science and religion provide different 'world-views'. The world-views of science and theology are able to be brought together in such a way that each respects the other as contributing to the 'whole story' of what is to be told about the world. This is called 'complementarity'[5]. In popular consciousness religion and science are contradictory for science has 'disproved' religion. In theology it has become customary to see theology and science, not as contradictory but as complementary.

These are some of the issues which are encountered in education. They are not the only ones. They are of particular interest to church schools, yet too often there has been no ministry at all from theologians to Christians working anywhere in education. Informal theology of education makes connections between theology and the needs of Christian educators. In this unit the informal approach is being adopted, and most of the problems identified in this section will form the agenda for the whole of the second part.

Activity C3

In activity C2 you were asked to comment on the adequacy of the list of beliefs which identified a theology as Christian. The present activity is about the adequacy of the above list of issues which might be central to an informal Christian theology of education. What would *you* have included in this list that isn't there? Is there anything in the list that *you* would have left out?

Comment on activity C3

Did you think that Christian teachers need guidance about matters of school discipline or classroom relationships? Or perhaps about whether there is any substance to the accusation that church schools or religious educators indoctrinate their children? There are chapters on both these subjects in *Christian Perspectives for Education*[6]. Did you think the distinctiveness of church schools in a secular state system should have been in the list? This is

---

[5] See e.g. John Polkinghorne, *One World - the interaction of science and theology* (London, SPCK, 1986), pp 89, 95, 106.
[6] Francis and Thatcher, *op.cit.*, chs 4 and 8.

excluded because a previous unit has already considered a range of problems associated with this pressing problem.

Would you have liked to see something in the list about Christian styles of management and leadership? This is undoubtedly an area of great concern and importance. The aim of this unit has been to introduce the possibility of there being a theology of education, at all. It has not been possible to deal with all the issues in such a short space. But if a possible Christian style of management had been included, it would have been one of the hardest issues to write about.

C3 Theology in context

So far we have looked at theology and education and seen that there are difficulties in bringing them together in something called the theology of education. But we are not quite ready to 'do' some theology of education. Having outlined some necessary features of Christian theology, we need to log some further features of the intellectual and social context[7] in which theologians and educators do their work.

Theology and religious studies

Since the 1960s religious studies has grown as a discipline separate from Christian theology. In several universities the new discipline has supplanted the older one. There are great gains for Christian theology as a result of the emergence of religious studies. As a result of religious studies we know much more about the religions of the world, together with their similarities and differences. We are in a better position to understand religion as a darker, disruptive, even destructive force in human life. Religious studies has enabled the study of religion, including the Christian religion, without commitment to religious beliefs or practices, only to the impartial methods that are necessary to the study. Because it investigates religions on a global scale and brackets out commitment to any of them, it is thought to be a more appropriate form of study of religion in an apparently 'secular', yet multi-religious world.

The danger of the very success of religious studies is that it has led to a displacement of the equally important content and methods of theology in schools, colleges and universities. There are clear differences between theology and religious studies. Christian theology is the systematic reflection on God and

---

[7] Hodgson (*op. cit.,* note 2 above) includes 'cultural history and theology', and 'cultural context (situation, social location)', among his list of five types of sources of theology (p 27).

belief in God, by Christians, for Christians[8]. It is a ministry, within the church, for the church, and the ministry of theology is that of enabling the people of God to have an informed grasp of their faith and to be able to communicate it to others. It takes place within the church, and it stands within one or more of the different Christian traditions. This is not to say that a Christian membership ticket is needed before the study of theology can be undertaken; only that the aims, and so the content, of the different disciplines of theology and religious studies are themselves different (even though they at many points overlap).

The most influential exponent of the discipline of religious studies in the last 30 years has been Professor Ninian Smart, who combines a vast knowledge of the world's religions with a sophisticated method for studying them. It is less well known that Smart is also an Anglican, and that in recent work he writes as a theologian offering a global Christian vision of reality or *darsana*. In his co-authored book *Christian Systematic Theology in a World-Context* (Smart and Konstantine, 1991), Smart combines theology and religious studies in a way that may offer a new start in the co-operation between them. This is a way that should be seriously considered by teachers and lecturers in both theology and religious studies.

On the one hand, the vision of reality that Smart and Konstantine commend is completely rooted in Christian belief in one God, Father, Son and Holy Spirit. They say[9]:

> Our vision flows from our feel for the Trinity. It is our sense of the social Trinity which explains how God is Love. This informs our whole viewpoint and ethos. We consider too that in surveying the sorrows of the world, which run like dark shadows through the beauties of the cosmos, only a God who is willing to come into our life and suffer in the world could contemplate the dread and wonderful task of creating us and all those other creatures who share the pains and risks of living in the light.'

This is a vision that begins from within a particular faith, and is offered as an expression of loyalty to it[10]. The global vision offered by theology is able to draw freely from religious studies. On the other hand, religious studies is[11]:

> quite independent of affiliations: it is in no way subordinate to Christian theology.... Its primary focus is the polymethodic exploration of religions and to some degree also secular anthropology, art history and various other methods or approaches to the study of religions, without fear or favour. It is thus an absurdity that often the study of world religions is placed institutionally under Christian divinity schools.... So in relating our Christian systematic theology to the milieu of religious studies we wish to affirm clearly that we are trying to make use of results independently arrived at.

---

[8] Nothing is said here about the structure, or different branches of theology. On this topic see Maurice Wiles, *What is Theology?* (Oxford, Oxford University Press, 1976).

[9] Ninian Smart and Steven Konstantine, *Christian Systematic Theology in a World Context* (London, Marshall Pickering, 1991), p 10.

[10] Smart and Konstantine, *op.cit.*, p 18.

[11] Smart and Konstantine, *op.cit.*, p 19.

This is an account of religious studies which both recognises its independence from theology and its usefulness for theology. Religious studies is a discipline which is equal to theology but different. Each has a vital task to perform, and each is able to assist the other. This is a positive, constructive statement of how the two disciplines stand, each in relation to the other.

Theology and culture

This sub-section suggests that teachers have to teach in a climate of unbelief and that this climate has a pervasive effect on what is expected of them. In *Christian Theology and Religious Education* the theologian Professor Daniel Hardy has warned in similar vein against the reduction of religion to culture[12]. Hardy addresses 'the diminished place of religious belief and commitment' in the whole of the western hemisphere. He links this diminution with 'the assimilation of religious beliefs and practices to the very tools which have been used to analyse them'[13]. He thinks that the methods used by religious studies have already caused us to lose, to fail to understand or appreciate the beliefs and practices of religion. Hardy's case is that 'religious beliefs and practices have - at least in some sense - a transcendent content but an innerworldly location'[14], and religious studies is in danger of missing them because it regards both of these 'as cultural in origin, and as such only human[15]. This is what he means by 'the cultural reduction of religion', the loss of appreciation of the full reality of God together with a loss of appreciation of how religious beliefs affect the human heart. The consequences of this neglect of transcendence are what Hardy calls 'deficient subjectivity' and 'deficient objectivity'. Together these make for a deficient religious education.

Deficient subjectivity arises from the deficient methods of study of religion. The human person (and not God) is given primacy 'as proponent and student of religious commitment and practice', and 'both believing and study are placed within the realm of human capability' (and so outside divine grace and illumination). Both the believer and the student become separated 'from the transcendent illumination of reason and religion'[16]. This is what deficient subjectivity means. It is an entrapment within a purely human understanding of religious phenomena, within a humanly-constructed (albeit religious) world. Deficient objectivity arises from the same deficient methods of study. Instead of God, phenomena pertaining to God take precedence, leading to a forgetfulness of divine being. For example, 'In the case of Christianity, it is often considered

---

[12] Daniel W. Hardy, 'Theology and the cultural reduction of religion', in Jeff Astley and Leslie J. Francis (eds), *Christian Theology and Religious Education: connections and contradictions* (London, SPCK, 1996).

[13] Hardy, *op.cit.*, p 16 (author's emphasis).

[14] Hardy, *op.cit.*, p 17 (author's emphasis).

[15] Hardy, *ibid.*, (author's emphasis).

[16] Hardy, *op.cit.*, p 19 (author's emphasis).

unnecessary to refer to the determining role of the trinitarian God and the fundamental structure of Christian religious theory and practices which understanding of God implies. The result is what can be called a "deficient objectivity"[17]. The perpetuation of these methods of religious study is certain to promote an inadequate and reductive religious education.

Hardy thinks 'these problems are so severe that the argument about the place accorded to religion or religious education is relatively unimportant'. He advocates a return to the appreciation of the 'worth-ship' of God where God and the human relation to God are explicitly acknowledged.[18]

> Worship designates worth or positive value, the honour or dignity which is inherent in the one in whom (or which) it is found. In the case of divine worship, worth-ship designates one in whom there is maximum value by virtue of the occurrence of the highest form of the fundamental 'transcendental notes' - unity, truth, goodness and beauty - which mark being as such.

When God is accorded the worth-ship which is God's due, everything, literally, which is other than God is seen in relation to God. God is constitutive for human life, and (if Hardy is right), religious studies places God last, not first, in its endeavours.

The contrast between Smart's and Hardy's approach to religious studies cannot easily be reconciled. Smart also wrote an essay for *Christian Theology and Religious Education*, and a reading of both of them together[19] provides a fine introduction to the tensions between religious studies and theology.

Activity C4

In the last two sub-sections we have touched on some alarmingly big issues in religious studies and theology. In this activity there are three questions about the content of what we have covered. The fourth question is a reflection about your experience as a teacher.

- On the basis of what you have read so far in this unit, what would you say were the main differences between theology and religious studies?
- What is Hardy's main worry about the impact of culture on belief in God?
- What did Hardy mean by 'deficient subjectivity' and 'deficient objectivity'?
- In your work as a teacher (and perhaps in your pre-service and in-service training) have you found evidence of the tendencies Hardy describes? If so, write down some of the areas and issues you have identified.

---

[17] Hardy, *op.cit.*, p 20.
[18] Hardy, *op.cit.*, p 32.
[19] Smart's essay, 'Global Christian theology and education' is chapter 1. Hardy's essay is chapter 2.

Comment on activity C4

First, the main difference between theology and religious studies is that theology presupposes the reality of God, while religious studies presupposes the reality of religion. A second difference is that theology serves the people of God who are engaged in the venture of faith. Religious studies serves students of religion who are engaged in the venture of understanding the diverse phenomena of religion. A third difference is that theology inherits several traditions of Christian thought about God which go back to the bible and attempt to release the resources of faith for every subsequent generation. Religious studies inherits the histories of all religions and attempts to release the resources of diverse knowledge about them.

Second, Hardy's main worry about the impact of culture on belief in God is that culture reduces belief in God to something else. Consequently it regards religion as a human phenomenon only, and belief in God becomes something optional and controversial.

Third, deficient subjectivity is the inadequate understanding of the human subject apart from God or the relation to God which is expressed in worship. Deficient objectivity is the inadequate understanding of the object of religious study once belief in God has been suspended in the quest for religious objectivity.

Fourth, evidence you have written down in answer to this question would help to make a lively tutorial. The second part of this unit takes up some of the areas which may be illuminated by Hardy's description of how culture impacts upon religion. You might want to argue that religious education syllabuses generally suspend belief in God and regard religion as a purely human phenom-enon or that religious education often turns into something else (like personal, social and moral education); or that collective worship is not worship, because the proper object of worship has been replaced by something else. You might think that your degree or training course (whether or not it included something called theology) was a cop-out because it shied away from the difficult task of relating the study of theology to the real needs of Christian teachers.

Theology and tradition

It is widely believed that Britain is largely a secular[20] society. Yet demand for places in church schools is strong, like support for religious education. But if

---

[20] Grace Davie argues convincingly that 'for the great majority of people' in contemporary Britain there is *both* 'a lack of attachment to religious organizations' which 'implies a lack of discipline in their spiritual orientation', *and*, for that reason, an openness 'to the widely diverse forms of the sacred which appear within contemporary society'. See her *Religion in Britain since 1945: believing without belonging* (Oxford, Blackwell, 1994), p 199. So it could be true that contemporary Britons are both less and more religious counterparts of 50 or 100 years ago.

there is a pervasive 'climate of unbelief'[21] in contemporary society, how does this society impinge on Christian institutions and people working inside it? What hope is there for passing on the tradition of faith if it has already been largely lost, and few people are even aware of the religious hiatus in their lives because they have not noticed its absence?

One of the most influential books in moral and social philosophy in the 1980s was Alasdair MacIntyre's *After Virtue*. MacIntyre took a pessimistic view of the forgetfulness of societies influenced by Christianity of their past traditions and roots. We shall only borrow from him the powerful thought-experiment with which *After Virtue* begins. The experiment will help us to reflect on the strange position of the believing church in the unbelieving world, or, more narrowly, the church school in a secular society, or religious education in a secular curriculum. These are the first two paragraphs of the book[22].

A Disquieting Suggestion

Imagine that the natural sciences were to suffer the effects of a catastrophe. A series of environmental disasters are blamed by the general public on the scientists. Widespread riots occur, laboratories are burnt down, physicists are lynched, books and instruments are destroyed. Finally a Know-Nothing political movement takes power and successfully abolishes science teaching in schools and universities, imprisoning and executing the remaining scientists. Later still there is a reaction against this destructive movement and enlightened people seek to revive science, although they have largely forgotten what it was. But all that they possess are fragments: a knowledge of experiments detached from any knowledge of the theoretical context which gave them significance; parts of theories unrelated either to the other bits and pieces of theory which they possess or to experiment; instruments whose use has been forgotten; half-chapters from books, single pages from articles, not always fully legible because torn and charred. None the less all these fragments are reembodied in a set of practices which go under the revived names of physics, chemistry and biology. Adults argue with each other about the respective merits of relativity theory, evolutionary theory and phlogiston theory, although they possess only a very partial knowledge of each. Children learn by heart the surviving portions of the periodic table and recite as incantations some of the theorems of Euclid. Nobody, or almost nobody, realises that what they are doing is not natural science in any proper sense at all. For everything that they do and say conforms to certain canons of consistency and coherence and those contexts which would be needed to make sense of what they are doing have been lost, perhaps irretrievably.

In such a culture men would use expressions such as 'neutrino', 'mass', 'specific gravity', 'atomic weight' in systematic and often interrelated ways which would resemble in lesser or greater degrees the ways in which such expressions had been used in earlier times before scientific knowledge had been so largely lost. But many of the beliefs presupposed by the use of these

---

[21] Adrian Thatcher argues this in 'The recovery of Christian education', in Francis and Thatcher, *op.cit.,* chapter 10.2.
[22] Alasdair MacIntyre, *After Virtue: a study in moral theory* (London, Duckworth, 1981), pp 1-2.

expressions would have been lost and there would appear to be an element of arbitrariness and even of choice in their application which would appear very surprising to us. What would appear to be rival and competing premises for which no further argument could be given would abound. Subjectivist theories of science would appear and would be criticised by those who held that the notion of truth embodied in what they took to be science was incompatible with subjectivism.

The purpose of sketching this imaginary world was to advance the hypothesis 'that in the actual world which we inhabit the language of morality is in the same state of grave disorder as the language of natural science in the imaginary world which I described'. While MacIntyre was interested primarily in the 'grave state of disorder' that had afflicted the language of morality, the imaginary world may be used to highlight the grave disorder in the language of theology.

Activity C5

Do you agree that there really are 'disquieting' parallels to be drawn between this imaginary world of science fiction and the real world where the language of theology and religion survives in fragments? Please write down some possible parallels between the world after the Know-Nothing party has left it and the actual world where you may have responsibility for the teaching of religious, and perhaps moral education.

When you have identified these points, the next step will be to assess how strong they are and whether they tell us anything about the place of religion in a secular society.

Comment on activity C5

Your list might have included points like the following ones organised under the two headings of science and religion.

Science	Religion
widespread ignorance about science	widespread ignorance about religion (and about morality)
the sense that much of the scientific past is fragmentary	the sense that much of the religious past is fragmentary
nobody realises that what they are doing is not science	nobody realises that what they are doing is not religion

teachers of science are not grounded in the traditions of science	teachers of religion are not grounded in the traditions of religion
children are being taught science but they are not learning science	children are being taught religion but they are not learning religion
rival theories of science are taught	rival theories of right and wrong are taught
people cannot agree about which theories are right	people cannot agree about which theories are right
conventional words like 'neutrino' are used but the beliefs assumed by them are lost	conventional words like 'God', 'right', 'wrong' are used but the beliefs assumed by them are lost

Some of these parallels will be rejected as unfair. Indeed they may be. The strength of the parallels may perhaps be assessed by the extent to which they support the contentions of Hardy that religious belief has been so reduced by culture, and that the damage inflicted on it is so grave that the place of religion in the curriculum is 'unimportant'. You may of course think that Hardy has overstated his case. If you have been able to make positive connections between the two worlds, perhaps you have already illustrated to yourself why it is that the language of theology is generally neither understood nor cared about, why the very possibility of something called 'the theology of education' is difficult to envisage, and why educators are unimpressed by the attempt of Christians to share their *darsana*.

In this section some suggestions have been made about the impact on Christian theology of religious studies and the broad intellectual background in which theology is set, and some of the possible effects on education. This background contains both resources and dangers for theology.

C4 Religious pluralism and religious education

In the second part of the unit we draw fully on the conclusions of the first part. Taking the informal approach to the theology of education discussed above, three problems which were identified as high on the agenda of Christians working in education will be considered. This discussion has prepared us for the prospect that there can be no easy accommodation between Christian theology and the social, cultural and intellectual background in which it is set, and to which schools, colleges and universities belong. This tension may be acutely felt by students on this course.

The extent of religious pluralism in Britain

In 1991, in England, Scotland and Wales, there were 51.8 million in the white ethnic grouping. All other ethnic groupings can be counted in thousands. There were 500,000 black Caribbeans, 212,000 black Africans, and 178,000 black 'others'. There were 840,000 Indians, 477,000 Pakistanis, 163,000 Bangladeshi, 157,000 Chinese and 198,000 Asians[23]. Many Afro-Caribbean people are Christian. Most Pakistani and Bangladeshi people are Muslims, who number between 900,000 and 1.3 million[24].

Britain is clearly a multi-cultural society but these figures show that 95% of the population is white. Substantial numbers of the remaining 5%, mainly black, are Christians. The moral (and theological) belief that all people deserve equal treatment and respect sometimes translates into the false statistical belief that there is something like equality of numbers between the different cultures represented in Britain. The multi-cultural approach to religious education often overlooks the actual proportions of religious minorities. The white majority may to some extent be labelled 'post-Christian'. But the most serious problem about differentiating between people on religious grounds at all, is that other differences are overlooked or altogether ignored. Yet these very non-religious differences turn out to be ones that are theologically more interesting.

People may just as easily be divided up by wealth and income. Division between people of different classes and social backgrounds has been, and to some extent remains, rooted in British society. Religious education is generally silent about the position and status of women within religions, yet the pervasive influence of patriarchy in all the religions might indicate that women across religions have much in common, i.e. oppression. There are minorities of people who are disabled, other minorities who are lesbian, bisexual or gay. These differences may actually be more acutely felt by these minorities than the kind of difference religious educators are keen to set before us. Religion is not a separate characteristic which can be conveniently separated from other differences. The suppressed problem for religious studies is whether religion is a genus, i.e. whether there can ever be something called religion which can be extrapolated from the broader social and cultural contexts within which the religion and the religious believer is set. There is considerable support among

---

[23] Steve Bruce, *Religion in Modern Britain* (Oxford, Oxford University Press, 1995), p 80.

[24] Bruce, *op. cit.*, p 79.

Christian theologians that no such genus even exists[25], yet this view is scarcely made available to students and teachers who do not study Christian theology.

Christian theology and the non-Christian religions

Whatever the answer might be to the question whether the differentiation of people by religious affiliation is misleading or unhelpful, it continues to be done, and nowhere is this more obvious than in religious education after the Education Reform Act. Syllabuses must 'reflect the fact that the religious traditions in Great Britain are in the main Christian whilst taking account of the teaching and practices of the other principal religions represented in Great Britain'[26]. A standard theological approach towards the non-Christian religions in the 1980s is to invoke the well-worn categories of exclusivism, inclusivism, pluralism[27]. An exclusivist is someone who holds that salvation is to be found exclusively in Jesus Christ. An inclusivist is someone who believes that salvation is exclusively in Christ but possible among the non-Christian religions because Christ is present among them. A pluralist is someone who holds that all religions are equally ways of salvation, or approaches to God or the Real.

There is merit in each of these positions, but in the 1990s and into the next century (when an adequate theology of religions will become an increasingly urgent task) it is necessary to go beyond all of them. They portray too easily the tendency to affix labels, to indulge in '-isms', to prefer theories to realities, and to ignore all other differences between people than religious ones. Neither does the term 'salvation' translate into ready equivalents outside Christianity. A fresh start can be made by beginning instead with the Christian doctrine of God, i.e. the Trinity, and acknowledging that religious difference is only one of many differences which must be explored if people are to be understood theologically.

Activity C6

The previous two sections have stressed that religious differences between people may be misleading. This activity is in two parts. First make a list of fairly obvious *non-religious* differences between people. Then consider

---

[25] For example, Milbank, Cobb and Thomas, all in Gavin D'Costa (ed.), *Christian Uniqueness Reconsidered: the myth of a pluralistic theology of religions* (New York, Orbis, 1990), pp 176, 81, 57.

[26] *Education Reform Act 1988*, s.8(3).

[27] For an introduction, see Gavin D'Costa, *Theology and Religious Pluralism* (London, SCM Press, 1986) and Alan Race, *Christians and Religious Pluralism* (London, SCM Press, 1983). D'Costa writes as an inclusivist, Race as a pluralist. A more exclusivist view is presented by P. Sookhdeo (ed.), *Jesus Christ the Only Way* (Carlisle, Paternoster, 1978) and A.D. Clarke and B.W. Winter, *One God, One Lord in a World of Religious Pluralism* (Cambridge, Tyndale House, 1991).

whether the differences you selected are greater than differences that *are* religious. (Don't worry if the reason for this activity is not immediately apparent: the next two sections also deal with religious difference.)

Comment on activity C6

Several of the obvious differences have already been mentioned previously. People are male and female, young, middle-aged, or old. They may be very rich or very poor, and their relative wealth will determine their economic power, freedom and opportunity. People are born into different cultures and are differently conditioned in different societies. Some people have no educational opportunities. People born in the present century may have wealth undreamed of in earlier times. The possession of good health constitutes a further difference.

The greater the list of differences, the more obvious it becomes that religious differences may at least be less significant than first thought. There are also huge religious differences between people within the same religion, as Christians know well. What may be needed is a theological account of differences, including religious ones, which actually unite people together.

The Trinity and religious pluralism

There has been a resurgence of work on the Trinity in the last 15 years, and previous neglect of it has led to a lack of awareness of its relevance to the problem of religious pluralism. The Roman Catholic theologian Gavin D'Costa has provided an outline of what a trinitarian approach to the world's religions would look like. The doctrine of the Person of Christ has traditionally and rightly been stressed in relation to the non-Christian religions, but the doctrine of the Person of the Spirit has rarely been understood in this context. The difference it makes to a theology of religions is profound. Beginning with Christ, D'Costa notes that Christians hold that 'God has disclosed himself in the contingencies and particularity of the person Jesus'[28]. But they also hold that 'the activity of the Spirit cannot be confined to Christianity'. The possibility of the presence of God the Spirit in the world's religions is capable of transforming Christian attitudes towards them.

The contrast between 'universal' and 'particular' helps us to understand the main point about a trinitarian theology of religions. There is a particular revelation of God in Jesus Christ, but there is also a 'universal activity of God

---

[28] Gavin D'Costa, 'Christ, the Trinity and religious plurality', in D'Costa, *op.cit.*, p 18.

in the history of humankind'[29]. This activity takes place through the Spirit who in Christian theology is, with Christ, fully God. 'Whenever and wherever God reveals herself, in a manner often unrecognised or misunderstood by Christians, this is the God who is disclosed in Christ.' But what can be recognised and understood is that 'God is love' (1 John 4.8) and the doctrine of the Trinity teaches that loving communion between the Persons in God is the heart of all reality, divine and human. 'A Christocentric trinitarianism discloses loving relationship as the proper mode of being. Hence love of neighbor (which includes Hindus, Buddhists, and others) is an imperative for all Christians.'

This account of how the Trinity helps us to understand the problem of religious pluralism is a fine example of a case where attention to the roots of Christian doctrine provides rich rewards. The account retains an emphasis on Jesus as the complete revelation of God while acknowledging the activity of the Holy Spirit beyond the confines of Church and Christendom. The Spirit also aids us in thinking and acting towards our neighbours in other religions with a Christian love which has not always been apparent inside the churches. The way Christians participate 'in Jesus' sonship', says D'Costa, is 'by living the pattern of his crucified self-giving love and being empowered and guided by the Spirit to instantiate this pattern within our differing socio-historical contexts. It is through this modality of love that we are called into communion with God. Hence, love of neighbour is co-essential with the love of God'[30].

D'Costa provides a trinitarian theology of religions which presses into service the renewed interest among theologians in the Holy Trinity. This emphasis has much enriched Christian theology in the last few years. In a global inter-religious context it recognises simultaneously both the finality of Jesus Christ as God's self-revelation and the revelation of the Spirit inside and outside Christian traditions bearing witness to the love which is found supremely in the mutual relation between Father and Son. In this way God is acknowledged both in the 'particular' tradition of Christianity and in the 'universal' history of humanity.

The Anglican theologian John Milbank[31] has drawn attention to the character of the Holy Trinity as a single divine life of Persons where each Person is different from the others, yet the difference between them is essential to the divine unity. In other words, in the divine life and nowhere else does difference contribute to the Love which is the Trinity in its being and operation. While differences between human persons may lead to conflict, violence and the misuse of power, only in God is difference made into communion. The Christian life is a summons to share in God's trinitarian life which is a kingdom of peace and love.

---

[29] D'Costa, *op.cit.,* p 19.

[30] D'Costa, *op.cit.,* p 20.

[31] John Milbank, *Theology and Social Theory: beyond secular reason* (Oxford, Blackwell, 1990), chapter 12.

Neighbour-love and the world religions

The doctrine of the Trinity provides Christians with a profound understanding of God's interaction with humanity. It is recognised, however, that the trinitarian approach to world religions may be unfamiliar. Nonetheless a similar position, i.e. the twin imperatives of loving God and neighbour but without an obvious trinitarian theology to support it, is clearly found in the teaching of Jesus. When asked about the criteria 'to inherit eternal life', Jesus replied that it is necessary to 'love the Lord your God with all your heart, and with all your soul, with all your strength, and with all your mind; and your neighbour as yourself' (Luke 10.27).

The lawyer who was in dialogue with Jesus at the time was vexed about the identification of 'neighbour'. Wanting to justify his question, he asked, 'But who is my neighbour?'

That, too, is our problem, for the more we allow ourselves to restrict the range of the term, the more we are able to place people outside the love we are taught to show them. But the reply of Jesus expands, and does not limit, the term. The lawyer is silenced by the parable of the good Samaritan. In this parable (Luke 10.29-37) the priest and the Levite do not even recognise the responsibility of neighbour-love to the traveller who 'was set upon by robbers'. It takes a non-Jew, i.e. a Samaritan, to recognise this. He was 'the one who showed him kindness' (Luke 10.37). Both the giving and receiving of neighbour-love are determined by human, not religious, considerations. Neighbour-love, like the work of Spirit, recognises no boundaries.

Activity C7

Several theological ideas have been kaleidoscoped together in the last two sections. Please go back over them and make a list of up to six of the main points that were made. Then ask yourself which of the ideas were new to you; which ones you agreed or disagreed with; and which ones you would like clarified more before you make up your mind.

Comment on activity C7

Some of the important points to emerge from the above activity may suggest that:

- religious differences have been generally over-emphasised;
- the presence of the Holy Spirit beyond the boundaries of church and Christendom has been under-emphasised;

- the doctrine of the Trinity has been seriously neglected;
- in the life of the Trinity the difference between the Persons contributes to their life of loving communion;
- the gospel is an invitation to share in the life of the Trinity;
- the love of neighbour is not confined to Christians, yet whenever and wherever it happens, Christ is present through the Holy Spirit.

C5 Spiritual and moral development

Church schools have a God-given opportunity to draw on the resources of faith in specifying and promoting what the spiritual and moral development of children amounts to. In 1994 the Department for Education stated 'The Government is concerned that insufficient attention has been paid explicitly to the spiritual, moral and cultural aspects of pupils' development, and would encourage schools to address how the curriculum and other activities might best contribute to this crucial dimension of education'[32]. If Christian theology cannot help here, it cannot help anywhere.

Humanism in religious guise?

A case for theological guidance in arriving at a practical understanding of spiritual and moral development may be made by considering the inadequacy of government guidelines on the topic. The government's discussion paper, published under the title *Spiritual and Moral Development*, marginalises God almost completely[33].

In another essay in *Christian Theology and Religious Education* Adrian Thatcher has subjected the portrayal of spiritual and moral development given there to sustained theological scrutiny and showed it to provide guidance which is importantly inconsistent with an overt Christian approach to these immensely important topics[34]. A reading of this essay is highly recommended. One of the suggestions Thatcher makes is that a society which has largely allowed its religious heritage to evaporate now expresses its regret by re-introducing former talk about spirituality and morality, while usurping the meanings that the Christian tradition once gave them.

---

[32] Department For Education, *Circular 1/94, Religious Education and Collective Worship*, (London, Department for Education, 1994), paragraph 1, p 9.

[33] National Curriculum Council, *Spiritual and Moral Development - a Discussion Paper* (April 1993), pp 2-3.

[34] Adrian Thatcher, '"Policing the Sublime": a wholly (holy?) ironic approach to the spiritual and moral development of children', in Astley and Francis, *op.cit.*, pp 117-139. See especially pp 120-130 for a detailed analysis of the concept of 'spiritual development' in the paper.

At this point MacIntyre's 'disquieting suggestion' (discussed above) is useful to us because it suggests discontinuity between the present generation's largely secular attempts to impart a religious and moral sense and the past traditions of doing these things which may by now be more or less irrecoverable. 'An "age of unbelief" might feel uneasy about its lost heritage. It might disguise its unbelief by borrowing the language of religion and employing it for different (and diversionary) purposes'[35], such as fostering the illusion that it respects religion, or blaming teachers for the alleged failure of children to discriminate between right and wrong.

The definitions of spiritual development offered in the government's publications do not draw on religious understandings of this term. That is why, in its attempt to provide neutral guidance, the Department of Education and Employment (its name will doubtless have changed again by the time this unit appears in print) has opted for a secular humanism which borrows the language of religion and imposes other meanings upon it. Borrowing Hardy's analysis (discussed above) we may say that here is a prime example of how religion gets reduced to culture, resulting in deficient subjectivity and objectivity. A flavour of this approach among the welter of literature which has recently appeared is the description of the scope of spiritual development offered to school inspectors[36].

> Spiritual development relates to that aspect of inner life through which pupils acquire insights into their personal existence which are of enduring worth. It is characterised by reflection, the attribution of meaning to experience, valuing a non-material dimension to life and intimations of an enduring reality. 'Spiritual' is not synonymous with 'religious'; all areas of the curriculum may contribute to pupils' spiritual development.

While there will be elements of this description of spiritual development which may be congenial to Christians, criticism of it will be confined to a single observation: the absence of God. What might we make of spiritual development if we began instead with some of the presuppositions of theology which we thought about in the foregoing sections?

Theology and spiritual development

A spiritual person is, in Christian faith, someone who is, at least to some extent, holy. Holiness is not measured by overt religious piety but by the extent to which one has oriented one's life towards the love of God and neighbour. Spirituality is about growth in, or into, the Christian life, and the Christian life

---

[35] Thatcher, *op.cit.,* p 132.
[36] *Framework for Inspection* (revised August 1993), cited in and endorsed by *Spiritual, Moral, Social and Cultural Development: an OFSTED discussion paper* (London, Office for Standards in Education, Feb. 1994), p 8.

is the love of God and neighbour. The OFSTED version of 'spiritual' just cited is hard to reconcile with the gospel version of it. OFSTED thinks spiritual development is about cultivating the individual's 'inner life'. A Christian account of spiritual development is relational, about our relationships with God, with our neighbours and ourselves, which are suffused with glimpses of divine love. OFSTED characterises it by reflection and 'the attribution of meaning to experience'. Unfortunately the latter term is almost impossible to make sense of, while the former, important though it is to religious faith (where it is generally called meditation), is primarily a mental act whereas a Christian account is about the development of the whole person in relation to God and neighbour. The command of Jesus is a 'holistic' one, reminding us that love requires the engagement of heart, soul, mind and strength[37].

The OFSTED approach to spiritual development is gripped by the notion of individuality and the problem of the individual's reflexive relationship to herself. While there is grudging admission of 'human interaction'[38] there is a complete lack in government literature of any mention of neighbour-love, or (to use an equally biblical word) justice[39]. In contrast it is open to Christians to illustrate what is involved in spiritual development by deploying the parable of the sheep and the goats (Matthew 25.31-46).

This parable of the sheep and the goats is unmistakable in its picture of what counts when the nations appear at the last judgement. 'When the Son of Man comes in his glory', those who 'have my Father's blessing', who are to 'take possession of the kingdom that has been ready for you since the world was made' (Matthew 25.34) are the people who ministered to Jesus when he was *incognito* among the hungry, the thirsty, the strangers, the naked, the ill, and the imprisoned. The spiritual discernment of the righteous was insufficient to save them from 'the eternal fire that is ready for the devil and his angels' (Matthew 25.41). That was because they did not recognise the identification of Jesus with the very people whom they had completely overlooked.

Neighbour-love and the crisis over values

Government accounts of moral development also do not mention the values of love or justice; neither does the simple notion of 'neighbour' appear among them[40]. As pupils 'develop a sense of morality', they[41]:

---

[37] See also Mark's version of the Great Commandments (Mark 12.29-31) where the commands are attributed to Jesus, not as in Luke, to the lawyer.

[38] OFSTED, *op.cit.,* p 9.

[39] Kenneth Leech demolishes these inward-looking and privatistic notions of spirituality in his *The Eye of the Storm* (London, Darton, Longman and Todd, 1993), especially chapter 1.

[40] National Curriculum Council, *op.cit.,* pp 4-5.

[41] OFSTED, *op.cit.,* pp 10-11.

should become more able to explore the place of reason in ethical matters and, as autonomous moral agents, acquire value-systems which are their own (rather than simply transmitted by others and accepted uncritically), together with the understanding that their behaviour and actions should derive from these beliefs and values.

The government's authors support the view that moral development is not about being in relationship but about being autonomous; that it is a matter of using reason, not about the engagement of the whole person; and that pupils should acquire their own independent value-systems, notwithstanding that such 'systems' might include the beliefs and values that white people are superior to black people, that a woman's place is in the home, that experiments with heroin injections are fun, and so on. All of this constitutes a grave matter of debate within the framework of public discourse that the government has initiated. From the point of view of a theological approach to moral development, it is obvious that neighbour-love has never even been considered. If an approach to morality had started here, the outcome would have been very different. Such an approach might have continued with the Sermon on the Mount (Matthew 5 to 7). A programme of moral development based on such sources is an urgent necessity.

Activity C8

The purpose of this activity is to demonstrate one of many possible connections that are able to be made between spiritual and moral development from a theological point of view. You are asked to read the parable of the sheep and the goats (Matthew 25.31-46) which was mentioned above and then write down your responses to the following prompts.

- With whom does the Son of Man identify in the parable?
- What was the fate of the righteous at the judgement, and why?
- What did the righteous fail to understand?
- What was the fate of the goats on the left, and why?
- What does the parable say about the religious basis of moral development?
- The parable provides one of the few pictures of the last judgement. What might it tell us about the judgement of non-Christian people?

Comment on activity C8

The first three questions are obvious enough. The Son of Man is found with the hungry, the thirsty, the strangers, the unclothed, the sick and the imprisoned. The righteous failed to understand that when they had visited Christ it was Christ whom they had visited. The fate of the goats is due to their inability to recognise that devotion to the king required revisioning the king's presence and serving him among the poor. Righteousness is found among the people who serve Christ through serving the needy.

The last two questions are harder to answer. Question 5 is intended to suggest that biblical faith always shows itself in self-giving action, and this suggestion confirms all we have considered in this unit about the love of God and our neighbours. In the language of the 1990s, this means that spiritual development is the basis of moral development. However else a secular society may wish to fill out the bare notion of moral development with content, Christian faith sees spiritual and moral development as inseparable.

The parable also confirms our earlier query about the usefulness of dividing people up according to religious differences. It may be significant that in the parable nations rather than individuals are being judged. The one difference that matters to the king is whether he was recognised and served among the groups of people who needed kindness to be shown to them. The parable affirms that the final judgement is about recognising and serving Christ among the needy, not about recognising him as a formal object of religious devotion.

Creation spirituality

When we asked earlier what Christian theology was, we built into the answer the belief that God was 'maker of heaven and earth'. What has come to be known as 'creation spirituality' is the discernment of God's presence in the natural world, and especially as that world is understood by the contemporary sciences, especially physics[42]. Creation spirituality is associated with Matthew Fox and in particular with his book *Creation Spirituality*. This is an essential read for anyone who wants to link spirituality firmly with the earth as God's gift. Fox writes[43]:

> Creation, then, at its core, is about relation. It is the spiralling, dancing, crouching, springing, leaping, surprising act of relatedness, of communing, of responding, of letting go, of being. Being is about relation. Eckhart says that 'relation is the essence of everything that exists' and that 'isness is God'. Thus all creation is a trace, a footprint, an offspring of the Godhead. Creation is the passing by of divinity in the form of isness. It is God's shadow in our midst. It is sacred. All our relationships are sacred. Native peoples know this. Jesus taught it.... Christians and other believers must learn anew the sacredness of creation. Without this, the 'first article of faith', we are lost.

Creation spirituality enables bridges to be built between Christian faith and environmental studies. It regards the pollution of the land, sea and air, and the

---

[42] See e.g. Angela Tilby, *Science and the Soul* (London, SPCK, 1993).
[43] Matthew Fox, *Creation Spirituality* (New York, Harper Collins, 1991), p 9 (my emphasis).

destruction of natural habitats as great sins against God. It locates the natural world as a source of spiritual discernment. While creation spirituality deserves more time than we can give to it in this unit, it is another example of a biblical and historical approach to spirituality which has been overlooked entirely by the secular curriculum-makers.

The Holy Spirit and human spirituality

Our work on the world religions led to the conclusion that the Holy Spirit is not confined to Christianity, and the 'fruits of the Spirit' are not confined to Christians. Smart and Konstantine (1991) speak of the Holy Spirit as unveiled 'in the transformed lives and creativity of men and women'. It is 'the dynamic power of the Spirit which enables human beings to grow and mature spiritually and to realize their creative potentialities through freedom'[44]. We might say that wherever there are traces of the mutual love between Father and Son, there is God's Spirit in the midst of us. Since God is the source of all Goodness, Truth and Beauty, we may say that wherever these 'transcendental' realities are glimpsed by us, there is the Creator Spirit showing them to us and enabling us to appreciate them. In this way there will always be a spiritual element to what the National Curriculum calls 'cultural development', since some of the inspiration that blows through art and literature, through music and sculpture, comes from a divine source.

C6 Collective worship

All teachers in the schools of Britain will have their own thoughts about school worship. Among the welter of official publications about worship, once again the theological dimension is crucially absent. In this section some suggestions will be made from a theological perspective.

Christian, corporate, or collective?

The government's circular *Religious Education and Collective Worship* makes the important distinction between 'corporate' and 'collective' worship. 'Worship', it says[45]:

---

[44] Smart and Konstantine, *op. cit.*, p 300.

[45] Circular 1/94, *op. cit.*, paragraph 57, p 21. For a trenchant criticism of the entire approach to worship adopted by the Circular, see John Hull, 'Can one speak of God or to God in education?', in Frances Young (ed.), *Dare We Speak of God in Public?* (London, Mowbray, 1995), chapter 2.

is not defined in the legislation and in the absence of any such definition it should be taken to have its natural and ordinary meaning. That is, it must in some sense reflect something special or separate from ordinary school activities and it should be concerned with reverence or veneration paid to a divine being or power. However, worship in schools will necessarily be of a different character from worship amongst a group with beliefs in common. The legislation reflects this difference in referring to 'collective worship' rather than 'corporate worship'.

It is unfortunate that there is a veritable pile of contradictions in this part of the circular. The distinction between 'collective' and 'corporate' is based on the assumption that the former is carried out (one hesitates to say 'offered') by a group which lacks common beliefs, while the latter has no such lack. Well, an aim of worship earlier in the circular was precisely 'to develop community spirit, promote a common ethos and shared values, and reinforce positive attitudes'[46]. Some common beliefs will be needed for this. The 'natural and ordinary meaning' of worship is not, for Christians 'concerned with reverence or veneration paid to a divine being or power'. If it were, any god, or perhaps the devil, would do. Christians worship the one God who is Father, Son and Spirit. The circular reminds us that the legislation requires collective worship to be 'wholly or mainly of a broadly Christian character', but such worship is of course corporate worship, not collective worship, because Christians are emphatically 'a group with beliefs in common'.

There is no intention here of unravelling these contradictions (the knot is probably untiable), only to introduce the missing theological dimension to this otherwise impoverished discussion of school worship (which may increase these contradictions further).

The uselessness of Christian worship

Christians worship God out of sheer gratitude for what God has done for them. Worship is the human response to God's saving initiative. They worship God for God's sake, and because God has become known to them through Jesus Christ by the Holy Spirit. As Douglas Davies says[47]:

> In Christianity worship is the human response to God's greatness, both in creating the universe and in providing salvation for humanity. In worship, men and women become aware of themselves as finite creatures on the one hand and as morally limited beings on the other.... From its first days as a new religion, Christianity has been a community of worshipping people. In very many respects worship came before theology, prayer before doctrine. An old Latin phrase, *lex orandi, lex credendi*, refers directly to this fact of Christian

---

[46]Circular 1/94, *op.cit.,* paragraph 50, p 20.
[47] Douglas Davies, 'Christianity', in J. Holm and J. Bowker (eds), *Worship* (London, Pinter Publishers, 1994), pp 35-6.

history that the law of prayer establishes the law of belief, or, in other words, that what is to be believed emerges from prayerful worship.

Worship could hardly be more central to the practice of faith and is, in more than one sense, logically prior to it. Since it is for God's sake, no other justification or purpose need be offered for it. That is why Jeff Astley speaks of its sheer 'pointlessness'. 'Worship is not for anything; it has no ulterior point or purpose - least of all an educational one. Religious people do not worship in order to do or become anything else, to teach or to learn. Worship is an end in itself.'[48]

The uselessness of worship, then, must be stated with some force, in deliberate contrast to the common, functionalist justifications (discussed below) which are likely to be offered for its continuation in schools. Worship is an exception (the most obvious one?) to the very many human activities which are instrumental or goal-directed; indeed the more one's life is filled with activities serving particular purposes or having to have a point, the greater the attractiveness of pointless worship. The distinction is not, of course, absolute. There are, we might say, 'derivative benefits' which follow from worship. Worship is also a learning experience. That is partly why the scriptures are read and sermons preached. Regular worship is likely to influence the characters of worshippers, or, as Westerhoff put it, 'liturgics' and 'catechetics' are intimately related[49]. Ultimately through worship one may expect to grow in love towards God and towards one's neighbours. All these outcomes may be desirable in themselves but attaining them is not why God is worshipped.

Worship and education

The maintenance of worship in schools is certain to attract criticism in a society which has largely cast off its religious heritage and has vocal religious and non-religious minorities within it. A counter-criticism, bravely developed by Brenda Watson, is to say that the aim of school worship must be educational. Its justification should lie, she argues, in the learning experience which worship offers pupils[50]. Worship is the key to understanding religion, and the key to understanding worship is participation. Since religious education uncontroversially involves finding out what religion is about, so worship is thought uncontroversially to be influential in bringing out religious discovery. So school worship must be compulsory (pupils would otherwise miss out on a valuable educational experience). The fact that worship is often badly carried out is an argument for investing in resources and training to do it better.

---

[48] Jeff Astley, 'The role of worship in Christian learning', *Religious Education* (79), p 244.

[49] J.H. Westerhoff, 'Liturgics and catechetics', *Worship*, 61, pp 510-16.

[50] Brenda Watson, *Education and Belief* (Oxford, Blackwell, 1987), pp 187-200.

Sometimes the educational justification for worship is combined with other supportive instrumental functions. Baroness Hooper, a government spokesperson, defended collective worship by claiming[51]:

> It is because such an act of worship can perform an important function in binding together members of a school and helping to develop their sense of community that we in this country make collective worship in schools a statutory requirement although other equally Christian countries do not do so. This educational value of worship must be clearly distinguished from confessional acts of worship which are properly pursued by practising Christians and members of other faiths.

The educational justification for school worship is now supplemented by another, what we could call the 'community-building' function. Faced with the challenge of supplying convincing functions which worship, in order to survive the criticisms of critics, must be seen to fulfil, the one supplied here comes in the fashionable language of community development. Collective worship binds people together, apparently so successfully, that the government has to legislate lest its success be impeded. Our concern here is not whether the community-building function of collective worship is successful, but with the deeper question about what happens to worship when functional justifications are offered for it *at all*.

The principal problem with functionalist justifications of school worship is that they exacerbate the tensions between Christian, corporate and collective worship which we have already examined. Given the distinctions between Christian, corporate and collective worship, it is hard to see how worship conducted under functional restraints can be worship at all. Worship cannot be useless: it has to have a use which outweighs its obvious divisiveness. If it is Christian (or Jewish, or Islamic) worship, it will be useless. If it is corporate or collective worship it will be useful. However, if it is collective worship, it is unlikely simultaneously to be Christian worship. This is both because it will be judged on whether or not it performs a useful function, and because (unlike corporate worship) there will not be a group offering it with 'beliefs in common'.

Armed with these distinctions it is easy to see that several irreconcilable contradictions are embodied in the legislation governing school worship and the circular which interprets it. This is reflected in the title of the National Society's report on school worship, entitled *Between a Rock and a Hard Place*[52]. In particular it is hard to see how acts of worship can be 'wholly or mainly of a broadly Christian character'[53] when they are distinguished from

---

[51] A. Brown and E. Brown, *Primary School Worship* (London, The National Society, 1992), pp 4-5.

[52] Alan Brown, *Between a Rock and a Hard Place: a report on school worship* (London, The National Society), 1996.

[53] Amplified further in Circular 1/94, *op.cit.*, paragraph 61, p 21.

corporate worship and assessed in educational terms. According to Zygmunt Bauman, one of the characteristics of the emerging 'post-modern' period is that we cannot but encounter irreconcilable conflicts and unresolvable differences and contradictions. An old Greek word, *aporia,* is used for such situations of contradiction[54]. A difference between modernity and postmodernity is said to be that the former wrongly believed such *aporiae* could be overcome: the latter acknowledges them, and encourages differences to be understood rather than submerged.

The suggestion to be made here is that Christian and secular understandings of worship may be helpfully understood as an *aporia.* There can be no agreement about such matters. If this is right, attempts to reconcile contradictory emphases in the literature on school worship is not going to succeed. They will furnish examples only of the habit of attempting a consensus where no such basis exists. In a pluralist society we might expect to encounter *aporiae* regularly. The impact of such an analysis on c*hurch* schools is considerable. They should be emphasising their distinctiveness with renewed confidence, not joining consensuses which cannot succeed in anything except the sacrifice of Christian particularity (which is exactly what many humanists and secularists want). Yet the recognition of difference must not be a pretext for confrontation.

If you find the notion of useless worship a convincing one, you will probably also have recognised its limitations. For example, worship offered to God for no other reason than the acknowledgement of God's worthiness can still be educational. The objection lies in the eclipse of the theological reason for offering it; not in the educational benefits that may derive from it.

I have suggested an approach of *holy irony* in such circumstances[55]. Holy irony (in the present context) is a combination of the acknowledgement that many of the trends affecting religious education and school worship are deeply contradictory, together with an acknowledgement that the same trends provide Christian teachers and church schools with unexpected opportunities for theologically-informed practice. The approach is ironic (since the opportunities provided were not wholly intended), and holy, since the opportunities provided can be turned into an increase in the love of God and of one's neighbour. And this, as we have seen, is the *raison d'être* of Christian involvement in education.

---

[54] Zygmunt Bauman, *Postmodern Ethics* (Oxford, Blackwell, 1993), pp 8, 11, 88-90.
[55] Thatcher,, *op.cit.,* pp 134-7.

The eucharist in collective worship

We noted earlier that in Christian faith Christ is present at the eucharist. David Attfield has written movingly[56] of his experiences of conducting a school eucharist at a Church of England inner city voluntary aided school, and from the theological point of view commended in this unit, this practice is much encouraged. Why conceal from children that act of worship which is most meaningful to Christians?

Provided that a school eucharist belongs to a broad tradition of Christian belief and is therefore not distinctive of any one denomination, it would not contravene the Cowper-Temple clause forbidding the teaching of anything distinctive of any denomination[57]. A church school will want to celebrate the presence of Christ in its midst in the way he himself commanded, since as Attfield rightly notes, 'any adequate educational presentation of the Christian religion must include holy communion'[58]. While a school eucharist will be celebrated for Christ's sake and for no other reason, there will be enormous 'derivative benefits' resulting from it. Not least among these will be the confident reaffirmation of the school's Christian identity. Christ is present in the school and is waiting to be acknowledged there, just as he is present among the community of the distressed. What better way to acknowledge and serve him where he already is?

Readers

You will find helpful much of L.J. Francis and A. Thatcher (eds) 1990, *Christian Perspectives for Education*, Leominster, Gracewing.

Bibliography

Astley, J. (1984), The role of worship in Christian learning, *Religious Education*, 79, 243-251.

Astley, J. and Francis L.J. (1996), *Christian Theology and Religious Education: connections and contradictions*, London, SPCK.

Attfield, D. (1993), Presenting the eucharist in a primary school, in L.J. Francis and D.W. Lankshear (eds), *Christian Perspectives on Church Schools*, Leominster, Gracewing, pp 141-147.

---

[56] David Attfield, 'Presenting the eucharist in a primary school', in Leslie J. Francis and David W. Lankshear, *Christian Perspectives on Church Schools* (Leominster, Gracewing, 1993), pp 141-7.

[57] Attfield, *op.cit.*, p 146.

[58] Attfield, *op.cit.*, p 145.

Bauman, Z. (1993), *Postmodern Ethics,* Oxford, Blackwell.

Brown, A. (1996), *Between a Rock and a Hard Place: a report on school worship*, London, The National Society.

Brown, A. and Brown, E. (1992), *Primary School Worship,* London, The National Society.

Bruce, S. (1995), *Religion in Modern Britain,* Oxford, Oxford University Press.

Clarke, A.D. and Winter, B.W. (1991), *One God, One Lord in a World of Religious Pluralism*, Cambridge, Tyndale House.

Cobb, J.B. (1990), Beyond 'pluralism', in G. D'Costa (ed.), *Christian Uniqueness Reconsidered: the myth of a pluralistic theology of religions*, London, Orbis, pp 81-95.

Davie, G. (1994), *Religion in Britain Since 1945: believing without belonging,* Oxford, Blackwell.

Davies, D. (1994), Christianity, in J. Holm. and J. Bowker (eds), *Worship*, London, Pinter Publishers, pp 35-62.

D'Costa, G. (1986), *Theology and Religious Pluralism,* London, SCM.

D'Costa, G. (1990) Christ, the Trinity and religious plurality, in G. D'Costa (ed.), *Christian Uniqueness Reconsidered: the myth of a pluralistic theology of religions*, London, Orbis, pp 16-29.

Department for Education (1994), *Circular 1/94, Religious Education and Collective Worship.*

Fox, M. (1991), *Creation Spirituality,* London, HarperCollins.

Francis, L.J. (1990), The logic of education, theology and the church school, in L.J. Francis and A. Thatcher (eds), *Christian Perspectives for Education*, Leominster, Gracewing, pp 20-35.

Francis, L.J. and Lankshear D.W. (1993), *Christian Perspectives on Church Schools,* Leominster, Gracewing.

Francis, L.J. and Thatcher, A. (eds) (1990), *Christian Perspectives for Education: a reader in the theology of education*, Leominster, Gracewing.

Hardy, D.W. (1996) Theology and the cultural reduction of religion, in J. Astley and L.J Francis (eds), *Christian Theology and Religious Education*, London, SPCK, pp 16-37.

Hodgson, P.C. (1994), *Winds of the Spirit: a constructive Christian theology,* London, SCM Press.

Holm, J.L. and Bowker, J. (eds) (1994), *Worship*, London, Pinter Publishers.

Hull, J. (1990), What is theology of education?, in L.J. Francis and A. Thatcher (eds), *Christian Perspectives for Education*, Leominster, Gracewing, pp 2-19.

Hull, J. (1995), Can one speak of God or to God in education, in F. Young (ed.), *Dare We Speak of God in Public?* London, Mowbray, pp 22-34.

Leech, K. (1993), *The Eye of the Storm,* London, Darton, Longman and Todd.

MacIntyre, A. (1981), *After Virtue: a study in moral theory,* London, Duckworth.

Milbank J. (1990), *Theology and Social Theory: beyond secular reason,* Oxford, Blackwell.

Milbank, J. (1990), The end of dialogue, in G. D'Costa (ed.), *Christian Uniqueness Reconsidered: the myth of a pluralistic theology of religions,* London, Orbis, pp 174-191.

National Curriculum Council (1993), *Spiritual and Moral Development: a discussion paper.*

OFSTED (1994), *Spiritual, Moral, Social and Cultural Development: an OFSTED discussion paper.*

Polkinghorne, J. (1986), *One World: the interaction of science and theology,* London, SPCK.

Race, A. (1983), *Christians and Religious Pluralism,* London, SCM.

Sookhdeo, P. (ed.) (1978), *Jesus Christ the Only Way,* Carlisle, Paternoster.

Smart, N. (1996), Global Christian theology and education, in J. Astley and L.J. Francis (eds), *Christian Theology and Religious Education,* London, SPCK, pp 7-15.

Smart, N. and Konstantine, S. (1991), *Christian Systematic Theology in a World Context,* London, Marshall Pickering.

Thatcher, A. (1996), Policing the Sublime: a wholly (holy?) ironic approach to the spiritual and moral development of children, in J. Astley and L.J. Francis (eds), *Christian Theology and Religious Education,* London, SPCK, pp 117-139.

Thatcher A. (1990), The recovery of Christian education, in L.J. Francis and A. Thatcher (eds), *Christian Perspectives for Education,* Leominster, Gracewing, pp 273-281.

Thomas, M.M. (1990), A Christ-centred humanist approach to other religions in the Indian pluralistic context, in G. D'Costa (ed.), *Christian Uniqueness Reconsidered: the myth of a pluralistic theology of religions,* London, Orbis, pp 49-62.

Tilby, A. (1993), *Science and the Soul,* London, SPCK.

Watson, B. (1987), *Education and Belief,* Oxford, Blackwell.

Westerhoff, J. (1987), Liturgics and catechetics, *Worship,* 61, pp 510-516.

Wiles, M. (1976), *What is Theology?* Oxford, Oxford University Press.

Young, F. (ed.) (1995), *Dare We Speak of God in Public?* London, Mowbray.

Belief and Practice

Belief and Practice

Unit A

Personal reflection

Dr Sheila Hunter

University College of St Martin

Lancaster

Contents

Introduction

Aims

After working through this unit you should be able to:

- show a familiarity with the process of critical reflection;
- support and inform reflection within academic study;
- articulate, analyse and evaluate your own beliefs and values;
- consider the effect of your own beliefs and values on professional practice.

Overview

This unit on reflection is the first of the core module *Belief and Practice*. In the course of your work in this unit you will have the opportunity to think about your own beliefs and their relevance to the context of the school in which you work and your role in that school. This unit will require you to undertake various types of activities designed to prepare you personally for work that you will meet in subsequent units. You will be expected to work through the unit in the order in which it is presented, as each section builds on the previous ones.

A1 The process

Reflection

One of the things you are asked to do is to keep a journal of your thoughts, feelings and ideas as you work through this unit. The aim here is to facilitate self-understanding. In subsequent units a journal may not be necessary, but as a method of recording your progress and your difficulties, it provides a helpful focus and a chance to be creative without being too self-critical.

The way in which we have been taught will often influence the way in which we ourselves teach. Parts of this unit are designed to help you think critically about your own learning and will encourage you to reflect on how you learn as an adult. You will be introduced to a range of methodologies which we hope will help you develop your own strategies for academic study as well as offering you insights into yourself as a learner and the influence of personal beliefs and values on that learning process.

The main focus of this unit is on you as a person and as a professional. It is concerned with beliefs and practice and therefore you will be asked to engage in critical reflection on three key areas.

Personal belief

For the purpose of working on this unit it is not expected that you embrace any *particular* personal belief. However, everyone has beliefs about themselves and the world in which they live, and it is the intention in this unit to enable you to spend some time reviewing your own beliefs and exploring how these might relate to working in a school.

Academic study

This may be your first encounter with academic study for quite some time, or you may be used to building academic study into your routine on a regular basis. Whatever your starting point, this unit should guide you towards sound study skills and help you to understand more fully the processes in which you are engaged.

School application

Although this unit concentrates on your personal beliefs and outlook, the purpose of the unit is to reflect on how these might affect your work in a school in whatever capacity. This might include working as a teacher, a headteacher, a governor, or as an ordained or lay minister.

Critical reflection

Throughout this unit you will be encouraged to engage with the process of *critical reflection* and to come to an understanding of the process.

Reflection upon your own beliefs and values can be a challenging, if not unsettling, activity and can sometimes be done more effectively with the help of another person. For this reason, and in order that you should have some support while you are working through this unit, we suggest that you should try to locate a 'critical friend'. This is a person with whom you would be comfortable to share your ideas, and whom you trust to help you see things more clearly. It is often best to choose someone who is not involved with your professional work but who nevertheless understands the context of schools and has sympathy with the work you are trying to do. You will occasionally be given exercises in the unit which require the help of a 'critical friend' and you will find further reference to the role later in the document.

A2 What is reflection?

The mind is a mysterious entity. It appears to be a product of the workings of the brain, though the connection between the two is uncertain and disputed. The view we take, and the view implied by the models we examine later in this unit, is that the mind is able to reflect the outer world, that it is able in some sense to make a mental copy of it, and also to reflect upon, that is to analyse or learn from, its own workings.

In this section we will be exploring the many meanings that the term 'reflection' might have and different contexts in which it is used. Before you are introduced to the meaning and use of *reflection* in the context of learning spend a few minutes writing down some ideas of your own.

Activity A1

Think of and write down some examples of different ways you might use the words 'reflect' or 'reflection' and then try to work out the different meanings these words convey. For instance, 'I could see my reflection in the water' and 'I reflected upon the problem'. How are these meanings related to each other?

Comment on activity A1

You may have thought of ideas to do with the physical sciences like, 'the light was reflected in the mirror' or more metaphorical uses like, 'her face reflected the enthusiasm of a novice' or 'he reflected deeply on his decision to emigrate'. You may also have thought of uses like 'the counsellor reflected the thoughts of the client back to her at the end of the session'. The strictly physical sense suggests light or an image being bounced back off a surface. The metaphorical sense suggest feelings or thoughts being bounced back off other people or from a facial expression or inside one's own head.

A psalm

Read Psalm 137. These are the thoughts of someone a long way from home. The person is reflecting on the experience of being forcibly removed from his homeland. We often reflect on significant experiences or events in our lives or the life of our community, nation or world. *Reflection is part of the process of making sense of experience.* It may be a conscious or subconscious activity and is likely to involve asking questions about ourselves or others, the world about us and events which happen, ideas, beliefs and values.

A poem

The poem below is an example of such questioning about the self, people's beliefs about themselves and the way others see them. It was written from a prison cell by Dietrich Bonhoeffer (1959), a German theologian executed in Flossenburg in April 1945 shortly before the war ended, and translated by J.B. Leishman.

> Who am I? They often tell me
> I stepped from my cell's confinement
> Calmly, cheerfully, firmly,
> Like a squire from his country-house.
> Who am I? They often tell me
> I used to speak to my warders
> Freely and friendly and clearly,
> As though it were mine to command.
> Who am I? They also tell me
> I bore the days of misfortune
> Equably, smilingly, proudly,
> Like one accustomed to win.
>
> Am I then really all that which other men tell of?
> Or am I only what I myself know of myself?
> Restless and longing and sick, like a bird in a cage,
> Struggling for breath, as though hands were compressing my throat,
> Yearning for colours, for flowers, for the voices of birds,
> Thirsting for words of kindness, for neighbourliness,
> Tossing in expectation of great events,
> Powerlessly trembling for friends at an infinite distance,
> Weary and empty at praying, at thinking, at making,
> Faint, and ready to say farewell to all?
>
> Who am I? This or the other?
> Am I one person to-day and to-morrow another?
> Am I both at once? A hypocrite before others,
> And before myself a contemptibly woebegone weakling?
> Or is something within me still like a beaten army,
> Fleeing in disorder from victory already achieved?
>
> Who am I? They mock me, these lonely questions of mine.
> Whoever I am, Thou knowest, O God, I am Thine!

Reflection requires that we engage not only with our thoughts but with our feelings, our attitudes, behaviours and beliefs.

Activity A2

Think of an event in the life of your local/national community and how that event has affected your life. Write down your thoughts and feelings surrounding this event.

Try working with the question raised in the poem: 'Who am I?' In particular give some thought to the questions raised in verse two: 'Am I then really all that other men tell of? Or am I only what I know myself to be?'

Comment on activity A2

With regard to the questions of the poem, you may have come to the conclusion that personal identity is both a product of our social environment (what is reflected back to us by others) and of our own internal awareness of private thoughts and feelings. The 'real' person is in both the outer and inner worlds, and many psychological models of personality recognise this (Jung, 1964; McLynn, 1996).

Reflection and learning

The intention of the first part of this unit was to introduce you to the idea of reflection in its widest sense as an activity which belongs to being human. The rest of the unit will now focus on reflection as part of the learning process in order to develop your understanding of yourself and others as learners and to apply this particularly to the more formal learning context of school.

Activity A3

Before we move on take some time to reflect briefly on an event/experience which belongs within your school context, e.g. an exciting and encouraging school/class achievement, a particularly memorable incident. Use the questions below to help you to reflect.

- What happened?
- What were your thoughts about this?
- How did you feel?
- Did anything change for you as a result of this?

Comment on activity A3

Now read the following statements about reflection and consider whether they help you to understand better your own experience of reflection. You may want to make one or two notes in your journal.

- Reflection is an active process of exploration and discovery which often leads to very unexpected outcomes.
- Reflection is not a single-faceted concept but a generic term which acts as a shorthand description for a number of important ideas and activities.
- Reflection is an important human activity in which people recapture their experience, think about it, mull it over and evaluate it. It is this working with experience that is important in learning.
- The adoption of a reflective approach is a choice which we can make or not as we wish, and is one which can be associated with the deep approach to learning (Boud, Keogh and Walker, 1985).
- Reflection as a mental process is usually thought of as an internal activity, carried out in solitude, for which the presence of other people is often an unwelcome distraction. In the physical world, however, reflection is a two-way process: without an appropriate 'reflector' it cannot occur at all.
- One of the most useful tasks we can perform as we seek to develop critical thinking in other people is to reflect back to them their attitudes, rationalisations, and habitual ways of thinking and acting. In doing this we function as a mirror, allowing individuals to view their own motivations, actions, and justifications as if they were those of others. This can be a powerful experience (Brookfield, 1987).

A3 What is critical reflection?

The last of the statements you have just read introduces the term 'critical thinking'. This unit will seek to develop the notion of critical thinking as part of the reflective process and will offer you opportunities to develop your own critical thinking and reflective skills.

Thomas Groome (1980) puts the words 'critical' and 'reflection' together and has some helpful things to say which we will explore in more detail later in this section. For the time being we will equate 'critical thinking' and 'critical reflection' since the reflection we are concentrating on at this point primarily requires thinking. Critical reflection according to Groome requires:

- *critical reason* to evaluate the present;
- *critical memory* to uncover the past in the present;
- *creative imagination* to envision the future in the present.

As we observed earlier in this unit reflection requires us to engage with both thinking and feeling. Critical reflection will also require us to engage with the past, the present and the future. The following exercise will help to introduce you to these elements of the reflective process.

Activity A4

Sketch a tree, showing roots, trunk and branches. The roots of the tree represent the past, the trunk represents the present and the branches represent the future. You are invited to use the tree to record some significant information about yourself as a *learner*. There are no right or wrong ways of doing this so please feel free to record whatever you wish in these three areas. It is probably best to start with the present and then to use this as a way of retrieving and reviewing the past.

For instance, you might wish to recall your first days at school and the good and bad experiences you had there. Were you rewarded by success or condemned as a failure? Do you feel you had ups and downs like everyone else? What did you enjoy about learning?

Can you make any connections between past, present and future which will help you to better understand the present and change the way you view the future?

Comment on activity A4

The image of the tree is simply a way of showing you how learning experiences are embedded within our whole personality system. You may have had an unhappy experience of maths at school and, as a consequence, always been shy of figures since then. Alternatively, you may have had very positive experiences as a young child and enjoyed learning, you may even have won prizes or received commendations at school, and this may have the long-term consequence of giving you confidence about learning new things and an appetite for knowledge. Certainly, it seems clear that the kind of labelling we received as children often stays with us for many years ('he's good with his hands'; 'she is very clumsy at sport').

In addition the kinds of work habits we cultivated as children (perhaps giving great attention to detail and neatness, perhaps enjoying working in silence, perhaps being happy when writing stories and totally caught up in our own fictional creations) may have stayed with us through to adulthood. If we enjoyed the sense of *achievement* given by work, it may be that we rush through to get to the end of what we have to learn. If we enjoy the *process* of learning, the developing sense of mastery of a new area or topic, then it is learning for learning's sake rather than the award or reward at the end that becomes our motivation.

Critical reflection in detail

Groome (1980) discusses critical reflection in detail. First, Groome points us to the role of reason. 'At the first level of reflection critical reason attempts to perceive what is "obvious" about the present.' Reason not only helps us to take note, to observe carefully and 'notice' in a new way that which we normally take for granted, it also helps us evaluate what we observe.

Implicit in this assumption is that the *critical* process is a *rational* process. This may lead us to ask questions about what we call reasonable. We would stress two characteristics of reasonableness here: what is reasonable should not be self-contradictory and what is reasonable should be supported by a common sense view of the world. It is not reasonable to say 'I want excitement and tranquillity at the same time' since this is self-contradictory and it is not reasonable to say 'I am worried that my thoughts are being read by aliens from Mars' since this is not supported by a common sense view of the world.

In Groome's account careful scrutiny of the present, however, requires that we also return to the origin of our present action, hence the importance of memory. The role of memory in critical reflection, according to Groome, is to discover the source of our thinking. Such remembering is not simply a calling to mind of the past but involves a critical engagement with the memory in such a way that the past can be scrutinised too and brought into a new relationship with the present and the future. Groome (1980) points out:

> A critically remembered past can be a basis from which to choose the present and its future. A 'forgotten' past, on the other hand, holds unconscious sway over the present and thus limits our freedom in shaping the future.

Bringing reason to critique our present action, and memory to discover the source of such action, moves us to the possibility of claiming the freedom to imagine and choose our future. It is here that, for Groome, the role of creative imagination becomes particularly important. Imagination is required if the future is not simply going to be a repetition of the past.

Activity A5

- Review in your mind the events of your day so far. (You may be doing this in the morning or the evening, it doesn't matter which except you will have a longer or shorter period to review.)
- Now identify half an hour of the period you have just reviewed and consider that half hour in more detail. Try to describe the events as if you were standing back and observing them from a distance. Pay attention to detail and try to record your *thoughts* and *feelings*. Use your journal to write your description.
- Go through your account and underline references to your thoughts and feelings. (*Example: I hate Mondays!*)
- Now examine the past to see what might lie behind these thoughts and feelings. (*Example: Monday is the day when everyone makes urgent demands on me after the weekend and I always end the day feeling exhausted and dissatisfied.*)
- Can you construct alternative futures, for example a future where you do not hate Mondays? (*Example: What kind of Monday would I like? Given the demands of my work is there any way that I can engage with the present which will help to create an alternative future for Mondays?*)

Comment on activity 5

Your activity should have made you more aware of your thoughts and feelings. You should have noticed that some of your thoughts are triggered off by external events, perhaps listening to the radio or reading the paper, and others triggered off by internal events. Perhaps tiredness generates gloomy thoughts or perhaps anticipation generates optimistic thoughts. You may have noticed how feelings and thoughts are intertwined so that feelings lead to thoughts and thoughts lead to feelings. Feelings may seem much more connected to physical state than thoughts. Tiredness, being hungry, being under pressure to fulfil deadlines may lead to feelings. Thoughts are a commentary on feelings, but they can be quite disconnected from feelings: they can belong to another world.

The journal should begin to show you how feelings may be built up over the course of many years. Feelings about Mondays arise because Mondays have, for years, been a day of stress and challenge.

Your attempt to construct an alternative future will depend on many personal factors. The alternative future may have shown you a paradox. The future is different but you are the same, yet you are not the same because you are now in new circumstances.

The half hour journal that you have written will also, if you have written down everything you thought and felt in that time, surprise you by the volume of your inner life. It ought to have reminded you that the outer life of action is only a small part of our total life.

Activity A6

Now use the same process, this time to reflect on a newspaper article. Look through a local or national paper and find an article/news item on an issue which interests you. Read the article carefully and:

- note the statements with which you strongly agree/disagree;
- note your *feelings* in response to these statements.

Now ask yourself the following questions:

- Why do I strongly agree/disagree with this statement?
- Why do I *feel* the way I do about these statements?

Examine past experiences/events to see if they influence/inform your present thoughts/feelings. Can you now contemplate a future which will not simply be a repetition of the past? How will you engage with those things with which you strongly disagree?

Comment on activity A6

You may be surprised to trace back your own feelings and reactions to particular news issues. The psychoanalytic researches carried out at the beginning of this century suggest that human beings tend to collect and cluster thoughts and emotions together into packages (sometimes called complexes) that can be unravelled by anyone willing to follow the associations to wherever they lead. The process of repression (used in a Freudian sense) suggests that unpleasant emotional experiences are 'pushed to the back of the mind' or to the unconscious, and it is these emotions which may be uncovered in your reflections.

On the other hand, you may consider that the case for psychoanalysis is not proven and that the most reflection can show is the immense intricacy of national and international events in the sense that there are multiple interconnections between economic, aesthetic, cultural and moral issues. Reflection may show you some of these connections as they present themselves to your mind.

It is important to remember that when Groome (1980) talks of 'critical reflection' he is not intending us to understand this as a destructive exercise intended to change current behaviour. Rather he is keen to point out that critical reflection 'affirms what is good and true in present action, recognises its limitations, and attempts to move beyond it'.

Activity A7

Now try some critical reflection for yourself. The first step is to decide upon an event or experience (preferably though not necessarily from the school context) which you would like to explore for yourself.

Take some time to write a description of the event/experience. Try to be as objective as possible, noting details and trying not to take anything for granted. If you were hearing someone else give this description what kind of questions would you want to ask them?

Next explore the situation a little further to see what influence past ideas, events, experiences, have had on the present event (uncovering the past in the present). Perhaps you are now coming to a better understanding of the present through uncovering the past. Do you have any ideas about how this better understanding might begin to shape the future? What would you really like to do if you could?

Comment on activity A7

We give this comment in the form of a case study about a teacher called Jean. This illustrates one way in which Groome's thinking can help us to understand the process of critical reflection in a practical context.

Jean found herself feeling uncomfortable about the outcome of a recent meeting to discuss the possibility of up-dating the hymn books used for the school worship. The books they were currently using had been in use for the past eight years and quite apart from the fact that they were looking rather worn, some of the staff thought that the contents were rather old-fashioned and out of date. There had been a great deal of disagreement at the meeting and it was clear that the subject aroused strong feelings among many of the staff including herself. Rather than succumb to the temptation to push the whole event to the back of her mind on the basis that she had little time to deal with it, she decided that it was worth setting aside some time to explore the situation for herself.

First of all she wrote a brief description of her own perception of the meeting and particularly her own role in it.

> Six of us gathered for one hour in the staff room after school. Two people could not come but one of them sent along ideas in a written note. Before the meeting another member of staff had sent off for some examples of alternative hymn books and these had been available for people to look through. The deputy head led the meeting and made it fairly plain that she supported the idea of getting rid of the present hymn books which she described as dull and dreary and contributed to the complaints about boredom from the children. This view was supported by two other teachers, one who was very new to the school and kept referring to the excellent hymn book that was used in the school that he had just left.

What Jean noticed most about the present situation was her own thoughts and feelings and the behaviour that these gave rise to. She noted her sense of anger at the comments made by the deputy head and felt resentful of the new teacher who was constantly making comparisons with his previous school. She also noted that she was resisting the efforts of those staff who wanted a change and this was becoming evident in her criticism of the books which had been brought for consideration and her insistence that just because something was new it was not necessarily better.

By looking carefully at the situation Jean had in fact noticed the obvious, that her behaviour was being driven by her feelings. So she decided to explore further. Jean then tried to identify why she felt this way. To do this she had to try to uncover the source of these thoughts and feelings. To do this required that she was perfectly honest with herself and face the importance of past events which now surfaced as she struggled to be objective about them. '*I* chose those hymn books!' 'I'd been in the school *five* years before I got to choose the hymn books!' 'The fact that people don't like the hymn books is an indirect criticism of me.' It became clear to Jean that it was thoughts such as these that were making her feel so angry and giving rise to the negative stance she was taking.

Jean's thoughts then turned to the pupils and she tried to focus what she wanted for them. She began to imagine the kind of hymn book that she thought would be ideal; it would be good to have that hymn because the children clearly like that, and it would be good to have some of the new hymns introduced in the last year or so which we have to put on the overhead projector. Gradually Jean began to see that the hymn book which she had chosen eight years ago no longer met her own ideals. Clearly she had some work to do!

A4 Methods and models

In this section we introduce the following four methods or models of learning.

- do-review-learn-apply (Dennison and Kirk, 1990);
- learning cycle (Kolb, 1984);
- pastoral cycle (Green, 1990);
- components of reflection (Boud, Keogh and Walker, 1985).

Learning is a life-long process. We are learning from infancy to old age and much of what we learn comes from doing. The old educational adage: 'I do and I understand' points to the importance of experience in the learning process, an importance backed up by the monumental researches of Piaget (Piaget, 1953, 1954; Sutherland, 1992). In the previous section of this unit you were encouraged to reflect on your or others' experience. In this section you will be introduced to a number of different frameworks for that reflective activity. This reflection, we maintain, is simply a conscious extension of the attempt to translate actions into concepts that occurs when children pass through the normal phases of cognitive development.

We will look at a number of methods or models describing the learning process and the role of reflection within that process. Dennison and Kirk (1990) make the following point.

> We are aware that learning occurs as a result of doing mainly because we can observe changes in behaviour and attitudes, and identify greater knowledge (in ourselves and others) following experience.

The term 'experiential learning' is a term widely used to describe *learning by doing* and it is a term which will be used in this unit. A common model used to describe the process of experiential learning is the 'learning cycle'. This part of the unit is designed to introduce you to variations in the learning cycle model and help you to become familiar with its usefulness in facilitating your own learning. Although the models to which we will introduce you may vary in certain respects, they all have one thing in common: they are founded on the importance of acknowledging the needs of the learner and focus on experience as the key to learning.

Do-review-learn-apply

Perhaps the simplest form of the learning cycle is that which presupposes that learning is initiated by the tutor organising an activity or experience for the students to participate in; this activity is then reviewed. Learning develops from the process of doing and reviewing and the learning is then applied, potentially in a range of situations. The do-review-learn-apply cycle was devised by the Development Training Advisory Group (Dennison and Kirk, 1990).

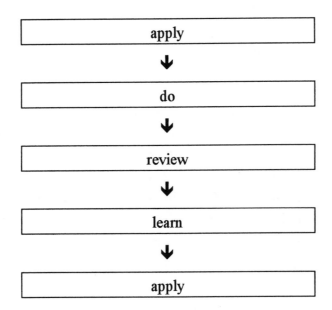

Learning cycle

Kolb's learning cycle (Kolb, 1984; Kolb and Fry, 1975) bears many similarities to the model above. It emphasises the role of experience, but Kolb points out that the learning cycle may begin at any stage and should be seen as a continuous spiral.

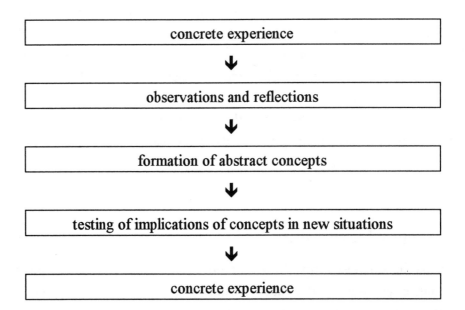

In Kolb's model (as in Piaget's) experience is translated into concepts or ideas as a result of a process of observation and reflection. These concepts are then used to inform our engagement with new experiences. The cycle has four stages:

- experience is the focus for observation and reflection;
- the observations and reflections move us back into new experience;
- the observations and reflections are built into a theory or abstract concepts;
- the theory or abstract concepts give rise to new implications for action.

In order to become effective learners Kolb argues that we need four different kinds of abilities corresponding to the four stages of the learning cycle.

Kolb's model has received critical attention from Jarvis (1995, p 70) who developed a much more complex model of the learning process which can be found in his more recent publications. However, Kolb's model has formed the basis of other models of the learning cycle, including that developed by Green (1990) whose model also owes much to the work of Paulo Freire and Juan Luis Segundo from South America.

Pastoral cycle

Green (1990) is interesting from our point of view because he seeks to introduce the idea of theology and theological reflection as something which belongs to ordinary people rather than exclusively to the academic theologian. This is important in the present context because there is a sense in which we are going to be involved in 'theologising' about education, or more particularly, about our own school situation. In other words, we may be asked to look at situations from the perspective of the teaching of the Christian faith and reflect on how that may alter the way we perceive events, situations, experiences, values or behaviours.

We need to point out that other kinds of theology, for example, systematic theology or dogmatic theology, start from the basic framework of truths and then interpret experience by extending or elaborating this framework (Barth, 1936 onwards). But the advantage of the reflective theology Green advocates is that it can help to explain apparently contradictory doctrinal positions. Thus, for instance, McGrath (1988) shows how the doctrine of the Trinity arises from the *experience* of the early church rather than from an attempt to reconcile competing theoretical ideas about Jesus and God.

Green emphasises the continual interaction between *action* and *reflection*.

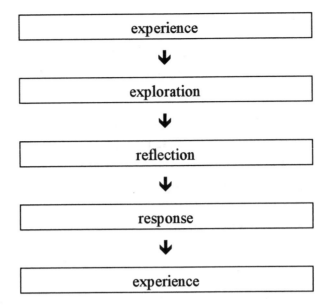

In Green's model *experience* is the starting point of theology and those undertaking the task are required to be as aware and conscious as possible of the feelings, emotions and impressions that the experience, which is the basis of the work, engenders. This period of engagement with the experience often takes the form of telling our own story and hearing others tell theirs. For Green, the reflective cycle is primarily a corporate process engaged in alongside others.

From this point of engagement the reflective process must move on from dealing with impressions to some more careful analysis of the situation. In the *exploratory* phase full use is made of a range of disciplines to try to come to a better understanding of the experience.

When the situation has been fully explored then Green's cycle moves on to reflection. Here Green's model differs slightly from the other models offered since he introduces the idea that in the reflective phase we bring the situation (or experience as we now understand it as a result of exploration) into relationship with the Christian faith. The reflection happens therefore in the light of our understanding of the Christian message.

Finally, the exploration and reflection require that we make some response. As a consequence of the exploration and reflection Green asks 'What does God want us to do?'

It must be understood here that Green is offering the reflective cycle as a method of doing theology, as a way of reflecting on the world from a very particular perspective. There will be units in this course which introduce you to concepts such as 'theology of education' and you may find yourself making use of Green's methodology as a means of thinking through a course of action.

Green devotes a chapter to each of the four phases of the cycle. The chapter on 'reflection' is particularly useful, for he draws attention to the importance of imagination in the reflective process and offers a helpful model with which to work.

Activity A8 (optional)

Read chapter 5 of *Let's Do Theology* by Green (1990). Try using the 'face to face' method of reflection described on pages 80-83.

Consider a situation where the school is rewriting its discipline policy.

- Under the heading 'facing the situation' note all the relevant items which you consider important to the present task.
- Under the heading 'facing the faith traditions' make a note of all the relevant Christian teaching you can think of relating to this issue.
- Look at each one of these in turn and then try to hold them together, let them as it were, confront each other.

Green's theory is that when we allow our everyday experience to be confronted by Christian teaching then a dynamic is created where we make an imaginative leap across the gap between the two and new insight is gained - there is some new learning. Make a note of any new understandings or insights that you have gained.

Comment on activity A8

We will not comment in detail on this activity since the whole process of bringing theology to bear on educational topics is discussed in a unit devoted to that topic by Professor Adrian Thatcher (see unit C of the module *History and Philosophy*).

Components of reflection

The final model we would like you to consider is one put forward by Boud, Keogh and Walker (1985, p 36). The model is set out in diagrammatic form and described in more detail below. However, it is important to remember that the process being described is unlikely to be as simple as the diagrams suggest and stages are unlikely to follow independently of each other as might be assumed from the diagram. As with all models, including those offered here, they are only models and are offered to try to clarify our understanding of the processes in which we are engaged. The left hand column shows kinds of experience, the middle column kinds of reflection and the right hand column the results of this experience and reflection.

This particular model pays more attention than the others to the actual reflective process and points to three stages or important aspects of reflection. These stages are referred to as: returning to the experience, attending to feelings, and re-evaluating experience.

Experience	Reflective process	Outcomes
behaviour	utilising positive feelings	new perspectives on experience
ideas	removing obstructing feelings	change in behaviour
feelings	re-evaluating experience	readiness for application

Returning to the experience

Boud *et al* (1985, p 27) point to the importance of recollecting in initiating reflection. They advocate:

> replaying the experience in the mind's eye, to observe the event as it has happened and to notice exactly what occurred and one's reactions to it in all its elements. It may be helpful to commit this description to paper, or to describe it to others. By whatever means this occurs the description should involve close attention to detail and should refrain from making judgements.

Attending to feelings

If the descriptive process has been detailed, then a careful account of the feelings raised by the experience will have been noted. Reflection requires, as pointed out earlier, that we pay careful attention to the affective (or emotional) dimension of experience. The feelings we note may be both positive and negative.

Utilising our positive feelings is particularly important as they can provide us with the impetus to persist in what might be very challenging situations, they can help us see events more sharply and they can provide the basis for new affective learning. Unless we believe in ourselves and our own capabilities we can constrain ourselves to such an extent that we deny ourselves learning opportunities and fail to extract what is available to us in any given situation (Boud *et al*, 1985, p 29).

It would, however, be foolish to believe that all feelings enhance our learning. There are likely to be those which interfere with our learning, creating barriers which prevent us from engaging fully in the learning process. Careful attention to the situation which is required in the first phase may alert us to those feelings likely to disable us. The danger is that we ignore such feelings rather than consciously seeking to discharge them as suggested in this model. As Boud *et al* (1985) point out:

> These issues need to be handled sensitively. They need to be resolved in a way that will remove their undesirable influence and will facilitate continued support for future leaning. They can be discharged by being expressed openly in a sustaining environment, for example on a one-to-one basis or within some kind of support group, so that an emotional obstacle can be removed through, for example, laughing, animated speech, anger or crying (Heron, 1982). Some people can discharge them, in the view of Rainer (1980), through forms of writing. Through such approaches learners can be freed from the mental bonds which were acting as constraints on them and they may be able to respond freely, flexibly and creatively once again. Not all authors, however, would regard discharge as the most appropriate avenue in the situations we consider. An alternative way is through transmutation of emotions through various meditative techniques (Heron, 1982).

Re-evaluating experience

Boud and his colleagues have identified four aspects of re-evaluation which contribute to effective reflection.

The first aspect of re-evaluation is known as *association*. This involves relating new information to that which is already known. It requires that we make connections between the ideas and feelings from the original experience with ideas and feelings which have emerged through the reflective process. These then have to be brought alongside existing knowledge and attitudes.

The new input linked with our existing knowledge and feelings can challenge us both intellectually and affectively. This aspect of reflection can lead us to the discovery that our old attitudes are no longer consistent with the new ideas and feelings, that re-assessment is necessary and, in the cognitive area, that our earlier knowledge needs modifying to accommodate new ideas (Boud *et al*, 1985, p 31).

The second aspect of re-evaluation is known as *integration*. The process of association brings together ideas and feelings which need to be examined for their relevance to us and integrated into a new whole where a new pattern of ideas and attitudes develops, and where new insight provides the basis for further reflection.

The third aspect of re-evaluation is known as *validation*. New patterns of ideas and insights which begin to emerge in the process of integration now need to be tested in reality. As Boud *et al* (1985, p 33) point out:

> We are testing for internal consistency between our new appreciations and our existing knowledge and beliefs, for consistency between these and parallel data from others and trying out our new perceptions in new situations... One of the techniques which can aid in validation is rehearsal. This can help us relate knowledge which we believe we have integrated to its application in our lives.

The fourth aspect of re-evaluation is known as *appropriation*. Such new knowledge that might come from this process and be integrated into our conceptual framework might also bring with it a further dimension, that it needs in some cases to be 'made our own'. Boud *et al* (1985, pp 32-33) say:

> Some learning can become so related to the self that it enters into our sense of identity and can have a considerable importance and become a significant force in our lives. Significant feelings can come to be attached to this type of learning and any learning experience which touches this area can give rise to strong emotions that may need to be taken into account in future reflection.... Appropriated knowledge becomes part of our value system and it is less amenable to change than other knowledge which we accept and work with but do not make our own to the same degree.

Activity A9

Read chapter 3 of *What Prevents Christian Adults from Learning* by Hull (1985). Now reflect on the ideas that are presented in the chapter.

First, return to the ideas. Make a note in your journal of the key ideas encountered in your reading, giving a brief account of what you understand them to be saying. Try rehearsing the arguments to a critical friend.

Second, attend to feelings. Try to acknowledge and record any feelings which this reading generated, for example:

- 'I felt confused by...';
- 'I felt excited by...';
- 'I felt anxious about...';
- 'I felt angry at....';
- 'I felt encouraged by...'.

Make a note of positive feelings which might help your learning, and negative feelings which might get in the way of your learning. How might you work with the latter to prevent them from disabling your learning?

Third, re-evaluate the ideas. Do any of these new ideas relate to what you already know? Can you see any connections? Can you see whether any of these new ideas might have a place in your current thinking? Is there any way in which these ideas might affect your professional role? Talk with your critical friend and test some of these ideas out.

Do you have a sense that any of these ideas are particularly important to your own personal thinking, beliefs and values? Are any of these ideas likely to affect you in a personal way?

Comment on activity A9

Hull distinguishes between certitude (or the feeling of being certain) and certainty (or the knowledge that the feeling is justified). The problem of adult religious learning arises from the need to throw old certainties away to make way for new ones. In psychological terms, we need to understand the 'defence mechanisms of the ego' and in sociological terms we need to understand the defence of 'belief structures' so that learning can be facilitated.

Psychology makes use of the concept of 'cognitive dissonance' where our beliefs seem to be in conflict with each other or with other belief systems. There are various ways of resolving the conflicts, one of which is to assume that, despite the disconfirming instances, the original beliefs are still correct. End-of-the-world groups who find their predictions unfulfilled reinterpret their beliefs to allow them to say that their expectations have been fulfilled in an unforeseen way. Hull's point is that, if Christian adults are to learn, they must not react in this head-in-the-sand way.

Psychology also makes use of the idea of personal constructs that enable us to categorise our mental world. Here Hull distinguishes between 'propositional constructs' that make affirmations without trying to cover all mental life and impermeable constructs that are not easily subject to change. Again, Christian education should help adults to develop their construct systems so that fresh views of problems can be taken.

To avoid having to learn new things, three strategies are normally used: to withdraw from conflict, not to think, or to suppress uncomfortable evidence. These strategies are worked out, according to Hull, institutionally and in church life.

The exercise we have suggested in activity 9 should enable you to understand your own position a little better and to help you change your ideas where necessary. But we need to enter a *caveat* against change for change's sake and we still need to weigh carefully evidence given to us, even if this evidence has led other people to change their views. If we do not do this, then we will not properly 'own' the new position we are being asked to adopt. Moreover, we should notice that Hull does not, and does not pretend to, offer a total learning theory. There is more to be said about learning than is contained in the topics of cognitive dissonance and personal constructs.

Reviewing beliefs and values

The tree exercise can be used to review your own beliefs and values. If you wish to, you may want to go through it for yourself again, this time noting the kinds of beliefs and values you hold and trying to work out where they come from and how they work out in your life.

We would expect many beliefs and values to be formed in childhood and to be modified, either by being held in new ways or by being seen in relation to large wholes, in later life. Research suggests (Kay and Francis, 1996) that young people often take their religious beliefs from the home, especially until adolescence, and the work of Fowler (Astley and Francis, 1992) follows the trajectory of faith and shows how it functions differently through different developmental stages. It is to be expected that personal faith will undergo transformations, sometimes being inclusive, sometimes being exclusive, sometimes being taken directly from respected people and sometimes being worked out on the basis of experience, especially where that experience is dramatic or tragic (e.g. after bereavement).

A5 Value audit

The final part of this unit is in four parts. *Knowing myself as a learner* and *How adults learn* are designed to introduce you to material intended to help you understand yourself as a learner. *Learning styles* and *The school situation* encourage you to apply your learning in this unit to the school situation. This last part is intended to prepare you for the next unit.

Knowing myself as a learner

A major theme in this unit has been the opportunity to engage with personal reflection and to begin to understand its processes. It has also been the intention of the unit to help you reflect upon your contribution as a professional person to the life of your school.

Both you and the school will embody certain beliefs and values. While your own beliefs and values may at times be in accord with those proclaimed by the school, sometimes they may not. Whichever is the case, both you as an individual and the school as a community must be helped to reflect on deeply held beliefs and values. As a teacher, headteacher, governor, minister or occupying some other role in relation to the school, you will have a key part to play in this reflective practice. If reflective practice has become part of your own personal, academic and professional routine, then you will be well placed to help others in this process.

As we pointed out earlier in the unit, this kind of work requires sensitivity and understanding. One important aspect of understanding is recognising that different people learn in different ways. There is not enough time here to go into all the complexities of learning but we considered it important that you have some insight into how adults learn and the potential differences in the way they learn.

How adults learn

If you have not done any reading in this area before you will probably find it helpful to start with chapter 3 of *Learning for Life* by Yvonne Craig (1994). In this chapter Craig lists ten factors which help adults to learn (notice the stress on adults here, not on the classroom and pupils). They are:

- *relevance*, when adult learners can see the point of what they are learning because it is related to their own lives and aspirations;
- *experience*, when what is learnt is checked against previously acquired knowledge, and this knowledge is not devalued;
- *variety*, when learners are given a mixture of learning environments and methods of teaching;
- *enjoyment* may come from all kinds of sources, but the important thing is that learning should, as far as possible, be made pleasurable;
- *study skills* can be imparted so that the learning process itself becomes easier - once we know how to make notes or where to find books other, more challenging, intellectual tasks are easier to accomplish;
- *acceptance* of other people in a learning group is important because it leads to acceptance of oneself and allows discussion to flow unhindered without a fear of unkind criticism;
- *tutoring skills* are a natural corollary of study skills and flow from good organisation;
- *individual progress* is affirmed appropriately and allows people to work at their own pace and to 'unlearn' as well as to learn;
- *opportunities* for putting learning into practice are vital because they generate confidence and immediately consolidate the value of the learning exercise;
- *nurture* of other people in a learning group is important since it gives an emotional rationale for learning, especially where learning is connected with a religious community and what has been learnt can be communicated to other members of it.

Adult learners have particular worries associated with their ages. Some adult learners may think they are too old to learn, though this is untrue. In experiments where two parallel classes have been run side by side, one made up of retired people and the other made up of young people, the retired people often did better. Other adult learners may think their memories are too bad to let them learn properly, but this may be mistaken since memories function best in a context of meaning (which is why we can remember stories more easily than a string of disconnected facts) and once meaning is grasped, memory often follows naturally.

Learning styles

In the section on Methods and Models Kolb maintained that effective learning requires learners to display four different kinds of abilities corresponding to the four stages of the learning cycle: experiencing, reflecting, theorising and action. Research suggests that, although we are able to develop sufficient levels of skill in all of these four areas, most of us have preferred ways of working and learning.

Yvonne Craig (1994), in her book *Learning for Life,* describes these preferred ways of working as pragmatist (do what comes to hand as circumstances dictate), reflector (happy in the world of ideas), theorist (happy to build ideas together into theories) and activist (who learn on the job in new situations). In this book on learning for life, Yvonne Craig produces a self-completion questionnaire to allow people to work out how to categorise themselves.

Pragmatists might say they:

- have a reputation for a no-nonsense direct style;
- think the key issue in any debate is whether something works or not;
- like to apply new ideas in practice as soon as possible.

Reflectors might say they:

- take pride in doing a thorough, methodical job;
- take care over interpreting data and avoid jumping to conclusions;
- like to reach decisions after weighing up all the alternatives.

Theorists might say they:

- tend to solve problems with a step-by-step approach;
- like to follow clear routines and logical thinking patterns;
- dislike situations that cannot fit a coherent pattern.

Activists might say they:

- take reasonable risks;
- find actions based on feelings are as sound as those based on thought;
- find new, unusual ideas more attractive than practical ones.

If you want to take this further read Craig (1994, pp 50-53) for a fuller version of this questionnaire. It is important to remember that such questionnaires are intended to give us indications, not 'put us in boxes'! They are intended to help us understand the way we work and learn rather than put us in a straight jacket. We all have to some extent a capacity for working and learning in each of the areas, but knowing where our preferences lie may explain to us why we find certain exercises easier than others or why some learning situations present us with particular difficulties.

Craig (1994, p 54) argues that activists learn best when they face a challenge and when they can be part of a team. Reflectors like to stand back from work and think before acting. Theorists learn best when they are offered a logical pattern of ideas. Pragmatists learn best when they are given skills to practise.

It may be that you have discovered that you are a reflector, in which case you will probably have found much of the work in this unit to your liking. If you are an activist, this unit might have presented you with some difficulties. This is not to say, however, that activists cannot reflect, but it may mean they have to work at it a little harder! Just to illustrate this point I will add a little anecdote. After introducing a group of students to the questionnaire I was confronted some weeks later by a student who, in response to an assessment item that I had just set, told me that she could not do it because it was not her preferred way of learning! The purpose of this kind of questionnaire is not to limit our learning capacities, but to help us understand them so we can develop them.

Though we have considered Craig's ideas in some detail, we need to alert you to the extensive amount of work that has been done on personality and learning and which is complicated by the various models of personality that have been used and the various kinds of learning that are possible (Whitehead, 1975; Pollard and Tann, 1994, p 155). Craig's set of categories fits well with the extravert-introvert distinction and could be assimilated to it. Thus the reflectors and theorists are introverts and the pragmatists and activists are extraverts. The introverts prefer to relate to the inner world of thoughts and feelings; the extraverts prefer to relate to the outer world of people, things and facts. The introverts are more cautious and the extraverts more inclined to take risks.

Pollard and Tann (1994, p 155) take a more cognitive approach and categorise learning styles according to their mental, rather than their personality, correlates. But, again, some of the features they distinguish might be amalgamated with Craig's scheme. For instance, a distinction is drawn between whole/serialist learners (the former trying to grasp a subject as a complete entity and the latter liking to work in cumulative steps); field-dependent/field-independent learners (the former making use of a general context to solve a learning problem and the latter preferring not to do so); scanning and focusing (the former tending to deal with a large amount of information at a rapid but perhaps superficial level for testing hypotheses, and the latter operating variable by variable). To take one example, it is obvious that the whole/serialist distinction would fit the pairing between theorists and reflectors.

The school situation

Throughout this unit we have tried to make connections with the school situation as well as encouraging you to reflect on personal and academic issues. If it is true that there can be no curriculum development without staff development, then the importance of the kind of work you have been asked to undertake in this unit will become obvious, not only for curriculum development but also for the development of the school ethos, its beliefs and values. Our personal beliefs and values, our professional roles and academic activity are not separate and unrelated areas but closely related parts of a bigger whole.

For this reason we have encouraged you to keep a journal. It is important that you use this as a working document where you can write freely, observe, reflect, theorise and contemplate alternative courses of action, both personal and professional. A minimum of twelve hours should be allowed over the whole duration of this unit to give you time for working in your journal. Remember the focus from your reflection is personal, professional and academic.

Certain of the required activities in this unit have asked you to articulate and examine your own beliefs and values. Many of the recent documents on religious education for Key Stages one and two require that pupils can give some account of their own beliefs and values and in some cases to begin to reflect on key beliefs, values, and behaviours. Such requirements demand that those involved in creating the learning environment in school are knowledgeable, experienced and practised in those areas where children are expected to perform.

We recommend that you make a habit of reflecting on key issues within the school, particularly issues related to the beliefs and values enshrined in the school. Careful articulation of the school's ethos requires the capacity for critical reflection on the part of the staff. If reflection is part of our personal discipline then it will become part of our academic and professional discipline also.

Pollard and Tann (1994) discuss reflective teaching in relation to the whole school. They consider three levels of reflection identifying:

- aspects of the learning process;
- techniques for monitoring the learning process and its outcomes;
- the social consequences of the learning process.

In the first level they include learning styles along the lines discussed above. At the second level, they consider conferencing (where an extended discussion takes place between teacher and child), logging (where children write down their thoughts about their learning experiences), questionnaires, mapping (where children draw 'maps' showing how what they have learnt fits together), marking (where teachers consider separate pieces of children's work in a sequence to discover whether there has been improvement) and testing (which can be used diagnostically). The third level deals with social values in the classroom engendered by teachers.

Pollard's research analysis of classroom comments led to the uncovering of three clusters of teacher values being communicated to pupils. These values related to:

- efficiency and productivity;
- social relationships;
- individualism and competitiveness.

Other values are implicit within the differentiation process because the basis of distinctions between children are largely under teacher control. Are teachers' rewards given to pupils for good behaviour or academic or social improvement or good work? Each of these bases implies a set of values that children come to understand.

In addition to the differentiation made by teachers, there are, within the school, differentiations made by pupils through their social networks. Pollard (1985) found a group of 'goodies' who were socially conformist hard workers, 'jokers' who were less conscientious but often more able than the first group and 'gang' members whose levels of academic achievement were low and whose behaviour often became disruptive. The reflective school will be aware of the social networks of pupils and try to mediate with them on the basis of the pupils' own sense of justice. In this way the academic work of each of the three groups will improve as the disruptive pupils become more satisfied and less inclined to disturb the learning environment of the rest.

Pollard and Tann (1994, p 170) suggest four basic strategies or policies for reflective schools:

- *listening to children* can be prioritised so that teachers gain access to pupils' perceptions and, at the same time, enable pupils to become more aware of themselves as learners;
- *being positive* with pupils enables teachers to encourage without condemning and to reinforce creativity and effort without overemphasising conformity;
- *challenging children* can stimulate their motivation and encourages teachers to avoid drifting into routine standards based on what is merely 'good enough';
- *acting fairly* is the basis for harmony within the classrooms, and it is a value that may become embedded in the life of the school.

Activity A10

Use your own journal to undertake one of the practical activities suggested by Pollard and Tann (1987, p 179). They recommend keeping a diary to monitor support, pressure and constraints arising from relationships with other staff.

Comment on activity 10

This is a private matter. What the exercise should reveal is the way some tensions with staff are accidental and non-repetitive while others are chronic. Where problems are chronic, it will be necessary to address these through institutional structures for change.

A6 Conclusion

Congratulations on reaching the end of this unit. You should now have some insight into the process of critical reflection and have some experience of this process as it relates to your personal, professional and academic life. Before you move on to your next task you might like to check your sense of learning through this unit.

- Has this unit helped you to understand the reflective process?
- Can you describe at least four methods or models of reflection and say to whom they are attributed?
- Have you used the opportunity these models provide to reflect on issues which relate to you personally, professionally and academically?

- Are you able to articulate and reflect on your own beliefs and values and relate these to others, especially the institutional beliefs and values of your school?

Readers

You will find helpful chapters in L.J. Francis and A. Thatcher (eds) (1990), *Christian Perspectives for Education*, Leominster, Gracewing.

Bibliography

Astley J. and Francis, L.J. (eds) (1992), *Christian Perspectives on Faith Development*, Leominster, Gracewing.

Barth, K. (1936-68), *Church Dogmatics*, Edinburgh, T and T Clarke.

Bonhoeffer, D. (1959), *Letters and Papers from Prison*, London, Fontana.

Boud, D., Keogh, R. and Walker, D. (1985), *Reflection: turning experience into practice*, London, Kogan Page.

Brookfield, S. (1987), *Developing Critical Thinking*, Milton Keynes, Open University Press.

Craig, Y. (1994), *Learning for Life*, London, Mowbray.

Dennison, B. and Kirk R. (1990), *Do, Review, Learn, Apply*, London, Blackwell.

Green, L. (1990), *Let's Do Theology*, London, Mowbray.

Groome, T.H. (1980), *Christian Religious Education*, New York, Harper and Row.

Heron, J. (1982), Education of the affect: the unexplored domain, in T. Habershaw (ed.), *Three Ways to Learn*, Preston, Standing Conference on Educational Development in Polytechnics, pp 31-46.

Hull, J. (1985), *What Prevents Christian Adults from Learning?* London, SCM.

Jarvis, P. (1995), *Adult and Continuing Education* (second edition), London, Routledge.

Jung, C.G. (ed.) (1964), *Man and his Symbols*, New York, Laurel.

Kay, W.K. and Francis, L.J. (1996), *Drift from the Churches*, Cardiff, University of Wales Press.

Kolb, D. (1984), *Experiential Learning*, New Jersey, Prentice Hall.

Kolb, D. and Fry, R. (1975), Towards an applied theory of experiential learning, in C.L. Cooper (ed.), *Series of Group Process*, London, John Wiley, pp 33-55.

Lankshear, D.W. (1992), *A Shared Vision: education in church schools*, London, The National Society.

McGrath, A.E. (1988), *Understanding the Trinity*, Grand Rapids, Zondervan.

McLynn, F. (1996), *Carl Gustav Jung*, London, Bantam Press.

Piaget, J. (1953), *The Origins of Intelligence in Children*, London, Routledge and Kegan Paul.

Piaget, J. (1954), *The Child's Construction of Reality*, New York, Basic Books.

Pollard, A. (1985), *The Social World of the Primary School*, London, Holt, Rinehart and Winston.

Pollard, A. and Tann, S. (1987) *Reflective Teaching in the Primary School*, London, Cassell.

Rainer, T. (1980), *The New Diary*, London, Angus and Robertson.

Schon, D. (1982), *The Reflective Practitioner*, New York, Basic Books.

Sutherland, P. (1992), *Cognitive Development Today: Piaget and his critics*, London, Paul Chapman Publishing.

Whitehead, J.M. (ed.) (1975), *Personality and Learning 1*, London, Hodder and Stoughton in association with the Open University Press.

Belief and Practice

Unit B

Reflection on context

David W. Lankshear

The National Society

London

Contents

Introduction

Aims

After working through this unit you should be able to:

- apply skills of reflection to roles in church schools;
- develop policy and action within the school context as a result of reflection.

This unit makes extensive use of policy and other documents produced by schools themselves. If you work as a teacher, you should not have difficulty obtaining such documents. Alternatively, you should be able to obtain school prospectuses, which often contain mission statements for example, from your local area education office or from your diocesan education office or from the reference section of your local library.

Overview

This unit takes six key documents relating to a particular school's practice and asks you to examine them critically and reflectively with a view to improving policy and, ultimately, practice. The documents are:

- the school mission statement;
- the school development plan;
- the school worship policy;
- the school policy for religious education;
- the school discipline policy;
- the appropriate syllabus for religious education used in the school.

In addition, you should be able to borrow:

- the relevant agreed or diocesan syllabus for religious education;
- *Inspection Handbook: for section 13 inspections in schools of the Church of England and Church in Wales* (Brown and Lankshear, 1995) or *Inspection Handbook: for section 23 inspections in schools of the Church of England and Church in Wales* (Brown and Lankshear, 1997)

The unit will invite you to explore the policy and practice of your school in the light of your reading. You should complete section *B1 School mission statement* first, but after that you could work through the other sections in any order.

Getting started

In order to begin your work, you will need to ensure that you have obtained the documents listed in the overview. One or more will be needed in all the sections that follow. You will only need to engage in this activity if your school does not possess the documents listed above.

Even if the school does possess the documents it may, in some cases, be inadequate. Not every school will have in place each of these six documents as separate papers. Some may be included in the *Information for Parents Booklet* published by the school.

Where no policy exists, or where it is inadequate, you should begin your work on this unit by writing down as many statements on the topic as you can which describe what your school does. Useful beginnings may be as follows.

- In our school we always...
- One of the main concerns of our governing body is....
- The parents of our pupils are particularly keen to...
- Nearly all our staff think it is important to...

From these statements and your general knowledge of the school you should now be able to identify statements which could form the basis of the aims section of a draft policy document for this area in your school. Notice, these statements will not lead you to construct the full policy, but only the first section dealing with *aims*. Write down two main aims, and distinguish in doing so between different Key Stages.

In practice this may provide the starting point for the development of a school policy. All these policies will be needed by an inspection team visiting your school for either an OFSTED or section 23 inspection.

B1 School mission statement

Writing in *Mission, Management and Appraisal*, Louden and Urwin (1992) introduce the concept of the school mission statement as follows:

> A 'mission statement' sets out the fundamental purposes and values of the school which are the basis for its actions, policies and relationships. It is the starting point for policy statements for all the main areas of school life, for development plans and for staff development and appraisal.
>
> Although the term 'mission statement' is widely used in business management and in public and voluntary services, in the context of church schools it may be open to misinterpretation. For example, it is occasionally and wrongly taken to imply that a school is setting out to evangelise its pupils. For this reason, some schools may prefer to use a different title here. What is important is that

church schools should clearly identify and state their basic values and purposes.

Waddington (1984) makes clear his expectation that every church school should have a theological understanding of its task. Extracts from this are reprinted in chapter 2.1 of *Christian Perspectives on Church Schools* (Francis and Lankshear, 1993), entitled 'No apology for theology'. Waddington offers ten points which, in his view, should distinguish a church school from other kinds of school. These points are all loosely derived from a trinitarian understanding of God as loving Father, as serving and teaching Son, and as creative Spirit. Such a God is not only disclosed through the events of salvation history, especially in the exemplary life of Jesus, but also implies the value of human relationships since the Persons of the Trinity exist in an eternal relationship with each other. Waddington's hallmarks of a church school are that it is:

> A *safe place* where there is no ideological pressure and yet Christian inferences are built into the ethos and teaching as signals for children to detect;

> An *ecumenical nursery* which builds from children's fundamental unity a sensitivity to difference, and the faiths of others;

> A *place of distinctive excellence* which is not just tied to what is academic but plainly linked to all aspects of the life of the school including the manual, technical, aesthetic and non-verbal;

> *Stepping-stones to and from the community*, for children, staff, parents and local interests; the school learns to be part of a local community, to share its concern and to be open to those who seek help, support and resources;

> A *house of the gospel* in which, starting at governor and staff level, there is a deliberate attempt to link the concerns of Christ's gospel with the life of the school, and to do this in educational terms;

> A *place of revelation and disclosure* in which the rigour of learning and the art of acquiring skill are seen as parables of the revelation of God and his continuous involvement in his creation;

> A *foster home of enduring values and relationships*, in which the selfless care and unlimited love of the Suffering Servant is the model for the life of the community;

> A *beacon signalling the transcendent* by the development of awe, mystery and wonder through the curriculum, exemplified in acts of corporate worship including contact with the Christian calendar and sacraments;

> A *place where you can see the wood for the trees*, for there are attempts to develop an integrated view of knowledge alongside sensitivity to the interests of others, as well as to cross traditional subject boundaries and carry out integrated projects in learning;

> A *creative workshop* which facilitates a thorough induction into cultural tradition and skills yet allows pupils to practise initiative, change and new direction as they shape their future.

Hull in his article 'What is theology of education?' (Francis and Thatcher, 1990, chapter 1.1) discusses a theoretical definition of the field by drawing on the disciplines of theology and of education and then proposes a taxonomy (or classification) of problems in the theology of education. He identifies three sets of principles:

- the problems of formal principles arising out of the relations between the disciplines education and theology;
- the problems of material principles relating to the subjects taught in the school classroom;
- the problems of pedagogical method since 'the methods of education are just as full of values and assumptions as anything else in education'.

He provides a detailed analysis of the first set of these problems, dividing it into two main sections: the problems arising from the formal principles of education and the problems arising from the formal principles of theology. Within this latter heading he has problems arising from confessional theology in which he includes denominational theories of education. Presumably he would place the publications from the Church of England on educational matters in this heading in so far as they contain theological content and assumptions. The article does not consider specifically the issue of church schools. It does, however, indicate the range of issues that a church school seeking to establish a theological as well as an educational rationale for its work will need to address. Moreover, it shows that theological insights may be applied both within and beyond the faith community.

Francis in his article 'Theology of education and the church school' (Francis and Lankshear, 1993, chapter 2.2) draws attention to the two models for a church school contained in the Durham Report (1970), namely the *domestic* and the *general*. The domestic model argues that the task of the church school is to provide a church education for the children of church members. The general model argues that the church exists to serve the whole community, Christian and non-Christian, in the name of Christ and that one of the ways in which it can do this is by providing schools to educate the whole community's children. An Anglican secondary school in a large town might well identify with the domestic model. A village primary school is more likely to identify with the general model. Many Anglican schools will find themselves partially identifying with both.

Francis then argues that these two models should be replaced by three theological frameworks held in tension. The first of his frameworks is the *theology of nurture*. He suggests that this theology has been well developed by Hull (1981). Francis' second framework is the *theology of service*. He claims that this is well understood by the churches and quotes Duncan (1988) as evidence of this theology as applied in the school context. His third framework is the *theology of prophecy*. In this he sees the church responding to the challenges of the secular theorists of education (e.g. Hirst, 1965) by using church schools to demonstrate the practical relevance of the Christian understanding of the task of education.

Activity B1

In the light of these comments in the preceding paragraphs and your reading of Hull's and Francis' articles you should now examine the mission statement of your school. Use the following questions to assist your reflection. Your response to the last of these questions will be needed later in this unit.

- Does the statement reflect a theology? If so, in what way?
- Does it reflect a theology which you can support?
- What aspects of the mission statement would you wish to retain in any future revision?
- What aspects would you wish to discard, and why?
- What evidence would you present to illustrate how the mission statement is reflected in the practice of your school?
- What evidence would you present to illustrate how the mission statement is not reflected in the practice of your school?
- Write in the wording of a mission statement that you would wish to see in use for your school. (We should make it clear that it is the job of the governing body of your school to produce the mission statement, and that all you are being asked to do is to write down the statement you would like to see if you had the opportunity to introduce it. In other words, this is an hypothetical mission statement).

Comment on activity B1

The mission statement may have an explicit comment like:

> Such-and-such a school is a Christian community within which the children are helped and encouraged to attain the spiritual, moral, social and cultural standards taught by the Christian church. Within the church family the school accepts each child with his or her own individual abilities and talents irrespective of cultural and ethnic origin.

Such a statement emphasises the Christian aims that guide the school but expresses these aims in an inclusive way without putting pressure on children. The theology here is that of loving one's neighbour, but it is a love that stems from the Christian gospel.

You may find such a statement and the theology that underlies it quite realistic and acceptable. It includes the notion that the school is a family, a place of close relationships and give-and-take. It does not conceptualise the child as a consumer and the parent as a customer in the educational market place. It does not depend on a political theory of constitutional rights. Rather it conceives of society as being made up of individuals and families and communities, an altogether simpler social model.

On the other hand, you may wonder whether an isolated non-Christian child might feel embarrassed and swamped. In the final analysis, you may decide that the wording of the policy must be seen in the context of the care and professionalism of teachers. Or you may consider that almost *any* theology is bound to have a boundary and to create a group of people who do not find it comfortable. But this problem is also one which applies to a political ideology and is, in the final analysis, unavoidable.

You may have ranged more widely in your discussion and included the theoretical considerations when theology, as a discipline, is applied to education as a discipline and you may have used Hull's mapping of the area to enable you to make differentiations. You may have included reference to the three kinds of theology identified by Francis and tried to show how these relate to Hull's principles and to your own documentation. For instance, you may have taken the view that a 'theology of service' can be expressed overtly in a mission statement and amplified in policy documents.

B2 Inter-pupil relationships

In the National Society Booklet *Looking for Quality in a Church School*, Lankshear (1992a) wrote:

> This is perhaps the area that is most commonly associated with the ethos of a church school. Often it is expressed in terms of 'caring and sharing'. It is therefore important that church schools have a clear understanding which goes beyond such a bland summary and which is expressed in terms that have clearer theological roots. Jesus was clear in his instructions to the disciples on this matter. 'Love your neighbour as yourself' - Matthew 22.39. 'This is my commandment: Love each other' - John 15.17 (NIV). Also important here is the Old Testament understanding of the nature of humankind. 'So God created man in his own image, in the image of God he created him; male and female he created them' - Genesis 1.27 (NIV). Everyone associated with the school is made in the image of God and is to be loved. This is the basis from which a church school should derive its human relationships, and anything less leads into an impossible compromise.
>
> The school will have a series of overlapping networks of relationship, which will include governors, staff, children, parents, church members and residents

of the community which the school seeks to serve. It is a significant challenge to create and maintain such networks in ways that reflect the gospel, and yet nothing less could or should be expected from a church school. Those who are in leadership roles have a particular responsibility to ensure that their personal example sets the appropriate standards.

The way in which schools encourage pupils to relate to one another is a crucial aspect of the quality of relationships that are created in a church school. The school's discipline policy has a part to play in the development of these relationships, particularly if it deals with rewards as well as punishments. Also vital are the values that the school promotes through worship, through displays, by the interaction in the classroom and playground and by the example that the staff sets.

You should now consider the inter-pupil relationships in your school in the light of your reading. You may need to undertake some careful observation as well as reflection. Watching how children behave towards each other as they leave school may sometimes reveal more about inter-pupil relationships than what happens inside the more closely supervised atmosphere of the classroom.

Activity B2

Are there policy documents or guidelines for your school that make it clear to all staff (not just teachers) what the school expects in terms of pupil/pupil relationships (e.g. policies on bullying)? List those that are relevant. Are these guidelines, if they exist, related to the mission statement, or observed in practice?

If no guidelines exist could they be derived from the school mission statement or your own mission statement (recorded in activity B1)?

Write down four statements that you would wish to see included in guidance for staff on inter-pupil relationships in your school.

Comment on activity B2

You may find that some policy documents (for instance related to sex education) are much more closely tied in to the mission statement than others (for instance the information technology policy). If the mission statement, as the one we have quoted in the comment on activity B1, specifically refers to the 'standards' of the Christian church, then you would expect its values to be echoed in those policies dealing with pupil-to-pupil and teacher-to-pupil behaviour. If, on the other hand, the mission statement emphasises the development of the abilities and aptitudes of pupils, you might expect to find this leads to policies that stress academic performance.

The observation of mission statement guidelines is likely to be hard to measure. If the headteacher and governors wish to remind the school community of the statement, then they would do well to include extracts from it in official communications between home and school and at special occasions, perhaps at the start of the school year or by giving awards and prizes on the basis of the statement's implied values. In practice, it is possible that the mission statement will become buried beneath the paperwork that keeps the school running and, especially if the statement contains ideas favoured by a previous headteacher or chair of governors, it is likely to be quietly ignored. Finally, as Marfleet (1996, p 165) asks, in a question that remains unanswered, 'Is the finished statement a fair reflection of the school's ethos, summarising what the school stands for, or is it intended to be an aspiration, an idea towards which the school is moving?'

B3 School worship

In *Open The Door*, Barton, Brown and Brown (1994) wrote:

> In all Anglican schools worship should reflect some of the essential features within the rich traditions of Anglican prayer and worship. Church schools cannot be expected to encapsulate all of that richness, but when planning worship it is useful to have an idea of the important areas to be explored at some time during a pupil's school career. This is appropriate in all phases of compulsory education as the pupils' growing maturity contributes to a broadening and deepening of their spiritual experience and understanding.

The suggestions below include some of the elements of the Anglican heritage which can be drawn upon over a period of time for use in school worship:

- using the bible as a source book for inspiration and learning;
- reflecting upon Christian symbols and their use in worship (e.g. bread, wine, chalice, cross and crucifix are symbols which lead to an understanding of the meaning of Jesus' death and resurrection);
- observing the cycle of the Anglican year: Advent, Christmas, Lent, Easter, Pentecost. This, with holy days, can provide the framework for a changing pattern of school worship;
- participating in the regularity and set order of Anglican worship (e.g. recognising the central significance of the eucharist while acknowledging the variety of other forms of worship);
- special services from time to time (e.g. welcoming new pupils to school or acknowledging the departure of older pupils);
- using collects as a focus for short acts of worship in small groups;

- identifying a collection of prayers, hymns and psalms which create a framework for worship within the school;
- learning traditional responses and prayers which express the essential beliefs of Christians throughout the ages;
- providing opportunities to discover the value of meditation and silence within the context of Christian worship;
- recognising that the Anglican Church has a strong commitment to ecumenism which may be expressed when members of other churches are invited to lead worship;
- experiencing the bond of community which encompasses gender, age, race and religious opinions (e.g. through the range of visitors who are invited to lead or attend school worship);
- sharing in a commitment to dialogue with other faiths, shown in the welcome we offer to all pupils and the celebration of shared values and beliefs.

The clear implication of this booklet and of *Inspection Handbook* (Brown and Lankshear, 1995, 1997) is that every Anglican school should have a worship policy document that reflects its trust deed and the Anglican heritage as well as the age, maturity and worship experience of the pupils. In the light of your reading, you should now reflect on the worship policy document of your school. If the school does not have a worship policy document you should use the statements about your school's worship that you created in activity B1.

Activity B3

How does your worship policy document reflect the mission statement of your school?

How does it reflect your own mission statement (recorded in activity B1)?

Barton, Brown and Brown (1994) identify eleven points that could be included in a school worship programme to ensure that it reflects the Anglican heritage. Given your school's current policy which three of the eleven points not now incorporated in the worship programme would be most straightforward to introduce?

What action needs to be taken in order to ensure that the policy on worship in your school develops appropriately?

Identify three steps that could be taken to develop the worship in your school within the next three months.

Comment on activity B3

There should be a reasonable match between the worship policy document and the mission statement simply because the school assembly is the place where the values of the school may be most explicitly expressed. If the school intends to promote or base itself on Christian doctrines, ideals and values, then the worship offered by pupils and staff may be stimulated by Christian moral teaching. If the school intends to offer a service to the community imbued with a sense of Christian reconciliation or concern, then the worship of the school may pick up and reinforce these themes.

The selection of three of the points made by Barton, Brown and Brown (1994) will depend entirely on what is appropriate to the school with which you are working. Similarly, the action that needs to be taken to ensure that policy on worship develops appropriately will vary from school to school. There may be a need for a staff discussion so that consensus can be reached. There may be the need for money to be found within the budget to allow a member of staff to be given time to prepare a cycle of assemblies. There may need to be a committee formed specially to co-ordinate assembly and music with the church calendar or with national curriculum work. Representations may need to be made by the staff to the governors, or *vice versa*, to ensure the maximum amount of support is given to the whole process of school worship. Each school will have slightly different ways of making decisions but it is important that these decisions are known and understood by all concerned and that sufficient time and thought is given for their implementation.

B4 Religious education

In *Religious Education,* Brown (1992, p 25) writes:

> For those fortunate enough to teach religious education in Church schools there should be a ready support for their endeavour. Whether the school is aided, controlled, special agreement or grant-maintained there should be a clear confident Christian ethos which will provide a firm platform for good teaching of religious education.
>
> In controlled schools where the agreed syllabus is taught governors should be able to support close links with churches and other local religious communities. The collective worship should complement the teaching of religious education for, distinctively in controlled schools, there is an interface between the Church of England and a cross-section of the nation's children (and parents). Whatever agreed syllabus is taught in the controlled school one would hope and expect religion to be recognised as important and therefore religious education to have a special place within the curriculum.
>
> In aided and special agreement schools religious education should be able to flower on the stem of the confident Christian ethos of the school.

The lack of any reference in the second and third paragraphs of the quotation to grant-maintained schools should not confuse the reader. The arrangements and regulations under which religious education is conducted in grant-maintained schools is determined by their previous status.

In *Looking for Quality in a Church School*, Lankshear (1992a, p 10) writes:

> Whatever syllabus is in use in the school, it must be an expectation of the church that in its own schools the quality of what is taught and learned will be particularly good in this subject. As in other areas of the curriculum, the children and young people will be encouraged to develop attitudes of openness and enquiry and to engage in a search for truth. In this way they will come to understand what they believe, and be in a position to enter into the joys and challenges of an adult Christian faith.
>
> There is evidence to suggest that, under the pressure of the introduction of recent reforms, this area of the curriculum has not received sufficient attention or support in schools generally, and possibly in some church schools. If this is the case, it will be expected that church schools would take urgent action to redress this balance.

For a controlled school the local education authority agreed syllabus provides the basis for the school's religious education policy document. In an aided or special agreement school similar support will be offered by the diocesan syllabus in all but a few Anglican dioceses. Before beginning the reflection in this section you should obtain and study the appropriate syllabus for your school. This should be available in your school. If it cannot be found, those who work in a controlled school should contact the local education authority to ask for a copy of the agreed syllabus, while those who work in an aided school should contact the diocese for information about the diocesan syllabus. If no diocesan syllabus is available for your diocese, you should ignore the reference to the external syllabus in the first question of activity B4.

Activity B4

Is there a policy document that demonstrates how religious education is to be conducted in the school in accordance with the appropriate external syllabus and in line with the school's mission statement?

Where does this policy document succeed in giving expression to the school's theological understanding of its purpose and where does it fail?

Where does the policy document succeed in providing support for the newly appointed non-specialist teacher and where does it fail?

Is the syllabus resourced at a level which suggests that the subject is being taken seriously in the school? What evidence would a visitor see of this?

What three steps could be taken to improve the teaching of religious education in the school in the next six months?

Comment on activity B4

The religious education policy document may need to explain the statutory requirements applicable to this part of the curriculum. It may also explain the SACRE machinery and the sorts of religious education offered in different categories of church school. It may also make reference to the SCAA model syllabuses, the DfEE guidelines issued from time to time and to the agreed syllabus in use in the school's area. It may deal with continuity, progression and differentiation in the classroom and give an outline of the Key Stage topics and time allocation set by the school. It may also deal with methods of teaching religious education and the policy on the use of visitors (for instance local clergy), assessing, recording and reporting of pupils' work, resources, interaction with equal opportunities policies and parental rights of withdrawal.

All this may or may not be related distinctly to the school's mission statement and, indeed, the mission statement may have been framed in the light of the practical needs and restrictions imposed by the classroom and wider context of religious education.

You should look at the second paragraph of comment on activity B3 for ideas about the introduction of change into an area of school life. As a result of your consideration of the school's religious education policy, you may have to use these ideas to improve resourcing, support for new staff and to make other improvements. Not all these improvements need involve spending money.

B5 Staff relationships

In *Schools of Reconciliation,* Chadwick (1994, p 57) pointed out: 'Christian schools above all need to retain the focus on the human being as an individual loved by God'. Her stress on the individual is salutary in the light of a tendency to see schools as institutions whose output is measured in league tables and cost-effective performance.

In *Looking for Quality in a Church School,* Lankshear (1992a, pp 16-17) expands on this theme:

The school will have a series of overlapping networks of relationship, which will include governors, staff, children, parents, church members and residents of the community which the school seeks to serve. It is a significant challenge to create and maintain such networks in ways that reflect the gospel, and yet nothing less could or should be expected from a church school. Those who are in leadership roles have a particular responsibility to ensure that their personal example sets the appropriate standards.

Within a church school the relationships that exist between the staff are not only a key factor in the way in which the school is managed, but are also the most important example to the pupils of the school's ethos in action. Key questions in this area include the following.

- What is expected of staff by the school, the church, and the community?
- Who sets these expectations?
- What happens when staff fail to meet these expectations?
- How is conflict managed?
- What policies exist to help and guide staff?
- What differences are made between teaching and support staff?

Activity B5

Within this aspect of your school's life explore the following issues.

- How is the school's mission statement reflected in the policies and practices of the school that relate to the staffing issues identified?
- What aspects of the school's policy or practice should be affirmed or developed?
- What aspects of the school's policy or practice should be reviewed?
- What aspects of the school's policy or practice would be challenged during a section 23 inspection (the inspection of the 'church' aspects of the school including worship, ethos, and in aided schools religious education)?
- How important is it that this aspect of the school's life is reviewed by the school within the next year?

Comment on activity B5

The expectations of staff should be set by the school's mission statement. That, at least, is where the expectations are most clearly articulated. So this leads us to a logically prior question: how is the mission statement drawn up? And the answer here is that it is drawn up by the governing body of the school which, by law, must represent the views of parents, teachers, the foundation (in this case the Anglican Church) and the local education authority. Thus the governing body is a democratic and representative body whose views ought, in theory, to reflect those of the local community, giving adequate weight to each shade of opinion.

When staff fail to meet the expectations laid upon them, there are mentoring, in-service training or, as a last resort, disciplinary procedures that may be invoked.

Conflict between staff and parents ought to be managed by the headteacher in consultation with the governing body. If the governing body does not agree with the strongly held views of staff about the need to exclude allegedly disruptive pupils, the teaching unions are likely to become involved. This certainly occurred in 1996 during the widely-reported disputes at The Ridings School and Manton Junior School. In these instances the unions withdrew their labour and forced school closure. The powers of local and national government to facilitate the resolution of such conflicts are considerable, though experience has shown that government wishes to avoid two things: being blamed for the breakdown in school life and spending fresh money to provide extra staff or special regimes for excluded pupils.

Other considerations will be related to the details of the documentation of the school you are studying and cannot, for this reason, be commented on here.

B6 Discipline policies

In *A Shared Vision*, Lankshear (1992b) wrote:

> One of the major themes of the gospel is the unique value of individual human beings and their importance in the eyes of God. Within a church school the basis on which human relationships are built will be this belief. Everyone in the school from the three year old just started in the nursery down to the head teacher is a uniquely valuable human being, whom God loves. They are all entitled to the love and respect which that fact demands. Attempting to organise a human institution on that basis can lead to complications.

> It is raining at lunch time, and everyone in the school is in need of more space than is available. Voices are raised in the school hall. You go to investigate the noise and find one of the dinner supervisors shouting at a child. There is some food spilt on the floor. The supervisor is claiming that the child threw it there, the child says it was an accident. The supervisor is at screaming point. The child is in tears. A hundred children are looking on. What do you do?

> It is much easier to answer the question if you are not trying to treat each individual as a unique human being loved by God. It takes less time if you do not try to find out why the child and the dinner supervisor had both got into that situation. By giving them time, you may find that you uncover deeper problems than those directly resulting from spilt food, and of course if you uncover problems you will need to take some time over them, even if only to listen.

Naturally there will be occasions when children break rules, are naughty, spiteful or disobedient. In these circumstances the school's approach to discipline will come into play. The principle that seems most appropriate to a church school is that the children should learn that doing wrong has consequences, which may include punishment, but that following these consequences, there is always forgiveness and reconciliation available. The sin is rejected, but the sinner is not. It is not simply a matter, in every case, of an instant response followed by a cooling off period and then everyone going on as if nothing has happened. This will be appropriate for some of the incidents that happen in the life of the school. At other times there will be more careful consideration, and more reflection on the reasons why an offence was committed.

Children need to be provided with a secure framework of expected behaviour, within which they can operate, and against which they can sometimes press. Therefore there will need to be some rules and these will need to be explicit to all in the school and as far as is possible consistently applied. At some time all children will transgress these rules, either through inattention, bravado or a deliberate attempt to establish whether the rules are still being upheld.

This is normal behaviour, and is usually easily dealt with. However there are two groups of children about whom teachers should be concerned. These are children who never break the rules, or break them so often that it seems to be a habit that the ordinary school sanctions cannot alter.

To summarise, Lankshear proposes that the discipline policy of the school should be based on the theological viewpoint adopted by the school. He suggests that the rejection of sin but not the sinner is a key factor and that there should exist an awareness of forgiveness and reconciliation built into the disciplinary process. He also suggests that schools should be concerned about two particular groups of children: those who persistently break the rules and those who never break them. He has developed these ideas further in *Discipline Policies in Church Schools* (Lankshear, 1997).

Activity B6

How does the discipline policy and practice in your school stand the test of being measured against these ideas? What aspects of it would you wish to see altered?

What action does your school take over those who persistently offend? If exclusions are used how is this reconciled with 'rejecting the sin but not the sinner'?

What action does your school take over those who never offend? Is there anything that should be done? How do they experience the existence of forgiveness and reconciliation if they never sin? How does your school reward good behaviour?

How does your school seek to ensure that *all* staff are aware of and apply consistently the school's discipline policy?

Comment on activity B6

The ideas outlined by Lankshear stress a separation between the pupil and the offence. The pupil, in a Christian community, is, so far as possible, to be shown consideration; the offence is to be condemned. There are various ways this may be done. Each time a pupil is admonished or disciplined, the basic distinction may be made. The distinction prevents a labelling of pupils: this is a 'bad' pupil, that is a 'good' pupil. Moreover, whenever discipline is administered, it may be done with an explanation so that the basis of the discipline becomes clear. Discipline and love can co-exist; it is because pupils are loved that they are disciplined.

It is not possible to comment on the detail of your school's discipline policy and you may, in addition, make use of other theological ideas held alongside the notion of separating the 'sin and the sinner'. For instance, your policy may stress the use of *proportionate* punishment or praise, that is, punishment or praise that is strictly proportioned to the relevant behaviour. Your policy may stress the need to ensure that disruptive behaviour that offends the whole school community or that interferes with the education of a whole class of pupils is treated more seriously than behaviour which, while naughty, only affects property (breaking a chair) or appearance (leaving the cloakrooms untidy).

The need to stress reconciliation is often best expressed when dealing with arguments that arise between pupils. Pupils frequently need to be taught to apologise to each other, to forgive each other (that is, not to harbour grudges) and to seek to become friends again. These lessons, though simple and basic, are often not taught by parents and may be presented as ways of solving inter-personal disputes by the school. This is particularly so since the televisual media rarely stress reconciliation; vengeance makes for more exciting drama.

Reward for good behaviour should be built in to school's discipline policies and schools may operate a 'star' system (a certain number of stars lead to a recognised privilege) or use a simpler less ostentatious method of praise. There is nothing wrong with using praise, public or private, as a response to pupils. Care must be taken, however, not to reward the same pupils over and over again, or to offer praise to some pupils for effort and to other pupils for achievement, since the basis for this distinction is not obvious to pupils and may appear to be unfair. The notion of reward may be theologically justified, though it is also arguable, on theological grounds, that 'virtue is its own reward' which needs nothing extrinsic to itself as a source of motivation.

The dispersal of school policy on discipline to all staff is probably best achieved on in-service training days and by staff meetings. Above all, staff need to appreciate that a discipline policy *works*, that it enhances education and produces a happy atmosphere in school.

Conclusion

In this last section you should review the notes that you have made in response to the previous sections. In light of the reflection and reading that you have undertaken you should now be in a position to identify those areas of your school's policy and practice which need review and those which need to be affirmed. In activity B1 you were asked to write a new, personal and hypothetical version of your school's mission statement. You may now wish to review that version further in the light of the detailed review that you have undertaken of aspects of the school's work and the reading that you have undertaken. If you feel your school's mission statement is in need of revision, then you may wish to revise it. How would you justify this new statement in terms of:

- a theology of education;
- a philosophy of education;
- the tradition and values of the school?

Readers

You will find helpful section 1.1 and chapters 4 and 5 of L.J. Francis and A. Thatcher (eds) (1990), *Christian Perspectives for Education*, Leominster, Gracewing, and chapters 2 and 3 of L.J. Francis and D.W. Lankshear (eds) (1993), *Christian Perspectives on Church Schools*, Leominster, Gracewing.

Bibliography

Barton, D., Brown, A. and Brown, E. (1994), *Open The Door,* London, The National Society and Oxford Diocesan Educational Services.

Brown, A. (1992), *Religious Education,* London, The National Society.

Brown, A. and Lankshear, D.W. (1995), *Inspection Handbook for Section 13 Inspections in Schools of the Church of England and Church in Wales,* London, The National Society.

Brown, A. and Lankshear, D.W. (1997), *Inspection Handbook: for section 23 inspections in schools of the Church of England and Church in Wales,* London, The National Society.

Chadwick, P. (1994), *Schools of Reconciliation,* London, Cassell.

Duncan, G. (1988), Church schools in service to the community, in B. O' Keeffe (ed.), *Schools for Tomorrow: building walls or building bridges,* London, Falmer Press, pp 145-161.

Durham Report (1970), *The Fourth R,* London, The National Society and SPCK.

Francis, L.J. and Lankshear, D.W. (1993), *Christian Perspectives on Church Schools,* Leominster, Gracewing.

Francis, L.J. and Thatcher, A. (1990), *Christian Perspectives on Education,* Leominster, Gracewing.

Hirst, P.H. (1965), Liberal education and the nature of knowledge, in R.D. Archambault (ed.), *Philosophical Analysis and Education,* London, Routledge and Kegan Paul, pp 113-138.

Hull, J. (1981), *Understanding Christian Nurture,* London, British Council of Churches.

Lankshear, D.W. (1992a), *Looking for Quality in a Church School,* London, The National Society.

Lankshear, D.W. (1992b), *A Shared Vision,* London, The National Society.

Lankshear, D.W. (1997), *Discipline Policies in Church Schools,* London, The National Society.

Louden, L.M.R. and Urwin, D.S. (1992) *Mission Management and Appraisal,* London, The National Society.

Marfleet, A., (1996), School mission statements and parental perceptions, in J.M. Halstead and M.J. Taylor (eds), *Values in Education and Education in Values,* London, Falmer Press, pp 155-166.

O'Keeffe, B. (1986), *Faith, Culture and the Dual System,* Barcombe, Falmer Press.

Waddington, R. (1984), *A Future in Partnership,* London, The National Society.

Belief and Practice

Unit C

Beliefs, values and practices of the Anglican Church

David W. Lankshear

The National Society

London

and

Revd Alex M. Smith

Liverpool Hope University College

Liverpool

Contents

Introduction

Aims

After working through this unit you should be able to:

- identify the main beliefs and practices of the Anglican Church and the ways in which they are expressed;
- appreciate the diversity of belief and practice within the Anglican Church and the reasons for this phenomenon;
- explore the beliefs and practices of the Anglican Church in relation to pupils' experience of church and school.

Overview

The beliefs, values and practices of the Anglican Church can be discerned from a number of different types of source material. We begin with a general overview of the beliefs of the Anglican Church and then focus more narrowly on those beliefs which are relevant to work in Anglican schools.

During the second part of this unit you will be presented with five issues associated with Anglican beliefs, values and practices. You will be required to investigate each of these using specified source material in the first instance. Each area has been chosen for:

- its relevance to an aspect of church/school conduct;
- the range of understandings within the church about the topic;
- the relevance of different types of source material.

C1 Beliefs and practices

The beliefs and practices of the Anglican Church stem from the Reformation and, before that, from the medieval church. As is well known, Britain was Christianised during the period of Roman occupation in the first four centuries of the Christian era and the establishment of the British church is documented by Bede whose *A History of the English Church and People* was completed in 731. The book begins with an account of Pre-Roman Britain and continues from the time of Julius Caesar, showing how the British church was affected by the Diocletian persecution. Surviving these convulsions, the church grew in strength and its saints, scholars and bishops played an important political and religious role in the life of the nation. The language of liturgy, Latin, was also the language of international diplomacy, the bible and some poetic literature.

The Reformation broke existing patterns and structures within the European church. While Roman Catholicism remained more or less uniform, Protestantism fragmented into its various national and denominational groupings. The radical Protestantism of the Swiss reformers (which was transplanted to Scotland) contrasted with the less radical Protestantism of Germany and England. Radical Protestantism adopted non-episcopal methods of church government, a view of the eucharist that was entirely commemorative and a form of baptism that was only open to professing believers and therefore not to young children. German Protestantism accepted the episcopacy, a view of the eucharist which, while denying transubstantiation, nevertheless believed that the body of Christ was present within the bread and wine, and a form of baptism similar to that operated by the Roman Catholic Church.

England was affected both by radical Protestantism (which remained alive and active within the Dissenting community and in Scotland) and less radical Protestantism. The Anglican settlement was ultimately seen as a 'middle way' between these competing positions. Anglicans accepted episcopacy and, indeed, gave prominence to the See of Canterbury, though at no stage was the Archbishop of Canterbury an Anglican Pope.

Thomas Cranmer

Archbishop Thomas Cranmer (1489-1556) embodies the initial Anglican position (Ridley, 1962; Buchanan, Lloyd and Miller, 1980). He was a fellow in Cambridge when Erasmus' *Greek Text of the New Testament* was published in 1516 and, after extensive study, was ordained as a priest in 1520. His study of Luther and the other reformers took place from 1521, though Cambridge banned all Lutheran books after 1520. He reported that from about 1525 onwards he began to pray for the abolition of papal power in England and he found himself thrust into the spotlight when it became clear that Henry VIII wanted a divorce. Cranmer suggested a solution to the king's problem: the king should take the opinion of the universities rather than the papal court. He prepared a thesis drawing upon scripture and the fathers to this effect and was called upon to defend his case before the universities of Oxford and Cambridge. Before he could do so, he was sent on a delegation to Rome, but it is not certain whether he was able to make his case there. By now, however, Cranmer was engaged in ambassadorial duties round the universities of Europe and it was here he met Osiander whose theological position was half-way between that of Luther and the orthodoxy of Rome. Despite the long-standing convention that priests remain celibate, his own willingness to move in a

Protestant direction was signalled by a marriage to Osiander's niece in 1532. When the previous Archbishop of Canterbury died, Cranmer was persuaded to succeed him in 1533. He declared the king's marriage invalid soon afterwards and then officiated at the wedding of Henry and Anne Boleyn.

Cranmer began to reshape the British church by promoting the publication of the English bible and introducing new liturgies and prayer books (1549 and 1552) and a set of 42 articles of faith (later reduced to 39) which were adopted by the Anglican Church and expressed its dogmatic position. The Thirty-nine Articles, as the *Book of Common Prayer* explains, were agreed in 1562 'for the avoiding of diversities of opinions, and for the establishing of consent touching true religion'. They begin by asserting the need for faith in the:

- Holy Trinity;
- incarnation and life of Christ;
- canon of scripture;
- Nicene, Athanasian and Apostles' creeds;
- original sin;
- human free will's limitations;
- justification through 'the merit of our Lord and Saviour Jesus Christ';

and they continue by reference to other matters of faith and conduct including the sacraments (or 'effectual signs of grace') of baptism and eucharist, the marriage of priests, homilies and the role of civil magistrates.

Cranmer, who was martyred for his Protestant beliefs in the reign of Mary, both by his disposition and his convictions, set a lasting stamp on the Anglican Church. He represented not only Protestantism's biblical and historical scholarship, but also tolerance, piety, humanity, adherence to the monarch and the sonorous beauties of the English language and, when necessary, a willingness to die for what is believed.

Activity C1

Consider briefly one aspect of Cranmer's life that you feel is relevant to the Anglican Church today. Write your conclusions on no more than a side of A4.

Comment on activity C1

You may have thought that Cranmer's flexibility and adaptability are relevant to today's church and you may have off-set this virtue with an awareness that there was a certain irreducible core of belief which was non-negotiable. You may consider that Cranmer's attitude, in turbulent political times when national alliances and deep-seated attitudes were unsettled, suggests a means of coping with change. Above all Cranmer returned to the scripture, but he was willing to interpret it in ways that were then untraditional, as, for instance, in his advocacy of the right of the king to divorce on what were Old Testament grounds, that Henry had married his elder brother's widow, and that this was contrary to Leviticus 18.16 and 20.21.

You may have thought that Cranmer's concentration on liturgy in a language understood by the uneducated is fundamental to the progress of the church today. Where the church is misunderstood, there is little chance of moral or spiritual influence. You may have thought that Cranmer's moderation, his willingness to balance extreme positions, shows how the Anglican Church should respond to the dilemmas that face her today, both in the field of education and in moral teaching.

If you wish to look at this subject further, and especially into the development of the prayer books written by Cranmer, you should read Proctor and Frere (1961) or Lowther Clarke and Harris (1932). Miller (1980, p 25) summarises the process by saying, 'the 1549 and 1552 Prayer Books were to be the basis of the 1662 *Book of Common Prayer*'. The standard exposition of the Thirty-nine Articles is given by Bicknell (1955).

Richard Hooker

Hooker (1554-1600) wrote the *Laws of Ecclesiastical Polity* in defence of the Elizabethan Settlement of 1559 against its radical Protestant and Roman Catholic opponents. He argued that ecclesiastical polity (or church order) should be deduced from scripture and nature together, but not from either separately. Scripture itself does not cover every conceivable instance about which human beings require a judgement to be made; scripture is sufficient for the ends for which it was instituted, which are to make salvation known, but not for the ordering of church life and conduct. Nature likewise speaks about God because the whole created order exhibits a general structure that is, in the last analysis, formed by the reasonable will of God. Since the will of God is reasonable, it may be discerned by reason, and is often expressed through a series of interlinked laws, where laws are conceived as general tendencies of things to behave consistently .

This dependence on scripture and nature (or reason) allows only a very limited role for tradition, but there is a logic in this position since tradition is only valid when it accords with scripture and reason; if it fails to do so, it is wrong; if it does so, it is redundant (McGrath, 1986). Nevertheless, tradition *does* have a positive part to play in justifying the existing order and rites of the Anglican Church. It is in matters of doctrine that tradition is insufficient.

The theological method Hooker devised is characteristically Anglican and, according to Avis (1989), he is 'unquestionably the greatest Anglican theologian'. His method allows for flexibility, is distinctly Protestant, and in the hands of later Anglican theologians, like Launcelot Andrewes (1555-1626) and Jeremy Taylor (1613-67), made room for an expansion in the appeal to tradition. As Andrewes wrote:

> one canon... two testaments, three creeds, four general councils, five centuries and the series of fathers in that period... determine the boundary of our faith.

The modern period

The development of Anglicanism in the following centuries up to the present may be simplified by saying that the three sources of theology, namely reason, tradition and scripture, issued in three broad wings within the church. The priority of *reason* led to the liberal (or broad church) section; the emphasis on *tradition* led to the catholic wing and the stress on *scripture* led to the evangelical wing. Each wing had periods of ascendancy, and there were complicating factors when the sources of theology were variously permutated or interpreted. Disputes or crises within the church may be understood as disagreements between the different wings (Neill, 1977; Sykes, 1978).

Partly for these reasons, it is helpful to view the essence of Anglicanism as being expressed in its liturgy rather than its developing theology. The liturgy is that which all Anglicans, whatever their theological stance, accept and by which their worship is offered.

In England, after extensive trials as Series 1, 2 and 3 Services, new liturgies were published in 1980 as *The Alternative Service Book 1980* and authorised for use. The new orders for holy communion (eucharist) were more complicated than those in the *Book of Common Prayer*. Two rites of communion were agreed and there were alternatives within each, as well as the possibility of making use of the pattern of the *Book of Common Prayer* in Rite A. Historical continuity was also maintained by the care taken in the preface to *The Alternative Service Book 1980* to state that:

> The doctrine of the Church of England is grounded in the holy scriptures, and in such teachings of the ancient Fathers and Councils of the church as are agreeable to the said scriptures. In particular such doctrine is to be found in the Thirty-nine Articles of Religion, the *Book of Common Prayer* and the Ordinal.

Vasey (1980) and Miller (1980) explain the complicated process by which *The Alternative Service Book 1980* was written, and Jasper and Bradshaw (1986) offer a commentary on the resultant text. Diverse theological views were treated in this way as explained by Vasey (1980, p 43):

> Wherever possible, forms of expression have been found which satisfy all views; this has often been done by returning to the language of scripture or by a re-examination of tradition. In cases where agreement has not been possible the matter has been left or forms of words which allow of different interpretations have been used.

The Alternative Service Book 1980 offers diversity-within-unity, and often the nuances of theological opinion implicit within liturgical variations are expressed by very small verbal alterations. But, in addition, the liturgical movement - a movement that started in the Roman Catholic Church at the end of the nineteenth century - that influenced the development of *The Alternative Service Book 1980* stressed the importance of intelligibility, congregational participation and simplicity as goals of modern worship, and this has had a further effect on the shape and texture of modern liturgies (Miller, 1980, p 27; Butler, 1988).

C2 A modern controversy

The first chapter of *We Believe in God* (Doctrine Commission, 1987) takes the view that the task of Christian education is a preparation for 'a lone quest of conscience, a sustained venture of prayer, a private journey' and also 'a common enterprise ... the shared receiving of a gift, a corporate experience of worship and a joint endeavour'. The themes of individuality and collectivity appear in the following illustration.

The Durham affair

Here are two passages taken from the book *The Durham Affair* by Ledwich (1985). They are:

- a petition presented to the Archbishop of York before the consecration of Professor David Jenkins as Bishop of Durham and after his appearance on the BBC 'Credo' programme in 1984;
- the Archbishop's reply.

The Petition presented to the Archbishop of York

In view of the recent statement made by the Reverend Professor David Jenkins, Bishop elect of Durham, on London Weekend Television on April 29th 1984, denying the Virgin Birth and the Resurrection of our Lord to be historical events and also that belief in Jesus as God made flesh is necessary for a Christian we, being communicant members of the Church of England, are grievously distressed by the prospect of a diocesan bishop of the church publicly professing and preaching such views, which are wholly incompatible with the teaching of scripture and the church. We, therefore, earnestly beg Your Grace to invite Professor Jenkins to affirm publicly that he believes the creeds as the church has consistently interpreted them; and that should he refuse, Your Grace will seriously question whether it is right to proceed with his consecration as a bishop.

In the *Credo* programme, produced by London Weekend Television and transmitted on the 29th April 1984, the Reverend Professor David Jenkins, Bishop elect of Durham was interviewed by Philip Whitehead. He was asked whether the story of the Virgin Birth of our Lord was historically and literally true. This Professor Jenkins said he did not believe. 'The Virgin Birth I'm pretty sure', he said, 'is a story told after the event in order to express and symbolise a faith that this Jesus was a unique event from God. Again, I wouldn't put it past God to arrange a virgin birth if he wanted but I very much doubt he would because it seems contrary to the way in which he deals with persons and brings his wonders out of natural personal relationships'. (The quotations from the programme are taken from the official transcript, issued by London Weekend Television.)

Later in the programme, Professor Jenkins expressed his view that there was no 'one event which you could identify with the resurrection'; but rather that it was 'a series of experiences', which convinced the apostles the 'very life and power and purpose and personality which was in him was actually continuing'.

Finally, in answer to Philip Whitehead, Professor Jenkins denied the necessity for a Christian to hold Jesus was God made flesh or that he was more than purely 'a great moral teacher and a divine agent', though the Professor, as an individual, appears to believe more than this about Jesus.

Now it seems to many Anglicans, clergy and lay people, catholic and evangelical, that the doctrines of the incarnation of God as Man in Jesus Christ, born therefore of his Virgin Mother, and the historical event of the bodily Resurrection from death, are indispensable doctrines of the Christian faith. Without them our Christian belief and our membership of the church are without content or purpose. To reinterpret these articles of the creed as mere helpful stories rather than real, historical events that have wrought our salvation is to substitute a new religion for the catholic faith.

Some academic theologians have, for many years, expressed views such as Professor Jenkins', and this petition is in no way intended to demand that their freedom of thought or expression be curtailed. But the Christian church has always accepted the limiting and liberating aspect of dogma; to be fenced around by doctrine that is revealed by the Holy Spirit and defined by the Church of Christ is not to be restricted, but to find new freedom within the structure of truth. We are not at liberty, therefore, to reinterpret the scriptures and creeds in a way which denies their content.

Furthermore the clergy, and particularly the bishops, have a special and sacred obligation to believe, defend, and sincerely teach these doctrines, without concession to the beliefs fashionable in any age. At the ordination of a bishop in *The Alternative Service Book 1980* Archbishop asks the Bishop-elect if he believes 'the doctrine of the Christian faith as the Church of England has received it', and if he will promise to 'expound and teach' that faith, which he will acknowledge as 'revealed in the holy scriptures and set forth in the catholic creeds'.

If Professor Jenkins, as Bishop-elect of Durham, can profess at his ordination belief in the creeds, yet interpret them as he has publicly done, it will reasonably be inferred by many that his views are compatible with the doctrine of the Church of England. This will constitute a major change in her official teaching, placing the seal of approval upon heresy as an alternative to the catholic apostolic faith; it will reduce both to the status of optional opinions within the church. The Church of England cannot seriously consider allowing such a development without undermining its credibility as part of 'the pillar and ground of the truth'.

This petition is therefore intended and organised as a plea to His Grace the Lord Archbishop of York to consider the very serious implications of proceeding with the ordination to the episcopate of Professor Jenkins.

The Archbishop of York's reply

Dear Mr Ledwich

I write to acknowledge receipt of your petition about the forthcoming consecration of Professor David Jenkins, and I wish to assure you that I understand the seriousness of the concern which has led you to promote it.

You ask for Professor Jenkins to make a further public affirmation of faith, though doubtless you are aware that in a written statement to the clergy of the Durham Diocese, issued on May 22nd, he said 'I shall unhesitatingly respond affirmatively before God, in complete good faith and in total dependence on his grace, to the question which the archbishop puts to a bishop-elect at his consecration, "Will you affirm your loyalty to this inheritance of faith as your inspiration and guidance under God in bringing the grace and truth of Christ to this generation and making him known to those in your care?"' 'The inheritance of faith' there referred to includes, as you well know, the scriptures, the catholic creeds and the historical formularies of the Church of England.

During the consecration service I shall ask him, 'Do you believe the doctrine of the Christian faith as the Church of England has received it...?' and from what I know of him personally and through his writings, I have every reason to believe that he will be able to answer this question affirmatively in complete good faith.

Apart from the recitation of the Nicene Creed during the eucharist these are the only explicit forms of doctrinal assent which the liturgy requires, and I see no valid ground for asking Professor Jenkins to make more declarations than the church has seen fit to prescribe.

If the petition implies that his sincerity in making these declarations is in doubt, then so serious a charge would need to be backed by evidence from his writing and other well considered expressions of belief. I note that none of those who have written to me, or who have in other ways complained about his appointment, have made any derogatory references to his numerous published works. Nor have his critics shown evidence of having acquainted themselves with his thought as a whole.

I must therefore reject your request. I note however that the petition raises three important questions of principle, on which some brief comments may be helpful:

1.   The first concerns the role of the mass media, and whether a bishop's orthodoxy should be judged by his writings, the general tenor of his teaching and his formal profession of faith, or by brief, unscripted and epigrammatic remarks made to the media. How important, in other words, is his media image, especially when it differs markedly from what he knows himself to be?

It can be argued that Professor Jenkins has been unwise in the manner he has expressed himself publicly. No doubt he will quickly learn that the way a bishop is heard differs from the way a professor is heard, and that the impression conveyed through the media may be more significant than what is actually said or left unsaid. In any attempt to communicate profound truths, public relations cannot be ignored. Nevertheless, it would be a strange reflection on the church's integrity if in so important a matter as the choice of a man to be bishop, it were to pay more attention to image than to the reality.

2.   Does the Church of England require its clergy to profess belief, not only in the catholic creeds, but also in a particular interpretation of them?

This is a question to which it would be difficult for any church, which takes seriously both the continuity of its faith and the processes of historical change, to give a definitive answer. The nearest that the Church of England has come to answering it is in its present Declaration of Assent, which invites a general rather than a particular and detailed affirmation.

The 1938 *Report on Doctrine* recognised that the creeds contain many types of statement in which the borderline between the symbolic and the historical dimensions cannot be precisely defined, and it explicitly affirmed a liberty of interpretation. It was careful, however, to stress that such liberty must not be taken so far as to undermine the historical basis of the gospel story - which story the creeds summarise and interpret - were such as to justify the gospel itself. To this extent the 1938 Report provides backing for the statement in the notes to the petition that 'we are not at liberty to reinterpret the scriptures and creeds in such a way which denies their content'. But, unlike the petition, the report did not conclude from this affirmation of the historical basis of Christianity, that everything stated in a historical form must necessarily be interpreted as literal history.

The 1981 Doctrine Commission Report, *Believing in the Church*, assumed a similar liberty of interpretation, and its use of the word 'story' to describe the content of Christian tradition deliberately kept open the same options which the 1938 Commission had been at pains to safeguard.

The case of Hensley Henson's consecration as Bishop of Hereford in 1918 provides an instructive illustration of the same theme. Henson was accused of doubting both the Virgin Birth and the bodily Resurrection of Christ. Archbishop Davidson asked him 'to profess faith in the creed, and that he declare himself to have no wish to alter the words of the creed on the Birth and the Resurrection', both of which Henson was prepared to do. Professor Owen Chadwick, in retelling the story, commented, 'To say that you have no desire to alter the historical wording of a clause is not to say that you believe the clause as your father believed' (Chadwick, 1983, p 141). In thus summarising what came to be known as 'The Hereford Scandal', he drew on a principle which even such brief notes as these can demonstrate as being characteristically Anglican.

3.   Is there a special obligation on a bishop, as a teacher and defender of the faith, to have a different standard of truth from that of other Christians? The question is not whether his faith is greater and more mature; it is to be hoped that it is. But insofar as certain historical events are affirmed to be true a bishop, like everyone else, must depend upon the historical evidence. His role as teacher, therefore, is not independent of the intellectual and spiritual task of the whole church, as in each generation it seeks to answer questions about the truth for itself. Within this total task of the church bishops and academic theologians have different roles, and often ask different questions, but it would surely be wrong to imply that as teachers they should have different standards.

A bishop's role as a defender of the faith is part of his corporate responsibility as a member of the whole episcopate, and is expressed synodically through some of the special powers conferred on the House of Bishops. Changes in the official teaching of the church on doctrinal matters involve elaborate procedures and widespread consultation, and cannot be inferred, as the petition suggests, from the opinions of a single bishop. Indeed, it is precisely the interplay between differing episcopal views which is one of the factors maintaining the comprehensive character of our church.

I make these general comments, not as in any sense a definitive answer to the questions, which are important and far reaching. The Church of England needs constantly to be challenged concerning the quality and integrity of its belief, and my hope is that your petition will encourage serious and widespread theological discussion. Such discussion cannot, however, alter the basic fact of this case, namely that Professor Jenkins is both willing and able to make the declarations required of him.

Yours sincerely

John Ebor

Activity C2

Where do you stand on the consecration of David Jenkins? Why?

Are there differences between Christian doctrine and the way it is believed?

What implications does your answer have for work in a church school?

The archbishop makes a distinction between the historical event, 'the story', and the symbolism that becomes attached to it. How does this have implications for teaching the faith to children?

The archbishop argues for the collective responsibility of the House of Bishops within which there are diverse views. In work with young people do church schools have an equivalent responsibility, in other words, should church schools *as a whole* convey the historical faith, but may there be differences of emphasis between them? If so, how might this work in practice?

Comment on activity C2

With the advantage of historical perspective, you have a viewpoint unavailable to the participants in the 1984 controversy. You will have noticed David Jenkins' political views, in the end, were probably more influential in the media than his religious views - he tended to support the miners in their struggle against Mrs Thatcher's government. To the extent that it is helpful for the Church of England to have spokespersons from the political right and the political left (so representing a balance in the minds of the population), it was helpful to have a bishop who spoke against the prevailing political orthodoxy.

The question that hangs in the air over the appointment of David Jenkins is whether a bishop, who has a special responsibility for doctrine and in the appointment of other clergy, should hold views which, while they may be perfectly valid in a department of theology, are less than transparently orthodox. The Archbishop of York's answer suggests that the whole of a person's theological output should be taken into consideration when an assessment is made of him or her and that, in the case of bishops, there is a sense in which the collective view of the House of Bishops holds sway over the individual opinions of its members. You may find the Archbishop of York's position realistic and with the merit of allowing individual freedom to co-exist with collective responsibility and the responsibilities of ecclesiastical office. On the other hand, you may take the view that if *all* bishops took non-traditional views, the balance within the House of Bishops would be unalterably shifted in a non-traditional direction. You might also think that, just as politicians and public figures, by virtue of their public role, are expected to hold views and uphold standards not expected of those who live outside the public spotlight, so bishops, in the age of an intrusive tabloid-dominated sound-bite media, forfeit some of the freedoms afforded to ordinary Christians.

You may have given thought to the distinction between a belief and the way it is held and interpreted. The relationship between a belief and the reality to which it refers is complex and belongs to the realm of philosophical theology and to language theory, both of which are outside the reach of this unit. The problem for most Christians lies in the interpretation of purportedly historical events in a symbolic mode. Clearly, if the historicity of an event is denied while its symbolic value is affirmed, we have a tension which is unlikely to be understood by children. The Archbishop's point here is pertinent:

> The 1938 *Report on Doctrine* recognised that the creeds contain many types of statement in which the borderline between the symbolic and the historical dimensions cannot be precisely defined, and it explicitly affirmed a liberty of interpretation. It was careful, however, to stress that such liberty must not be taken so far as to undermine the historical basis of the gospel story - which story the creeds summarise and interpret - were such as to justify the gospel itself.

There are implications here for teaching the Christian faith to children, but these implications need also be taken in conjunction with the findings of child psychology which are dealt with in the module on *Spiritual and Moral Development*. In brief, it is clear that the beliefs expressed in the Thirty-nine Articles and affirmed in the scripture are likely to be held by children in less symbolic ways than those advanced by David Jenkins. But it is also clear that many adult Christians are likely to hold these beliefs in less symbolic ways than those advanced by David Jenkins. This implies that the teaching given to children should be such as will admit, but *not require*, development in a symbolic direction.

The overall presentation of the Christian faith by Anglican schools is, in a sense, a collective responsibility, but the parallel with the House of Bishops is inexact, especially since church schools are of two kinds (controlled and aided) and operate with distinct theological frameworks (as specified by the *Durham Report*), whereas the bishops are a much more homogeneous body.

C3 Initiation

In their article 'Changing trends in Anglican confirmation', Francis and Lankshear (1993, pp 64-76) wrote:

> Theologically within the Church of England there are two rather different views regarding the nature of the sacrament of confirmation. Each of these two views carries different practical implications for the way in which the sacrament is regarded and for the age groups among whom it is administered.

> The first view regards baptism as the total and sufficient sacrament of Christian initiation. This case is argued, for example, by Buchanan (1986) and the General Synod report *Christian Initiation* (Ely, 1971), which stated that:

>> In the period covered by the New Testament we have no firm evidence that any rite resembling confirmation was regularly practised.

> According to this view the baptised person may be admitted to communion prior to confirmation (Dennis, 1985). Such a view removes any pressure for

early confirmation and allows confirmation to be regarded as a rite of adult commitment. According to this view the future for confirmation may be seen to be increasing among adults rather than among teenagers.

The second view regards baptism as, in some senses, incomplete without confirmation. The case is argued, for example, by Mason (1891) and Dix (1946) and has recently been re-emphasised by the General Synod paper, *Christian Initiation Matters* (House of Bishops, 1991), which states that:

> the Church of England has never accepted that baptism is the sole and complete rite of Christian initiation when administered to infants.

According to this view the baptised person should not be admitted to communion prior to confirmation. Given the current tendencies for young Anglican to be present in the adult Sunday congregation rather than in separate Sunday Schools (Board of Education, 1988), and the growing centrality of eucharistic worship in the Anglican churches (Francis, 1985), this view generates pressure for early confirmation. According to this view the future of confirmation may be seen to be increasing among children rather than teenagers.

Thus according to these authors the Anglican church uses confirmation for two distinct purposes. These are rites concerned with admission to communion and with commitment to the faith. For adults who seek confirmation there would appear to be little conflict in these purposes and they may be appropriately combined, although many would argue that adult baptism should be sufficient for both the purposes above.

When the nurture of children in the church is being considered, it is argued that there is a tension between these two purposes of confirmation. A child being brought up in a church which has the eucharist as its main celebration may desire full admission to the service when he or she is aged eight or nine, but, in order to gain this admission, will need to undergo confirmation at an age when it is impossible to give a faith commitment similar to that which might be made after reaching maturity. There is therefore a conflict which is only resolved if the young person's wish to participate fully in the eucharist coincides exactly with his or her ability to make the mature faith commitment expressed in confirmation.

You should find out the policy operated by the church to which your school is attached over the age of confirmation. You should then read through the confirmation service in both *The Alternative Service Book 1980* and the *Book of Common Prayer* and the rubrics that relate to the service.

Activity C3 (optional)

How has your church interpreted the rubrics? How does the policy on confirmation affect the work of the school? On what basis would a regular eucharist in your school be justified in the light of your church's policy on confirmation?

Comment on activity C3

Children will become unhappy if the eucharist is an occasion when they are divided from each other. Some children, having previously lived in another parish, will have been confirmed early, and they may be admitted to the eucharist. Others, of the same age and the same spiritual and intellectual maturity who have not been confirmed, will be excluded. Children who are not given an opportunity to be confirmed will resent the privileges of those who are. One way to try to solve this conundrum is to admit to full participation in the eucharist those who are confirmed and to allow others to come forward for a blessing. But this may be unsatisfactory. In any case it is probable that a regular eucharist will benefit the school community most obviously if everyone, pupils, parents and staff, know and appreciate the policy on admission to it. There must be some minimum age and some minimum requirement for admission to full participation in the eucharist. As long as the age and requirement are applied with scrupulous fairness, grounds for complaint and for disunity should be reduced to well-nigh zero.

C4 Attitudes to children

In 1988 the Church of England published a report to the General Synod entitled *Children in the Way* (Board of Education, 1988). This report was received by synod and commended to dioceses and deaneries for discussion. It was accompanied by a video which introduced many of the topics in the report. The report contained a list of recommendations, which were as follows:

Chapter 1

1.   The church should seriously consider what priority it places on serving the needs of all children in our contemporary society. Parishes, deaneries and dioceses should acknowledge their responsibility: to learn from those already involved in social work with children; to investigate particular local pressures on children; to establish practical ways of contributing to children's support and enrichment.

2.   PCCs should carefully consider the suitability of new leaders to whom they delegate responsibility for work with children of the parish.

Chapter 2

1.   Parishes, deaneries and dioceses undertaking children's evangelistic missions should examine the appropriate basis for them, with special reference to follow up work, family involvements and peer group pressures.

2.   The church, nationally and locally, should actively support the efforts of uniformed groups to evaluate the moral and spiritual aspects of their work with children.

3.   Parishes should consider how they can effectively support the best traditions of Christian marriage and family life, while affirming their active and sensitive concern and care for all for whom this is not a reality.

4.   Boards of General Synod should include the consideration of children's needs and experience in their Reports to Synod whenever this is appropriate.

5.   The Board of Mission and Unity and the Board of Education should explore as a matter of urgency appropriate ways to enable children and leaders to respond to a multi-ethnic society.

Chapter 3

1.   PCCs, whenever possible, should plan at least one venture for the coming year in which adults and children are involved together in learning and exploring what it means to be followers 'in the Way', and should develop a continuing pattern for learning together.

Chapter 4

1.   The Board of Education should commission an appraisal of the research into faith development and its implications for Christian nurture.   Further research is required into the critical stages of transition and growth in a child's spiritual development, and the appropriate support to be offered by the church to parents and children at these times.

2.   A resolution of the issue of communion before confirmation is required as a mater of urgency.

3.   The Board of Education and the Liturgical Commission should examine the need for new liturgies to serve all-age worship, and in particular for a form of eucharist suitable for when children are present.   There should be full consultation with leaders and parents of young children.

4.   Funding should be sought for a field officer, responsible to the Board of Education, to promote experiments, produce resources and disseminate information relating to all-age learning.

Chapter 5

1.   Parishes should review the support they offer to those who lead their education work, with particular reference to: realistic finance for resources; regular training; personal support and development.

2.   Those responsible for ministerial training should review the adequacy of their consideration of children in the church and society. The possibility of liaison with professionals in teacher training departments in universities and in higher and further education colleges should be considered.

3.   The training of leaders for all-age learning should be explored by Diocesan Education Committees in conjunction with the recommendations about developing leadership in *Faith in the City* and the guidelines suggested in *Called to be Adult Disciples*.

4.   Diocesan Education Councils should reassess their staff and resources in the light of the training and assistance which will need to be offered to parishes to implement the recommendations of this report.

Of the recommendations in chapter 4 the first was met by the publication of *How Faith Grows* (Board of Education, 1991). The second featured as an issue in the synodical debate on initiation in 1992 but is still unresolved. The third recommendation has not been actioned although a draft eucharistic prayer for use when children are present was submitted to Synod in 1996. Along with five other drafts for alternative eucharistic prayers it was rejected by the Synod. The funding for a field officer has not been available and has ceased to feature in the draft budget for the Board of Education.

If the response to the recommendations has been disappointing there have been a number of aspects of the synodical process which have been encouraging. An amendment to the original resolutions in Synod was introduced by a private member which drew attention to the large numbers of children who had no contact with the church. The Synod approved the creation of a working party to produce a report on children's evangelism, *All God's Children* (Board of Education and Board of Mission, 1991).

Children in the Way was debated in every diocesan Synod and most deanery Synods discussed the report. It triggered considerable work on worship appropriate to an 'all-age' congregation and a number of publications not only from the Church of England itself.

The report contained a chapter on the extent to which children were in contact with the church. This was the first reporting of a major survey undertaken by Francis and Lankshear into this topic. Further reports from this survey have been published by the National Society under the following titles: *Continuing in the Way, In the Evangelical Way* and *In the Catholic Way.* (Francis and Lankshear, 1991, 1995a, 1995b). In 1996 the Church of England published the report *Youth A Part* (Board of Education, 1996) which explores issues related to work with the fourteen to twenty-five year olds. *Youth A Part* contains some preliminary results from a replication of the 1980s study by Francis and Lankshear.

The intention of these reports is to stimulate discussion and review within parishes, deaneries and dioceses on how the church should be working to attract children and young people and nurture them in the faith. Try to obtain at least one of these reports and study it with two contexts in mind.

Activity C4

How does the parish to which my school is attached undertake its work with children and young people? How do the reports indicate that it might develop its work?

'All-age worship' has become something of a cliché. In many churches it seems to have degenerated into a service for children to which parents and grandparents come. There are rarely teenagers or single people present. The result is still one service for 'adult' Christians and another for those who are, or who think as if they are, children in the faith. Is this a fair critique of all-age worship or is it a caricature promoted by two confusions: by identifying adherence to the *Book of Common Prayer* with the essence of Christianity; by identifying all modern liturgical developments with compromise?

Teachers frequently assert that none of their children are in contact with a Christian church. To what extent do the surveys conducted by Francis and Lankshear reported in these publications challenge such statements, bearing in mind that the authors focused exclusively on the Church of England?

Comment on activity C4

An analysis of the situation in your school, or the school you are studying, will be unique. You may have discovered that the parish has analysed its own situation carefully, made a sensible range of provisions, and is in contact with many young people. On the other hand, the situation may be rather less dynamic. As *In the Evangelical Way* and *In the Catholic Way* show, the provision may be driven, or appear to be driven, by a theological position: evangelical parishes offering a range of activities for young people while delaying confirmation and catholic parishes providing earlier confirmation and drawing, or attempting to draw, young people into eucharistic worship.

In attempting an evaluation of all-age worship in your parish you would do well to provide a systematic description of what goes on. If the worship is well thought out, it may be quite complicated and try to balance the competing needs of different sections of the congregation by varying the mix of liturgical components according to a prearranged plan. Try to distinguish between the pattern of all-age worship provision and the way it is carried out. It may be that the pattern is good but that its conduct is marred by poor communication skills; conversely, good communication skills may make a simple liturgy appeal to the whole age range (for instance, in the way a good carol service touches everyone).

You may well need to carry out your own survey of contact between young people and the church in your area. If you collect figures similar to those collected by Francis and Lankshear (1991, 1995a, 1995b), you will be able to assess your area against a national baseline. If you want to carry out a survey, talk to your tutor before doing so since this could become an assessable task.

C5 Role and expectations of the priest

The parish priest has a key role in every parish and in any church school attached to the parish. Starting from the services for ordination you should explore the expectations that the church has of its priests and in particular consider how those expectations can be met within the context of a church school.

In the *Book of Common Prayer* the tasks of priests, over and above those given to deacons, are:

- administering doctrine and the sacraments;
- driving away erroneous doctrines and ministering to the sick;
- being diligent in prayer, reading and studying scripture;
- ensuring that their lives and those of their family are an example to the congregation;
- maintaining quietness, peace and love amongst all Christian people;
- obeying the bishop.

In *The Alternative Service Book 1980* the tasks to which priests commit themselves are:

- accepting the discipline of the church;
- being diligent in prayer, reading and studying the scripture;
- fashioning their lives and those of their households according to the way of Christ;
- promoting unity, peace and love amongst Christian people;
- making Christ known to all.

Comparison between the two service books raises the following questions.

- Are the tasks expressed or implied different in the two books?
- What does the church expect of its ordained ministers?

- What do you expect of your parish priest? Does it correspond with the contents of the church services?
- What might a school expect from its parish priest? Does it correspond with the contents of the church services?
- Does the parish exist to help the priest do his/her job or does the priest exist to enable the parish to do its job?

Activity C5

When you have read the ordination services use Lankshear (1996), *Churches Serving Schools*, to explore how the priest's role is interpreted and developed within them.

It would be helpful to discuss your responses with the priest of the parish in which your school is placed. You should now be in a position to reflect on the following questions.

- In the light of your reading how can the school enable the priest to fulfil his or her role?
- To what extent is it realistic to expect the parish priest to be chair of governors, worship co-ordinator and teach some of the religious education? Are these the key priorities for priestly ministry?
- How can the priest help the school to carry out its responsibilities and obligations?

Comment on activity C5

You may have found that the school, depending on its type and religious education syllabus, can invite the priest into school for religious education lessons, assemblies, question and answer sessions, lunchtime clubs, offer teaching in religious education that is specifically geared to common Christian practices (lessons on the Lord's prayer or the eucharist) take the children to services in the church as part of the life of the school (a Christingle service, perhaps) or as part of an education programme designed to see churches as working places. All kinds of possibilities are available. For instance, in one town money has been put up by a church benefactor for a competition for the best carol written by children each year. This stimulates children's writing, but also stimulates their thinking about the meaning of Christmas. In all these ways the school can help the priest to widen his or her ministry, a width that may also embrace staff as well as pupils. After all, if the *Book of Common Prayer* enjoins 'administering doctrine and the sacraments' and *The Alternative Service Book 1980* enjoins 'making Christ known to all', the priest can only succeed in these tasks if he or she is granted a hearing in the community.

Parish priests vary enormously in their ages, skills and experience. Some will enjoy giving regular time each week to the schools in their parish. Others will find the task unappealing and one for which they do not feel fitted. Undoubtedly it is possible to function as a chair of governors, religious education teacher and worship co-ordinator, but many priests will feel happier with only one of these roles, or prefer only to do all three for a limited period of time. If parish priests wish to be involved in the life of the school, then they should be acquainted with the demands and details of school life, and it may be necessary to receive additional training. Certainly, most priests would agree that care of the spiritual development of the young should be one of their ministerial priorities.

The obligations of a school to its pupils are wide. They range from delivery of the National Curriculum to helping children with special needs. A good parish priest, especially if he or she is in contact with a range of charitable and local authority provision, can provide human or monetary resources in emergencies or in mediating in disputes that threaten the harmonious functioning of the school. Furthermore, a priest can offer the church building as a resource for non-religious curriculum areas, whether related to local history or geography or specialised subjects like the design of roofs. The priest who has gifts in this area may also be able to help staff by working with local SACREs or attending or giving in-service training.

C6 Eucharist

Within the Anglican Church there has been a significant move towards the eucharist as the focal point of Sunday worship week by week. The eucharist has become more important in recent years even in churches where morning and evening prayer or a family service are still the services attended by the largest numbers of members of the congregation each week. The implications of this development for Christian initiation have already been explored to some extent earlier in this unit. What implications might these developments have for worship in school? How should a school respond to them?

Activity C6

Using the *Book of Common Prayer* and *The Alternative Service Book 1980,* identify the key elements in a eucharistic service. Draw up a list of these elements in the sequence in which they usually occur in the service. Then reflect on the following issues.

- What is the church doing when it celebrates the eucharist?
- What is the church enabling itself to do in this service?
- What is the church doing at the offertory?
- Where is the joy of it all, especially for children?
- How could a church school introduce its pupils to these elements?

Comment on activity C6

The church in celebrating the eucharist is giving thanks for the offering of Christ's life for our salvation and appropriating the benefits of this offering to go out and serve God. Within this general description of the eucharist, there are emphases of a liberal, evangelical or catholic nature that the wording of the liturgy will bear. The liberal interpretation will stress the symbolic nature of Christ's offering as an example for human beings to follow; the evangelical interpretation will stress the substitutionary and propitiatory death of Christ on behalf of the sinner and in which the sinner places his or her trust; the catholic interpretation will stress the presence of Christ within the bread and the wine and their offering to God for human sin.

The church is offering to God the products of human labour (often money) as a way of giving thanks for all that God has given to human beings. In other words, the offertory is not simply a voluntary collection of money to repair the church roof! Such a conclusion is established by the point at which the offertory comes within the eucharist: it takes place near to the preparation of the bread and wine.

Children can understand that God loves them and what Christ did for them. This can make them glad. In other words, it would be wrong to argue that children are incapable of real spiritual discernment and genuine religious emotion. But, the initial joy for children in attending church services usually rests in the people they meet and the activities they participate in, and many of these activities, like singing or learning, can be fun.

C7 Psalms, hymns and spiritual songs

Priests and church musicians often remark on the inappropriateness of the hymns chosen for weddings and funerals. One reason for this might be that, for many people the hymns and songs that they have sung in school or church as children form a key resource available for them to use in their subsequent adult religious expression. The words of such hymns could be a basis from which they explain or express their faith. If this is true, the selection of hymns and songs for children to use in school and church may have a significant effect on their subsequent beliefs. Great care needs to be taken by adults charged with choosing hymns for children. In this area of exploration you are asked to examine the words of some of the most commonly used hymns and songs in the church school and parish with which you are most closely connected in order to explore aspects of the underlying theology.

Activity C7

Obtain a list of the hymns, psalms and other spiritual songs used in the school and the church. From these select the ten most frequently used. Using the words of these hymns and songs only, identify what children are learning about the person of Jesus and his relationship with God; the church - its beliefs, practices and traditions; and God as Creator.

Assume that children learn all the words of these hymns and songs and apply meanings to them that are in common usage. If you identify gaps between your understanding of Christian teaching on these issues and the content of these songs examine the hymn book for other hymns that could be added to the repertoire to develop a better balance.

In practice what could you do to improve the selection of hymns and songs in your school?

Comment on activity C7

Your comments will depend on exactly which hymns and songs you use in the school you are studying. Words such as 'son', 'saviour', 'redeemer', 'Lord', 'friend', 'brother' are often used and many people have difficulty in disentangling the ordinary use of these words from their theological meaning. For example, a redeemer is literally anyone who redeems something (that is, buys it back having previously owned it). When Christ is called redeemer, that meaning has theological resonances and theological complications. If Christ is 'buying back' human beings, when did they first belong to God, how were they lost and to whom is the price paid? An understanding of how Christians think about Christ *can* be gained from an understanding of the literal meaning of a word, but very often further explanation is necessary. Children may fasten on the simple and literal meaning of a word and apply it to Jesus, or the church or God as creator. They may also do their own theological thinking and arrive at strange conclusions. The module *Spiritual and Moral Development* explores these issues more thoroughly.

There is a huge variety of songbooks and hymnbooks on the market and so you ought to be able to find something suitable for your school. Alternatively, or in addition, the use of an overhead projector allows you to introduce new songs without expenditure on new books. Make sure you do not break copyright, and one of the easiest ways of doing this is to pay a music publisher a single blanket payment for the use of OHP slides which may be used as many times as you like. You may find the formation of a choir or the introduction of music practices allows you to improve your selection of hymns and songs.

Readers

J. Astley, L.J. Francis and C. Crowder (eds) (1996), *Theological Perspectives on Christian Formation*, Leominster, Gracewing, gives an excellent introduction to Christian formation as a whole, but does not deal specifically with the doctrines and practices of the Anglican Church.

Bibliography

Avis, P. (1989), *Anglicanism and the Christian Church*, Edinburgh, T. and T. Clark.

Bede (731/1968), *A History of the English Church*, Harmondsworth, Penguin.

Bicknell, E.J. (1955), *The Thirty-nine Articles* (third edition), London, Longmans, Green and Co.

Board of Education (1988), *Children in the Way*, London, The National Society and Church House Publishing.

Board of Education (1991), *How Faith Grows*, London, The National Society and Church House Publishing.

Board of Education and Board of Mission (1991), *All God's Children?* London, The National Society and Church House Publishing.

Board of Education (1996), *Youth A Part*, London, The National Society and Church House Publishing.

Buchanan, C. (1986), *Anglican Confirmation*, Bramcote, Grove Books.

Buchanan, C., Lloyd, T. and Miller, H. (eds) (1980), *Anglican Worship Today*, London, Collins Liturgical Publications.

Butler, P. (1988), From early eighteenth century to the present day, in S. Sykes and J. Booty (eds), *The Study of Anglicanism*, London, SPCK, pp 28-47.

Chadwick, O. (1983), *Hensley Henson: a study in friction between Church and State*, Oxford, Clarendon Press.

Dennis, J. (1985) *Communion Before Confirmation?* London, CIO Publishing.

Dix, G. (1946), *The Theology of Confirmation in Relation to Baptism*, London, SPCK.

Doctrine Commission (1987), *We Believe in God*, London, Church House Publishing.

Ely, Bishop of (1971), *Christian Initiation*, London, General Synod of the Church of England.

Francis, L.J. (1985), *Rural Anglicanism: a future for young Christians?* London, Collins Liturgical Publications.

Francis, L.J. and Lankshear, D.W. (1991), *Continuing in the Way*, London, The National Society.

Francis, L.J. and Lankshear, D.W. (1993), Changing trends in Anglican confirmation, *Journal of Empirical Theology*, 6, 1, 64-76.

Francis, L.J. and Lankshear, D.W. (1995a), *In the Evangelical Way*, London, The National Society.

Francis, L.J. and Lankshear, D.W. (1995b), *In the Catholic Way*, London, The National Society.

General Synod (1995), *On The Way; towards an integrated approach to Christian initiation*, London, Church House Publishing.

House of Bishops (1991), *Christian Initiation Matters*, London, General Synod of the Church of England.

Jasper R.C.D. and Bradshaw, P.F. (1986), *A Companion to the Alternative Service Book*, London, SPCK.

Lankshear, D.W. (1996), *Churches Serving Schools*, London, The National Society and Church House Publishing.

Ledwich, W. (1985), *The Durham Affair*, Welshpool, Stylite Publishing.

Lowther Clarke, W.K. and Harris, C. (1932), *Liturgy and Worship: a companion to the prayer books of the Anglican communion*, London, SPCK.

McGrath, A.E. (1986), Reformation to enlightenment, in P. Avis (ed.), *The Science of Theology* (vol. 1), Grand Rapids, Eerdmans, pp 107-229.

Mason, A.J. (1891), *The Relation of Confirmation to Baptism*, London, Longmans, Green and Co.

Miller, H. (1980), Service books in the Church of England: authors and influences, in C. Buchanan, T. Lloyd and H. Miller (eds), *Anglican Worship Today*, London, Collins Liturgical Publications, pp 24-29.

Neill, S. (1977), *Anglicanism* (fourth edition), London, Mowbray.

Proctor F. and Frere, W.H. (1961), *The Book of Common Prayer, with a rationale for its offices*, London, Macmillan and Co. Ltd.

Ridley, J. (1962), *Thomas Cranmer*, Oxford, Clarendon Press.

Sykes, S. (1978), *The Integrity of Anglicanism*, London, Mowbrays.

Vasey, M. (1980), The church's role in worship, in C. Buchanan, T. Lloyd and H. Miller (eds), *Anglican Worship Today*, London, Collins Liturgical Publications, pp 38-43.

Philosophy of Religious Education

Philosophy of Religious Education

Unit A

The legal basis for religious education

Dr William K. Kay

Trinity College

Carmarthen

Contents

Introduction

Aims

After working through this unit you should be able to:

- understand the historical basis of the law relating to church schools;
- understand the provisions of the main laws relating to church schools;
- understand the role of SACREs;
- understand the basics of the process of inspection.

Overview

The whole process of understanding the law in relation to religious education in church schools is only possible if one also understands:

- how law is made;
- how law is enforced.

Unfortunately, what complicates this understanding is the gradual evolution of society as a whole. We begin at the start of the nineteenth century and we arrive at the last part of the twentieth century. The process of law-making, the speed of communication, the complexity of local administration and the influence of the church have all changed in the period under review.

You will be asked to work through an account of the changes made to the law relating to church schools and religious education since 1945 so that you can see what the issues are, in so far as possible what the 'mind of Parliament' was on the occasions when it deliberated and why some matters are left to local discretion and others are dealt with at a national level. In matters of law, detail is important; but detail is usually informed by general principles, and we want you to explore and grasp these principles.

In 1996 two Consolidation Acts were passed bringing together all the educational legislation affecting schools passed between 1944 and 1995. Since 1 November 1996 all references to *current* law affecting schools should be made to these two Consolidation Acts, to legislation passed before 1944, or to new legislation passed subsequent to the Consolidation Acts. Because this unit sets out to provide an historical overview, references will be made to the original acts between 1944 and 1995.

A1 General theory

According to the general theory, those who are allowed to vote elect representatives who make rules, or laws, which apply to everyone. Because the parliamentary system has evolved over many years, it also contains non-elected people, for example hereditary peers and bishops, who represent broader long-standing interests which are not directly related to the voting figures of the last general election. Nevertheless, the non-elected house, the House of Lords, may always be defeated by the House of Commons so that, in general, the Lords simply exercise a scrutinising, amending or delaying role with regard to the laws framed in the Commons.

In respect of the churches, if a large number of voters are churchgoers, or elect representatives who are churchgoers, then the laws which are passed will take into account the wishes and interests of churchgoers. The churches receive no particular privileges in the House of Commons. When we look at the law as it applies to church schools, we need to be clear that this law has been passed in the same way as any other law. It expresses, so far as may be, the 'will of the majority' and not the will of a minority, or of the sovereign, or of an unelected and domineering House of Lords. Moreover, as we shall see, the major law which summarised, developed and regularised much of the legislation that had preceded it, namely the 1944 Education Act, was passed by a coalition government, that is, a government made up of all the main political parties acting together for the good of the nation.

How law is made

Before a law is presented to parliament the ideas that it contains have to be developed and turned into legal language. In the past this has been done by using a two stage process. First, the government publishes a *Green Paper* which sets out its ideas for discussion, consultation and debate. At this stage it is open for all interested parties to make their views known. Second, the government publishes a *White Paper* announcing its formal policies following the consultation process. Policies that do not require legislation can be implemented following a White Paper. If legislation is needed the next stage is for a Bill to be drafted. In recent years this two stage process of consultation has often been compressed, but the 1944 Education Act provides a good example of the system in full operation.

In essence, statute law is made by being passed by both houses of parliament. In detail, a Bill is introduced by a member of parliament with the support of twelve named members of the Commons[1]. This is the Bill's first reading.

The Bill is then published in preparation for the second reading which is the occasion when it is debated by the House of Commons. At the end of the debate a vote of all those present takes place. If the Bill receives a majority vote in its favour, its financial implications will be considered before it passes through to the committee stage where it is examined in detail clause by clause and may be amended[2]. The committee which examines the Bill in this careful way is made up of MPs matching the proportions of their parties in the House of Commons. This gives the government of the day a majority on committees as well as on the floor of the whole House. The committees follow the seating arrangements and procedures of the whole House: a committee's chairman[3] has the same powers as the Speaker.

After this there follows a report back to the Commons. Here the amendments made at the committee stage can be discussed by any member of the Commons. If no amendments have been made, the report stage is omitted. The third reading involves a debate on the wording of the Bill in the stage that it has now reached, that is, with amendments brought in at the committee stage and any others which have been brought in at the report stage, though the Speaker will use well-recognised procedures to avoid a repetition of the substance of the debate which took place at the second reading. From here, if the Bill has not been defeated, it passes to the House of Lords, where it passes through a similar procedure (though without any consideration of financial implications). Assuming that the Lords vote in the Bill's favour, it may pass through for Royal Assent and so becomes law. Royal Assent has not been refused since 1707 and so is considered a formality. But if the Lords vote down the Bill, then it can still be passed by the Commons for Royal Assent within a period of thirteen months[4]. If, as is more common, the Bill is amended in the Lords, then only the amendments are passed back to the Commons for consideration. The Lords' amendments must be agreed by the Commons before the Bill becomes law. If they are not agreed, then the amendments may

---

[1] A Bill may originate either in the Commons or the Lords, though usually in the Commons. It passes through the same stages whichever House it originates in, but if it originates in the Lords then all the stages in the Lords are completed before the Bill is passed to the Commons.

[2] It was common till 1882 for Bills to be considered in a Committee of the Whole House of Commons (Jennings, 1957, p 268). At this point standing committees were introduced against Cabinet opposition by Mr Gladstone. After 1907 the Standing Orders of the House of Commons were changed and the present system was established (Jennings, 1957, p 269). Nevertheless a Committee of the Whole House remains a procedural possibility and is used for urgent or uncontroversial Bills to save time.

[3] The terms 'chairperson' and 'chairwoman' are not at present used formally by parliament (Silk and Walters, 1989, p 130).

[4] The rule is 'any Bill (except one to extend the life of a parliament, i.e. to postpone a general election) which passes the Commons in two successive sessions (whether or not a general election intervenes) can be presented for Royal Assent without the agreement of the Lords, provided (a) there has been a minimum period of one year between the Commons giving it a second reading for the first time and a third reading of the second time, and (b) that the Lords have received the Bill at least one month before the end of each of the two sessions' (Silk and Walters, 1989, p 147).

be amended before being passed back for reconsideration by the second House. Complicated though this sounds, the basic principle is easy to grasp: every clause of every Bill, including its amendments, must be agreed by both Houses. In this way what started as a *Bill before* Parliament has become an *Act of* Parliament. Further details are given by Griffith and Ryle (1989) and Silk and Walters (1989).

How law is enforced

If law is broken, then it is enforced by the police. But if it is not clear that law has been broken, then the two parties will attend the court and the court will decide whether or not there has been a breach in the law. Sometimes the matter may be in dispute because there are genuine misinterpretations as to the law's meaning and, in these instances, the will of parliament, insofar as it can be gleaned from verbatim reports of parliamentary debates, will be helpful to the courts. Clearly, however, what is decided in London, though in theory it may apply equally at every point within the United Kingdom, may not in practice be enforced with the same vigour where local police, magistrates or officials are deliberately dilatory.

Activity A1

Organise a debate with a class of children and, at the end of the debate, take a vote. To try to make the debate realistic and important ask the children to discuss a subject which affects them all. For example, should they all have school dinners? Ask some children to speak in favour and others to speak against. Then take a vote.

Reflect on the activity. Are there any things you learnt which would help you to understand the problems of making law on a large scale for a nation of many million? List the problems with democratic law-making. List its advantages.

Comment on activity A1

You may have found that all kinds of problems occur with law-making, for example:

- some children do not understand the issues;
- some children do not think they should obey rules for which they did not vote;

- some children would like to eat dinner sometimes: they want flexible rules, but such rules are more difficult to draft;
- some children found they did not have enough time to say what they wanted because others did all the talking;
- some children wanted a secret vote and others wanted an open vote.

All these problems can be transferred to the larger-scale democracy. Lack of understanding, unwillingness to accept rules even after a vote (think of the poll tax riots), complexity of drafting and filibustering (talking so as to prevent other people having a chance to express their views in the allotted time) may all be seen.

On the other hand, there are advantages to democratic law-making, for example:

- the system is essentially fair; everyone can vote as they choose;
- the system allows law to be changed after it has been made;
- the system is likely to produce rules which everyone will abide by because everyone had a chance to make them.

A2 The situation before 1944

It is necessary to work through unit A of the module *Church Schools: history and philosophy*, to understand the full historical background to church schools prior to 1944. However, in brief, a 'dual system' was in operation in which church schools and county schools existed side by side. Though church and county schools were distinct and had different origins, they were organised under the same local authorities and treated together as a single system. For some purposes, notably the inspection of religious teaching, they were distinct, but for many others there was little or no difference.

An historical perspective on education in England and Wales is made confusing by changes in terminology in successive legal enactments between 1870 and 1902. The 1944 Education Act distinguishes between 'county' schools and 'voluntary' schools, and this terminology is retained in subsequent Acts. County schools were those established by public money from the beginning or had at some stage been handed over by a voluntary body to the local education authority. The buildings of voluntary schools were usually owned by charitable bodies and their use regulated by a trust deed. For the sake of simplicity this module uses the terms 'voluntary' and 'county' throughout.

In addition, the term 'dual system' is sometimes only strictly applied following the 1902 Education Act, but the seeds of duality were present in the

1870 Education Act and it would not be inaccurate to think of the dual system as dating from then. All schools within the dual system may be referred to as 'maintained' schools since they are maintained by public money.

During the period from 1870 onwards almost all county schools included religious worship and religious instruction on their premises, though this was not a duty placed on teachers by law and parents might, on grounds of conscience, withdraw their children without penalty from either of these activities. Voluntary schools also conducted religious worship and carried out, if they wished, denominational religious instruction subject to the same 'conscience clause'. Religious activities within church schools were, however, inspected by inspectors nominated by church authorities.

A3 The 1944 Education Act

Before the 1944 Education Act came before parliament there had been both a Green Paper and a White Paper on the subject of the structure of education after the war. During a two year consultation period there were many meetings between the minister and representatives of the churches. There was a voluminous correspondence on the subject, much of it involving the Archbishop of Canterbury. By the time the Bill reached parliament, the churches were largely in agreement with the proposals that it contained.

As we shall see the Act introduced several changes which have become a permanent feature of the dual system. In essence:

- church schools within the dual system could choose either controlled or aided status (explained later);
- religious education was made up of two components, collective worship and classroom instruction;
- in all schools (except the aided category), classroom instruction was given according to an agreed syllabus.

For the purposes of this unit, only those features of the 1944 Education Act which are currently relevant to schools are discussed. Some features, once they were introduced in 1944, continued more or less unchanged until today. Other features were slightly altered. The information given in this unit is intended to be practical and useful, but occasionally it is not possible to avoid historical details. A summary of the current position is given at the end of this unit.

Parliamentary debate

The debate on the 1944 Education Act took place in the spring of 1944. The Act was very extensive in its provisions but the main part of the debate only took two days (Iremonger, 1948, p 577). There was, of course, discussion on the matter of collective worship. Some Members of Parliament took the view that it was impossible to compel worship. 'The act of worship is an interior thing which cannot be enforced by an external authority' said Mr Harvey (Hansard, 397, 2396). Others worried about the effect of the legal requirement on teachers. 'I entirely agree that, when it comes to a question of religious worship, we really must stand for the greatest freedom of the teacher, and incidentally for the children' (Mr Richards, Hansard 397, 2397). Such a point was answered by Mr Nicholson who asked 'Would it not be better if my hon Friend considered the question from the point of view of the children rather than the teachers? What I am anxious to ensure is that every child shall have the opportunity of daily collective worship provided and I think the schools should be compelled to provide that opportunity' (Hansard, 397, 2396). In effect, what most worried some Members of Parliament was not that worship was already taking place in schools, indeed they approved of this, but that what was then a voluntary but near universal practice should be made a legal requirement. Mr Butler's answers to the objections which were raised was that the right of withdrawal removed any element of compulsion. He said (Hansard, 397, 2402):

> The later provisions of the Clause indicate that a parent who desires his children not to join in this act of worship, is not obliged to cause the children to attend. Therefore, it is not a compulsory act of worship, or a compulsory church parade, as some people imagine. It is a collective act of worship which carries on the present practice... to have used alternative words would have made the situation rather too vague for me to be able to satisfy all those who are interested in this matter.

Butler was supported by members who had spoken at public meetings up and down the country about education. Mr Colegate, for example, said (Hansard, 397, 2410):

> I have had large meetings in my constituency... if there is one feature in this Bill which is more popular than any other it is the actual Clause we are discussing today. I venture to say that if you could have a plebiscite of parents today 95 per cent would vote for that Clause as it stands.

Despite Butler's assurances, the matter was taken to a vote. Of the 141 votes cast on this occasion, 121 were in favour of making collective worship a legal requirement.

There was also discussion about agreed syllabuses. Again, it was not the principle of Christian teaching in school which worried Members of Parliament, but whether undenominational and basic teaching through an agreed syllabus was adequate. Mr Thomas, for example, said (Hansard, 397, 2433),

> the agreed syllabuses are not in themselves evil. What is in them is nearly always good. I would rather have the religion that is envisaged in this clause than no religion at all, but it does not fill me with any enthusiasm and it is not going to help the cause of religion.

A more fervent view was expressed by Mr Nicholson who argued that (Hansard, 397, 2437):

> the very existence of a free state depends on the general acceptance of the thesis that man is the child of God, that every individual man must be treated with dignity as a soul precious in the sight of God.

It is impossible to summarise adequately all that was said on these occasions. The impression given by the House of Commons during the 1944 debate and substantiated by its votes on individual clauses was of extensive support for Christian influence in education. Indeed, 224 members of both Houses of Parliament had signed a declaration calling for a strengthening of Christianity in school, including the requirement of daily worship (Souper and Kay, 1982, p 13). Iremonger (1948, p 577) pointed out that nearly twenty of the thirty-one speeches were largely concerned with the religious issue and that 'no more than twenty votes' could be mustered for an amendment against the collective act of worship. The handling of the main clauses of the Bill was not narrowly political because, though Mr Butler was a Conservative, the Parliamentary Secretary who worked with him in piloting the Bill through the Commons was Mr Ede, a Labour member.   Occasionally Welsh Noncon-formists objected to what they saw as advantages being given to Church of England schools but, as Mr Ede pointed out (Hansard 397, 2451):

> One of the effects of the coming of the controlled school is that the head teachership is relieved from a religious test and becomes available generally to the teaching profession. That is a consideration which has weighted very much in drafting the controlled school status and in giving to the controlled school the financial advantages which are conferred by this Bill.

Moreover, as Butler pointed out, Free Church leaders supported the Bill.

What the debate showed was that the legislation was carefully considered, thoroughly discussed inside and outside parliament and supported by a national coalition government. Because the 1944 Education Act was the product of a government containing both Labour and Conservatives within the same administration, it may be considered a specially good expression of the democratic process.

Categories of church school

Section 15 of the 1944 Education Act stipulated that voluntary schools should belong to one of three categories: controlled schools, aided schools or special agreement schools. The special agreement schools (of which there were less than 200) were those which had made special agreements with local education authorities under the 1936 Education Act and functioned in many respects in a way similar to aided schools. Church schools could make an application to belong to the controlled or aided category. All but two Roman Catholic schools opted for the aided category, but the Church of England schools were much more varied in their choices.

In controlled schools the mangers or governors[5] were not responsible for any expenses in maintaining the school, neither the salaries of staff nor the costs of buildings or equipment. In aided schools the managers or governors were responsible for capital expenditure on alterations required by the local education authority and for expenditure on external repairs. The local education authority became responsible for all running costs, including staff salaries, interior repairs to the building, the maintenance of playgrounds and playing fields and for the erection and maintenance of buildings used exclusively for school health services and school meals (Dent, 1944, p 23).

Although managers and governors were responsible for particular areas of expenditure in aided schools, they did not have to raise all the necessary money themselves. Until 1959 they had to find half of the money needed. The proportion was successively reduced to 25% in 1959, 20% in 1967 and 15% in 1974.

Differences between aided and controlled schools are expressed in the composition of the governing body of each. In an aided or special agreement school two-thirds of governors were 'foundation governors', that is, appointed by the voluntary body owning the school. In controlled schools only one third of governors were appointed by the voluntary body. Therefore, in aided Anglican schools there is a built-in majority of church appointees on the governing body; in controlled Anglican schools, this is not the case. In effect the advantage to the church in having greater influence over what happens in a school is off-set by the extra funds which have to be provided from voluntary sources. As we shall see, the composition of governing bodies was changed by the 1980 Education Act and the 1986 Education Act (No 2).

Differences between aided and controlled schools are expressed in the denominational education they offer. The differences are complicated, but the principle is simple. In aided schools religious education may be entirely

---

[5] Between 1944 and 1980 primary schools were managed and secondary schools were governed. Governors had more extensive powers than managers. After 1980 all schools were governed.

denominational, in controlled schools religious education in the classroom is subject to the agreed syllabus (see below) though with the option of special denominational religious education if that is requested by parents. In order to provide denominational religious education 'reserved' teachers may be appointed for this purpose. All teachers are appointed by the local education authority and may only be dismissed by the local education authority but governors in controlled and special agreement schools have a voice in the appointment of 'reserved' teachers and may lay down special conditions for their appointment. In aided schools, however, the teacher(s) appointed to give denominational religious instruction may be dismissed by the governors without the consent of the local education authority. In the case of all other teachers, the function of the local education authority and the governors is regulated by the school's articles of government. Again, though the detail is complicated, the principle is straightforward: the entire purpose of controlled or aided status might be undermined by unsuitable denominational teaching but as much protection as possible against wrongful dismissal is given to teachers who carry out this function.

Both controlled and aided schools offer denominational school worship. Aided schools offer denominational religious education, though if the parents of children attending aided schools wish their children to receive instruction according to the agreed syllabus, the school must make this provision if the children cannot conveniently attend a school where that syllabus is in use.

Aided schools and special agreement schools normally make use of a syllabus recommended by the diocese for schools of these types within its area. Schools which wish to use the religious education syllabus of another diocese or denomination[6], or indeed the agreed syllabus, are at liberty to do so. The matter is in the hands of the governors of individual schools. Similarly, the governors are also responsible for an aided school's collective worship. Some Anglican aided schools have regular but infrequent celebrations of the eucharist to which parents are invited and some may 'worship as a school' in the local parish church (Durham Report, 1970, p 255).

A detailed consideration of how the law affects different categories of church schools is provided by Department for Education and Employment (1994) and by Duncan and Lankshear (1996).

---

[6] For example a Church of England school might wish to use the syllabus prepared by a Roman Catholic diocese.

Components of religious education

When the structure of the 1944 Education Act is examined and when the debate in parliament is analysed, it is clear that religious education within the dual system was seen as having two components: religious instruction and collective worship. Section 25 of the 1944 Education Act is headed 'Religious Education in County and Voluntary Schools' and paragraph 1 of this section stipulates that 'the school day in every county school and in every voluntary school shall begin with collective worship' and paragraph 2 continues 'religious instruction shall be given in every county school and in every voluntary school'. Remaining paragraphs within this section deal with matters relating to withdrawal of children on grounds of conscience or the provision of another kind of religious instruction during the period of withdrawal. Section 26 stipulates that in country schools religious instruction shall be given in accordance with the agreed syllabus 'which shall not include any catechism or formulary which is distinctive of any particular religious denomination'.

The terminology used in these sections is revealing. Religious *education* includes religious *instruction*. Education is conceived of as having a didactic element. It is also conceived of as having an experiential element conveyed in worship. A later analysis in the Durham Report (1970, paragraph 298) explained the rationale for this conceptualisation: 'just as artistic capacities cannot be developed without being exercised, by painting pictures or making music, so religious understanding cannot be developed without an experience of worship'.

Role of the agreed syllabus

Within any particular local education authority the controlled and county schools are similar to each other in the religious instruction they offer. This is because both make use of the same syllabus. The 1944 Education Act extended and gave legal force to the concept of the 'agreed syllabus' which had been used in a few counties on an *ad hoc* basis since 1924. The agreed syllabus is, therefore, a document backed by statute. For this reason all well-prepared agreed syllabuses make it clear which of their stipulations are legally obligatory and which are illustrative or optional. The 1944 Education Act defined the procedures by which these syllabuses were to be drawn up and placed the obligation for drawing them up on each local education authority. Each syllabus was the work of four committees and each committee had one vote. Syllabuses were only adopted after receiving all four votes. The four committees represented interested parties: one included representatives of any 'religious denominations' which the local authority considered should be present; a second included representatives of the Church of England (except in

Wales, where the Anglican church has no separate committee, but joins the religious denomination committee); a third included representatives of teachers; the fourth included representatives of the local authority itself. A modification to the membership of one of the committees was, as we shall see, made by the 1988 Education Reform Act.

Activity A2

A game of football may be described as an attempt by two opposing teams to kick a ball between their opponents' set of goal posts. Yet the rules of football cover all kinds of eventualities like the size of the pitch and the penalties for the various kinds of infringements.

Only when the general aim of the game is kept firmly in mind do the rules make sense. What were the aims of the 1944 Education Act with regard to church schools and religious education?

Comment on activity A2

The aim of the 1944 Education Act was to allow schools within the dual system to function together harmoniously and to deliver Christian teaching within the bounds set by conscience clauses covering parents and teachers. There were other aims to the 1944 Education Act relating to the provision of free schooling for all, raising the school leaving age and providing education appropriate for pupils' aptitudes and abilities. In many areas these issues contributed to the decision to focus Anglican church schools on the primary age range. Given the political furore associated with church schools before and after the 1870 Education Act, the settlement reached by the 1944 parliament was one that allowed a much wider spread of agreement within and between churches and their associated political affiliates than had been possible previously.

A4 The 1980 Education Act

Section 1 of the 1980 Education Act turned school managers into governors. Sections 6, 7, 8 and 9 of the 1980 Education Act dealt with admissions to schools and gave parents far greater powers of choice than had previously been the case. The Act also required governing bodies or the local education authority to publish an admission policy for each school.

A5 The 1986 Education Act (No 2)

Section 1 of the 1986 Education Act (No 2) required that every county and voluntary school should have an instrument or, in lay language, a document 'providing for the constitution of the governing body of the school' and articles 'in accordance with which the school is to be conducted (to be known as the articles of government)'.

This law required governing bodies of county and controlled schools with less than 100 pupils to have two parent governors, two governors appointed by the local education authority, one teacher governor, the headteacher (unless he or she decides not to take this post) and either two foundation governors and one co-opted governor in the case of a controlled school or three co-opted governors in the case of a county school. It is the appointed governors who co-opt the co-opted governors.

The controlled school's foundation governors therefore occupy two out of the nine possible places. In schools with between 100 and 299 pupils, the figures are changed slightly and foundation governors occupy three out of twelve possible places. In schools between 300 and 599 pupils foundation governors occupy four out of sixteen possible places. And in schools of more than 600 pupils foundation governors occupy four out of nineteen possible places.

While the 1986 Education Act (No 2) changed the constitution of the governing bodies of controlled schools, it did not change the constitution of the governing bodies of aided schools. These remained as they were in the 1980 Education Act. Therefore, in aided and special agreement schools of fewer than 300 pupils, there is at least one local authority governor[7], at least one parent governor, at least one teacher governor, and the headteacher (unless he or she chooses not to be a governor). In schools of more than 300 pupils there must be at least two teacher governors, otherwise the numbers are the same. The number of foundation governors is flexible, but it must be such as to ensure that they will out-number the other governors. If there are eighteen or fewer governors, the foundation governors must have a majority over all other governors of two, and of three where there are more than eighteen on the governing body.

---

[7] And in areas where there is a minority authority the same rule applies.

A6 The 1988 Education Reform Act

Church schools: aided, controlled and special agreement

The Education Reform Bill was introduced first in the House of Lords. Although it contained no proposal to change the nature of church schools, unless they chose to become grant maintained, the provision affecting school worship and religious education in county schools proved to be contentious. Eventually a compromise was reached before the Bill went to the lower house.

The parliamentary debate in the House of Commons concerning voluntary schools was good tempered and achieved consensus without a vote. The debate took place on 23 March 1988 and lasted about two hours. There were changes to the curriculum as a whole and to the way agreed syllabuses were drawn up (see below), but the basis on which the different categories of school were able to offer either denominational or non-denominational religious education was not altered.

Some Roman Catholics, however, perceived an indirect challenge to the role of church schools within certain geographical areas, posed by the proposal to create grant-maintained schools. The major problem here was that grant-maintained schools might operate admissions policies that could upset the religious ethos of denominational schools by forcing them, in the interests of viability, to accept large numbers of pupils who would not identify with that ethos. Section 86 puts in place an obligation on grant-maintained schools which seek significantly to change their religious character to gain the approval of the Secretary of State.

So far as other aspects of the religious education at grant-maintained schools is concerned, section 88 relates to the use of any agreed syllabus which falls to be reconsidered according to the 1944 Education Act procedures. The agreed syllabus conference is required to consult the grant-maintained school's governing body before making any recommendations and exempts non-agreed-syllabus religious education at grant-maintained schools from inspection.

Sir Hugh Rossi in the debate said that church authorities might be forced to 'admit up to a standard number of pupils' which would create 'an entirely new situation and would leave protection of the denominational character of church schools to the good will of local authorities'. Moreover, intolerable burdens could be placed on church authorities 'to incur expenditure in maintaining places not required to meet the needs of their own communities' (Hansard, 130, 400). Alternatively the opposite problem might arise and church authorities might have difficulties in maintaining 'a viable network of schools for their communities as a whole if individual schools are able to withdraw too easily from the maintained sector' (Hansard, 130, 400). The results of this discussion appear to have been incorporated within sections 29 and 30 of the 1988 Education Reform Act. They offered protection to aided (and special agreement) rather than to controlled schools by allowing the governors of these schools to make arrangements with local education authorities 'in respect of the admission of pupils to the school for preserving the character of the school' (section 30).

Religious education

The 1988 Education Reform Act, like the 1944 Education Act, uses the overall heading 'Religious Education' to cover sections dealing with collective worship and religious education. A footnote in circular 3/89 from the Department of Education and Science (which was then the government department in charge of education) attempts to clarify the matter in the following way:

> The Education Act 1944 used the term 'Religious Education' to encompass Religious Instruction, Collective Worship and Religious Education generally. The Education Reform Act refers to 'Religious Education' in place of 'Religious Instruction' and separately to 'Collective Worship'; all previous legislation has been amended accordingly.

Yet, the reference to collective worship in the 1988 Education Reform Act is no more separated from the heading 'Religious Education' than it is in the 1944 Education Act.

During the 1988 debate, collective worship was certainly mentioned and supported[8], but the main concerns of the speakers, who represented both the main political parties, were directed towards the content of religious education and whether or not religious education would be one of the subjects included within the National Curriculum. Parliamentarians foresaw that, if it were not, its importance in the classroom would never live up to the importance attributed to it by law. Kenneth Baker, then Minister of Education, rejected the argument that religious education should be included within the National Curriculum on two grounds: if it were included, the content of religious lessons would have to be determined, as with other subjects, by a secular committee, the National Curriculum Council; second, it would be difficult to allow the withdrawal of pupils, on the grounds of conscience, from a National Curriculum subject.

With regard to the *content of religious education* Mr Coombs argued that 'religious education should be ... Christian-based' (Hansard, 130, 404). Mr Beith pointed out that 'an understanding of religion, especially the Christian religion, is essential to an understanding of the society, history and heritage of

---

[8] Notably by Sir Rhodes Boyson (Hansard, 130, p 411).

these islands' (Hansard, 130, 405). Mr Raison declared that 'it is wholly impossible to understand British culture without a knowledge of the bible and, I would add, the *Book of Common Prayer*' (Hansard, 130, 408). Sir Rhodes Boyson contended that 'religious education must not be a parade round a museum of religion.   There must be faith... religious education must be a foundation or core subject, and the churches, Her Majesty's Inspectorate and the local authorities must ensure that it is taught' (Hansard, 130, 413).   Mr Baker, replying for the government, agreed that 'a fundamental part of any religious education syllabus should be the Christian faith.   That faith was brought to these islands by St Augustine and it has woven its way through our history' (Hansard, 130, 426).   Nearly all these speakers also believed that religions other than Christianity should be taught.   Only Sir Rhodes Boyson made specific suggestions about how this should be done.   He recalled that, in the school where he had been headmaster, local religious leaders had been invited to come in to teach pupils the faith of their parents.

Role of SACREs

The content of religious education has, from 1944, been regulated in county and controlled schools by agreed syllabuses.   The mechanism for production of these syllabuses had not been used as actively as the government wished and, in any event, the syllabuses to be produced by the new National Curriculum Council[9] would take on a shape and style suitable for the new Key Stages in the child's education which the 1988 Education Reform Act recognised (section 2).   For these reasons, and because religious education would look outdated if it failed to reformulate itself during the general overhaul of the curriculum, each local education authority was required to set up a body specially relevant to religious education.   This body is the SACRE, or Standing Advisory Council on Religious Education (section 7.6; section 11).   The respective clauses in the Consolidation Acts are 387 and 390.   Although prior to 1988 local education authorities had power under the 1944 Education Act to establish these councils, few had exercised this power.

A SACRE must be constituted by every local education authority with the duty of advising 'upon matters connected with religious worship in country schools and the religious education to be given in accordance with an agreed syllabus' (section 11.1.a.).   These matters include the methods of teaching, the choice of materials and the provision of training for teachers.   The SACRE should be properly resourced by the local education authority and, if a majority

---

[9] Since replaced by SCAA, the School Curriculum and Assessment Authority, which also incorporates the School Examination and Assessment Authority.

of the non-LEA groups on the SACRE asks the local education authority in writing to reconsider its agreed syllabus, it must establish a conference for that purpose. The SACRE, in other words, can set the pace of reform despite its advisory role (Circular 3/89, paragraph 28).

The SACRE consists of four groups of people, each of which has one vote for decision-making purposes:

- Christian and other religious denominations as in the opinion of the authority reflect the principal traditions of the area;
- the Church of England (except in Wales);
- such associations representing teachers as in the opinion of the authority ought to be represented;
- the authority itself.

In Wales, it should be noted that because the Church of England is not established, it has no right to a committee made up solely of its own members. Instead representatives of the Church in Wales (that is, Anglicans) will be placed on the first committee listed above.

However, where there is a separate Church of England group, the Church of England may not be represented in the 'Christian and other religious denominations group'. The SACRE may also include co-opted members, but these may not vote. Among matters to be voted on is the timing of decisions for reviewing the agreed syllabus. The drawing up of an agreed syllabus shall be by the convening of a conference for that purpose according to schedule 5 of the 1944 Education Act, thus demonstrating continuity with previous legislation. The SACRE must report annually (Liell, 1988).

Circular 3/89 points out that the composition of SACREs and that of agreed syllabus conferences is very similar. The difference lies in the fact that there is no provision for co-opted members or members representing grant-maintained schools to be part of the conference. What is clear, however, is that the 'other religious denominations' are likely to include non-Christian groups. This was not an assumption implicit in the 1944 legislation.

The syllabuses which conferences make 'shall reflect the fact that the religious traditions in Great Britain are in the main Christian whilst taking account of the teaching and practices of the other principal religions represented in Great Britain' (section 8.3). The content of agreed syllabuses is therefore expected to give prominence to Christianity. In Wales the dimension of Celtic Christianity must be taken into account.

Section 9 of the 1988 Education Reform Act perpetuates the right of parents to withdraw children either wholly or partly from religious education and collective worship. If parents wish their children to receive religious education of a kind not provided by the school, these pupils may be withdrawn from school during such periods of time as are 'reasonably necessary' for this kind of religious education to be given. Various provisos ensure that this permission to withdraw is not used to avoid school attendance.

With regard to collective worship, the provisions are altogether more complicated. This is because it is assumed that pupils belonging to a non-Christian religion may wish to worship together on the school premises. With regard to the *content of worship*, however, the 1988 Education Reform Act lays down that it must be 'wholly or mainly of a broadly Christian character' although this wording should not be understood to apply to individual acts of worship but to the pattern of acts of worship in 'any school term as a whole'. Subject to these considerations the collective worship shall be appropriate to the age and aptitudes of pupils and their family backgrounds. Such worship may also be organised more flexibly than before in the sense that the requirement for the whole school to worship together at the start of the school day is now dropped. Sub-groups of pupils may worship together and this need not take place at the beginning of the day. Also, where the SACRE so determines, either any county school or any class or description of pupils in a county school may participate in collective worship which is *not* distinctive of any particular Christian or other religious denomination but which *is* distinctive of another faith (section 7.6.a and b). The school should apply for this 'determination' to the SACRE.

The government's intentions are clear enough and though they have been criticised (e.g. by Hull, 1989) the drafting allows schools considerable leeway with making arrangements for large groups of pupils who wish to pursue non-Christian worship while, at the same time, encouraging Christian worship for spiritual, moral and cultural reasons. These reasons are included within the first paragraphs of the 1988 Education Reform Act (section 1.2.a and b) where the remainder of the Act's provisions for the curriculum are set within the context of a broad governmental intention to promote the 'spiritual, moral, cultural, mental and physical development of pupils' and to prepare them 'for the opportunities, responsibilities and experiences of adult life'. Religious education in the classroom and collective worship in the assembly hall are intended to play their part in the attainment of these general objectives; parental right of withdrawal is respected while giving schools more than optional guidelines in religious matters. Moreover, despite the tendency towards the centralisation of the control of education which the 1988 Education Reform Act represents, the principle of local direction of religion (through SACREs) is carefully retained.

Worship in voluntary schools continues to be determined by governing bodies after consultation with the headteacher (see Circular 3/89, paragraphs

31, 33). In voluntary schools collective worship shall be in accordance with the school's trust deed or, if there is no trust deed, in accordance with the school's tradition before 1944. This means that, even though there is not a majority of foundation governors on the governing bodies of controlled schools, denominational worship may still be provided in such schools.

Finally, collective worship is normally held on the school premises, though in the case of controlled schools, if worship off the school premises is occasionally deemed appropriate, it may only take place in addition to the daily statutory act of collective worship (Circular 3/89, paragraph 32).

Activity A3

Briefly compare the 1944 Education Act and the 1988 Education Reform Act in respect of church schools and religious education. What are the differences and similarities?

Comment on activity A3

The similarities lie in the continuation of the main categories of voluntary school (aided, controlled and special agreement) and the continuation, with modification, for the procedures for drawing up agreed syllabuses, whose role remains unaltered. The differences lie in:

- the clear inclusion of non-Christian groups in agreed syllabus conferences;
- the monitoring and reforming role of SACREs and their enduring existence;
- the powers of SACREs over the determination of collective worship;
- the greater flexibility of the 1988 stipulations relating to collective worship;
- the requirement that the content of worship should be broadly Christian;
- the acceptance that, after a SACRE determination, non-Christian worship is acceptable in maintained schools;
- the freedom that church schools have in respect of worship since this is determined by governing bodies in consultation with the headteacher according to the trust deed or pre-1944 tradition;
- the creation of grant-maintained schools.

A7 The 1992 Education (Schools) Act

The 1992 Education (Schools) Act lays down the ground for inspection of schools in England and Wales. The opening section deals with the appointment of a Chief Inspector of Schools and other inspectors who are to serve as staff to the Chief Inspector. All these appointments are crown appointments made by Order in Council. As the 1992 Education (Schools) Act makes clear these inspectors are distinct from 'registered inspectors' whose appointment is on a different basis and described in sections 9, 10 and 11 of the Act.

The second section of the 1992 Education (Schools) Act sets out the general duties of the Chief Inspector, and these include keeping the Secretary of State informed about the quality of education, the educational standards of schools, the financial resources made available to schools and the 'spiritual, moral, social and cultural development of pupils'. The third section gives the Chief Inspector the right to inspect any school in England and to monitor the work of registered inspectors. The fourth section gives the Chief Inspector the duty of:

- making an annual report to the Secretary of State, who 'shall lay a copy of it before each House of Parliament';
- making reports with respect to other matters which fall within the scope of his functions;
- arranging for any reports brought under this section to be appropriately published.

The Inspectorate for Wales operates identically and is described in sections 5, 6, 7, and 8. These inspectors in Wales are known as OHMCI inspectors.

Section 9 gives the Chief Inspectors the duty, through registered inspectors, to inspect county schools, voluntary schools, special schools, grant maintained schools and some independent schools, city technology colleges and maintained nursery schools.

For the purposes of this unit, it is important to note that voluntary schools fall within the category of schools liable to inspection by registered inspectors. These inspectors are concerned with those things described above in the second section of the 1992 Education (Schools) Act but *not*, as section 13 indicates, the 'denominational education' of voluntary and grant-maintained schools.

Section 13 explains that 'denominational education' in voluntary and grant-maintained schools means 'religious education given otherwise than in accordance with an agreed syllabus'. Inspection of this aspect of the life of such schools is the responsibility of the school's governing body. In the case of controlled schools, it is the foundation governors who choose the denominational inspector and in other cases (i.e. aided, special agreement and grant-maintained schools), it is the whole governing body which chooses the denominational inspector. As paragraph 5 makes clear, the person chosen by the governors need not be a 'registered inspector'. However, the frequency of these inspections is at the discretion of the Secretary of State and the inspections are liable to the same period as section 9 inspections, i.e. every 4 years. Such inspections (paragraph 7) shall report 'on the quality of the denominational education provided by the school for pupils to whom denominational education is given by the school' and these inspectors may be assisted by such persons as they think fit.

The exact definition of 'denominational education' has been further clarified in subsequent enactments. The 1992 Education (Schools) Act left confusion over the inspection of collective worship and this led to an amendment in the 1993 Education Act (section 259) which makes section 13 of the 1992 Education (Schools) Act read: 'it shall be the duty of the governing body of ... any voluntary school ... to secure that the content of the school's collective worship is inspected under this section'.

In summary, then, *all* voluntary schools are subject to section 13 inspections. In controlled schools this inspection covers:

- collective worship;
- social, moral, spiritual and cultural education if this is requested by the governing body (nevertheless spiritual, moral, social and cultural education is also still inspected under section 9).

In aided and special agreement schools this inspection covers:

- religious education;
- collective worship;
- spiritual, moral, social and cultural education.

Schedule 2 part 2 of the 1992 Education (Schools) Act gives further information about inspection of denominational education. Written reports on the inspection, within a specified period of time, must be sent, together with a summary, to the governing body of the school concerned. It is then the duty of the governing body to make the report and its summary available to members of the public and to provide a copy of these to 'any person who asks for one'. It is also the duty of governors to take reasonable steps to provide every parent of a child at the school with a copy of the summary of the report.

Once the report has been delivered and publicised, it becomes the duty of the governing body to prepare an 'action plan' of the action they propose to take in the light of the report and the period within which they propose to take it. This plan must be sent to the person who appoints the school's foundation governors and to the local education authority or, in the case of grant-maintained schools, to the Secretary of State. The action plan shall also be made available to members of the public and reasonable attempts must be made to circulate it to parents. Subsequently the governors' report should include reference to the 'extent to which the proposals set out in the plan have been carried into effect'.

The procedures for reporting on section 13 inspections mirror almost exactly the procedures for reporting on section 9 inspections. In each case reports must be prepared and submitted with a summary within a specified period of time, must be made available to governors and the public, especially parents, and are the basis of action plans, the implementation of whose proposals must be monitored through the governors' report. Schedule 2 part 1 deals with these matters.

Voluntary schools, therefore, find themselves subject to two kinds of inspection, an OFSTED inspection (or OHMCI in Wales), carried out by registered inspectors, which looks at everything except denominational education (section 9 inspections) and an inspection by an appointee of the governors (section 13 inspections) which only looks at the denominational education. Under the Consolidation Acts, section 9 inspections became known as section 10, while section 13 inspections became known as section 23. Both sorts of inspection produce reports which must be made widely available and which must result in action plans prepared and monitored by governors.

It should be noted that section 9 inspectors of all kinds of voluntary schools may comment on whether arrangements for school worship comply with the law. They may also appraise the contribution of school worship to the spiritual, moral, social and cultural education of pupils.

In the case of aided schools, where parents have withdrawn their children from religious education or where religious education is taught according to the agreed syllabus, the arrangements will be inspected under section 9 (Brown and Lankshear, 1995).

Activity A4

In your opinion might there be a conflict between section 9 (now called section 10) and section 13 (now called section 23) inspections? Would action plans be better monitored by the local education authority rather than by school governors?

Comment on activity A4

It is not easy to cover spiritual and moral education under section 9 without referring to denominational education, which is the prerogative of section 13. Moreover, if requested to do so, section 13 inspections can take in spiritual, moral, social and cultural education. Consequently there might be a conflict between the priorities set by action plans resulting from the two sets of inspectors' reports. The governing body may need to balance competing recommendations.

If action plans were monitored by local authorities, this would enormously increase the advisory or inspectorial staff of local authorities and would be likely to cause conflicts with independent-minded school governors. On balance, and in keeping with the other powers of school governors, it seems wise to keep action plans within the purview of the governing body of each school.

Readers

You will find helpful sections 5.1 and 5.2 of L.J. Francis and D.W. Lankshear (eds) (1993), *Christian Perspectives on Church Schools*, Leominster, Gracewing,.

Bibliography

Brown, A. and Lankshear, D.W. (1995), *Inspection Handbook: for section 13 inspections in schools of the Church of England and the Church in Wales*, London, The National Society.

Dent, H.C. (1944), *The Education Act 1944*, London, University of London Press Ltd.

Department for Education and Employment (1994), *School Governors: a guide to the law*, London, DfEE.

Duncan, G. and Lankshear, D.W. (1996), *Church Schools: a guide for governors*, London, The National Society.

Durham Report (1970), *The Fourth R*, London, The National Society and SPCK.

Griffith, J.A.G. and Ryle, M. (1989), *Parliament: functions, practice and procedures*, London, Sweet and Maxwell.

Hull, J.M. (1989), *The Act Unpacked*, Birmingham Papers in Religious Education No 1, University of Birmingham and the Christian Education Movement.

Iremonger, F.A. (1948), *William Temple: Archbishop of Canterbury, his life and letters*, London, Oxford University Press.

Jennings, I. (1957), *Parliament*, Cambridge, Cambridge University Press.

Liell, P. (1988), *The Law of Education: special bulletin Education Reform Act 1988*, London, Butterworths.

Silk, P. and Walters, R. (1989), *How Parliament Works* (second edition), London, Longman.

Souper, P. and Kay, W.K. (1982), *The School Assembly Debate: 1942-1982*, Southampton, University of Southampton.

Philosophy of Religious Education

Unit B

A rationale for religious education

Gaynor Pollard

University College

Chester

Contents

Introduction

Aims

After working through this unit you should be able to:

- develop a rationale for religious education;
- demonstrate the relationship between religious education, school worship, spiritual, moral, social and cultural development, and the ethos of the school;
- give examples of fruitful co-operation between religious education and other subject areas;
- work out a professional rationale for religious education relevant to your context.

Overview

The purpose of this unit is to help you to develop understandings of the place and purpose of religious education in the school curriculum, and the relationship between religious education and other curriculum and pastoral areas.

The place and purpose of religious education has been debated sporadically since the 1960s. The positive result of the debate is that religious education has been kept in the public eye and subject to rigorous educational thinking. The negative results have included confusion amongst teachers, who may be troubled about the varied and often mutually exclusive expectations placed on them. The exclusion of religious education from the National Curriculum (see unit A of the module *History and Philosophy*) has also made it difficult for teachers to make connections between this subject and the rest of the curriculum.

In this unit you will address some of these issues by considering suitable aims and objectives for religious education, and by undertaking a study of how religious education contributes to the rest of the curriculum and to the ethos of the school. You will be expected to:

- consider some of the expectations of religious education, from a variety of sources;
- explore the links between religious education and those areas of school life which are often connected and sometimes confused with it: spiritual, moral, social and cultural development, school worship, and the ethos of the school;

- evaluate the importance of curriculum documentation that stresses links between different areas of the school curriculum and the school community;
- consider the ways in which religious education may support and be supported by subjects of the National Curriculum.

This unit is based firmly in classroom practice and, if you are a teacher, you are encouraged to use the exercises and reflections to evaluate your own practice and to research amongst your colleagues to discover good models for collaboration. Practising teachers will often be the most fruitful source of good ideas to enhance the learning of pupils. You will also be asked to do some reading and reflection in the area of the theory that underlies good practice, in particular to become clear about what you are trying to achieve and how you might assess whether you have accomplished this or not.

You will find that it is impossible to produce a rationale that will please everybody concerned with your school. This is so in every area of the curriculum, but is particularly relevant in religious education. The important point to remember is that everything you propose should have a well thought-out *educational* basis. Although your work will be informed by theology and religious studies, and will take account of the beliefs, values and practices of faith communities, this unit will concentrate on the needs of pupils in church schools, drawn as they are from a variety of social and cultural backgrounds.

By the end of the unit you should be in a position to lead a discussion on possible rationales for religious education in your school, and to have an understanding of the positions of others who do not agree with you.

B1 Issues and aims in religious education

One of the most important preconditions of success in any project is to understand what you are aiming to achieve. This can be complicated in RE, where there seem to be many interested parties, all with a different idea of what a successful programme might look like. I once received a report on RE from my daughter's primary school with the brief comment: 'Hannah is a very polite girl'. I was pleased to hear this, as it was not a description I would normally associate with her, but it informed me that success in the school's RE programme was available through social behaviour. There was no indication of the importance of spiritual development, knowledge of religions, understanding of religious ways of life, or anything else that I might have expected to see.

This anecdote illustrates the necessity for each school to make a relevant assessment of pupils' attainment in this area. Each school needs to have a clear view of why it is teaching the subject, what it hopes each pupil might achieve, and to have put in place the means to monitor and evaluate the success of the programme.

During this section you will examine some of the issues involved in developing a rationale, or an educational justification, for teaching religious education. There will be many factors that you will have to take into account, not least the statutory basis of the subject. Educational programmes depend upon team-work, and the rationale you devise will need to be put before a variety of groups connected with the school before it could be implemented as a school policy. During these negotiations it is worth keeping in mind the processes you used to reach your present point of view, in order to discover at what point other people differ from you in their opinions, and whether these points are negotiable or not. In this section you will consider:

- the purposes of teaching religious education;
- the practical parameters of religious education;
- the contribution of religious education to spiritual, moral, social and cultural development;
- the contribution of religious education to the ethos of the school;
- the taught curriculum and the school's foundation;
- the role of religious education as the conveyer of information about religions;
- the purpose of progression;
- skills development in religious education.

The following comments give the views of four people concerning religious education. These views express those typically held by parents and carers of children. They demonstrate the kind of tensions that lie in the background of religious education.

> As a parent, I expect the school to teach my son Christian values. We don't go to church ourselves, but I wanted him to go to a church school so that he would learn how to behave properly. That's what religious education is all about really, isn't it? Learning how to look after other people's feelings, and to show respect.

> As a social worker I believe pupils should find out about all kinds of religious beliefs. When they become adults they will need to know about all kinds of beliefs and practices. We should introduce different ways of thinking to children as soon as possible in their education. The world has opened up, and they need to be able to grasp that this causes difficulties between people. The most important task of religious education is to enable children to deal with difference, without resorting to violence.

> As a regular churchgoer I believe we should emphasise that this is a church school where the children should be nurtured in the Christian faith. They need to feel safe and secure about their own identity and culture, before they can cope with different ideas. Teaching a range of religions, as if they all had equal validity, just causes confusion amongst young children. If church schools don't

teach religious education like this, then they are betraying the trust that the church places in them. Even if the children are not interested in Christianity at school, it still gives them a grounding that they can always turn to later.

As a humanist I think some of our children attend church schools because of the way education developed in this country. In this day and age it should be irrelevant to the content of their learning. Since county schools follow agreed syllabuses in religious education which cover a range of religions, studied in an objective way, church schools should be doing the same. Muslims haven't been allowed to open Aided schools, so why should Christians and Jews be allowed to?

Practical parameters for religious education

It is clear that there is a wide variety of opinion on religious education, including expectations that are mutually exclusive. Different categories of school may legitimately have different emphases. There are, however, basic legal parameters that must be taken into account in any programme of religious education operated in any particular school (see unit A in this module). In addition there are practical parameters to the subject, conditions which must be fulfilled to allow effective teaching to take place:

- religious education should occupy not less than 5% of curriculum time, excluding time spent in the act of worship;
- religious education should receive the same resources as other subjects enjoying the same amount of curriculum time. This includes pupil resources and the provision of teachers who are able to teach the syllabus confidently. In a church school, this may also mean providing in-service training for clergy who are involved in the religious education provision.

When resources are allocated for religious education who makes the decision? In practice, interested parties will include:

- governors with responsibility for safeguarding the terms of the trust deed;
- local education authorities, when the local agreed syllabus is being taught;
- members and officers of the Diocesan Board of Education;
- local clergy and members of the church;
- the school's co-ordinator for religious education;
- teachers, who will be responsible for day-to-day teaching;
- pupils.

Activity B1

Read the statements below and ask yourself, 'To what extent can I agree with this as a purpose for religious education?' Take a piece of paper and note the statements with which you agree strongly and those with which you disagree strongly. After this, add in any statements which you have thought of that are not included in this set. Ask yourself why you hold the views you do. What are the reasons for your strong feelings in response to some statements? Here are the statements:

- to nurture children in the Christian faith;
- to study information about religions;
- to help in the search for meaning and purpose in life;
- to make children aware of their own cultural heritage;
- to learn about the bible;
- to give children a secure grounding in morals;
- to enable children to master skills;
- to give children options in religious choices;
- to enable critical thinking;
- to enable spiritual development to take place;
- to encourage tolerant attitudes;
- to enable children to hear the Gospel;
- to enable children to think deeply.

Now examine any 'not sure' answers, and write down why you feel ambiguous about these areas.

Comment on activity B1

We have not designated this an activity which might be assessable because it is so personal, but we think you should clarify your own views about the purposes of religious education. We recognise that you may have a series of views, some of which may seem to be incompatible with each other, or appropriate on different occasions. For instance, you might think that a faith-nurturing aim is appropriate for young children in church schools but not appropriate for older children in county schools.

Spiritual, moral, social and cultural development

Since the 1988 Education Reform Act, all schools have been required to assume a responsibility for spiritual, moral, social and cultural development of their pupils. In Part 1, section 1 (2) under a heading entitled 'The Curriculum' the Act states:

> The curriculum for a maintained school satisfies the requirements of this section if it is a balanced and broadly based curriculum which:
>
> (a) promotes the spiritual, moral, cultural, mental and physical development of pupils at the school and of society; and
>
> (b) prepares such pupils for the opportunities, responsibilities and experiences of adult life.

This emphasis on spiritual development is a new one in the maintained sector of British education and was reinforced in the 1992 Education (Schools) Act. These Acts do not attach the responsibility for spiritual, moral, social and cultural development to any particular curriculum or pastoral area, which has left the questions of where and when and how this might happen in schools an open one.

Many church schools cannot rely on their pupils sharing a common world-view or belief system, and need to spend time thinking through what spiritual development might mean in their context, and the role of religious education in this.

Activity B2

Read one or both of the following discussion papers from the School Curriculum and Assessment Authority: *Spiritual and Moral Development* (SCAA, 1995) or *Education for Adult Life: the spiritual and moral development of young people* (SCAA, 1996).   Then consider these two questions.

- What do you think are unrealistic expectations of schools in this area?
- How would you define spirituality?

Comment on activity B2

You might have found that the terminology is much vaguer than for other tasks assigned to schools. For instance, *Spiritual and Moral Development* says that spirituality has to 'do with relationships with other people and, for believers, with God' but it goes on to say that it has to do with 'our universal search for identity' and has many aspects included 'beliefs', 'a sense of awe, wonder and mystery' and feelings of transcendence as well as 'self-knowledge' and 'creativity'. You may well feel that it is impossible to know whether a child has feelings about the transcendent or what the child's relationship with God is.

You may also wonder whether the child's creativity with paint is relevant to spirituality or a simple talent for design and an eye for colour. You may feel that a child has a clear sense of identity as a supporter of Manchester United but you may feel that this has little or nothing to do with spiritual values.

You may also feel that the amalgamation of spiritual and moral development is confusing since creativity and transcendence may be entirely personal and solitary while morality is always to do with other people.

On the other hand, you may conclude that it is realistic for schools to help children become aware of the existence of others (by pastoral care and insisting on fairness) and that it is possible for children to learn to reflect on their experience either in class or in collective worship. You may also find that, if spirituality is defined in terms of relationships, then it is logical to link these with moral education and morality in general. *Spiritual and Moral Development* says that spiritual and moral development may be promoted by the 'ethos of the school' and you may consider that, though this is vague, it is meaningful and that the examples given in relation to religious education are illuminating. Religious education asks children to consider ultimate questions about life, death and absolutes.

If you have read *Education for Adult Life*, you may feel that it gives greater prominence to personal and social education than it does to religious education; that values have been included and religious beliefs omitted; that citizenship education has appeared; that moral development is tied to a school's ethos rather than to the curriculum; that the assessment of spiritual development is problematic but worth further consideration; that ethical debates now often appear in a scientific context. Many of these implications are presently unrealistic since they would require changes to the teaching given in, say, science or the replacement of religious education with personal and social education.

Ethos of the school

Many teachers feel that the church school should be an example of a Christian community or family. Mission statements often make claims for a 'caring' and 'harmonious' ethos, which appears to preclude conflict, and this perception of Christian ethos may encourage teachers to prefer harmony at the expense of progress.

The church school is often in a special position to establish good links with the home since the parish in which the school is situated may cover or overlap to a considerable extent with the school's catchment area. Certainly, with regard to Roman Catholic schools, one of the strengths recently identified

(McLauglin, O'Keefe and O'Keeffe, 1996) has been dependent on the 'extended role' of the teacher, allowing him or her to meet with and support children in social, sporting and extra-curricula activities that build up relationships that benefit classroom interaction.

Those who take risks, make mistakes and get things wrong, may find that they perceive a mismatch between what goes on in the school and what they are teaching about the Christian life in religious education. The same considerations apply to pupils. Those who have strong moral feelings (perhaps about animal rights, for instance) may find themselves marginalised by other pupils or by teachers.

These difficulties may be addressed by an understanding of the Christian view of the world that emphasises, not only its beauty and harmony, but also its state of fallenness and need of God's grace. This theological insight can be carried over to religious education, in an exploration of the ways in which Christians and others address social and personal problems.

In some cases church schools emphasise their commitment to Christian values and ethos, yet put very few resources into the curriculum for the teaching of religious education. The clear message is then that, although Christian values are important, core and foundation subjects of the national curriculum take precedence over a consideration of religious claims. This position, tricky in any school, is indefensible in a church school.

Activity B3

Read *Looking For Quality in a Church School* by Lankshear (1992), particularly the section on religious education. Then consider these two questions.

- How may the quality of religious education be improved?
- How may this improvement make an impact on the ethos of the school?

Comment on activity B3

Lankshear outlines several objective measures that can be taken by a school. These include good, clear documentation (including a school policy on religious education), adequate staff training (as much training as for any of the foundation subjects of the National Curriculum), adequate resources (in terms of books and equipment), adequate classroom time (especially when it is integrated with other subjects and in danger of losing its identity), enthusiastic teaching (particularly from specialist staff) and support from governors and parents (which results in good all-round communication).

The ethos of the school is likely to be subtly changed by giving religious education the support and profile it needs. Although religious education is not the same as moral education, where there is religious education, there will often be a concentration on pastoral care, honesty and the moral values implicit in the great religions.

Taught curriculum and school foundation

Academic subjects other than religious education are sometimes referred to as 'the secular curriculum'. This is a misleading term which seems to suggest that the Christian foundation of a church school has no effect on teaching in National Curriculum subjects. No academic areas are value-free, and all schools must consider their total educational provision in the light of their Christian foundation. A neglect of this task could leave religious education in a kind of ghetto of learning, and at a considerable disadvantage. Christian theology relates to all aspects of knowledge and learning, and it is worth drawing pupils' attention to this at appropriate moments.

In *A Christian Vision for State Education*, Cooling (1994) writes about finding a basis for education in a plural society. Since this situation applies to many church schools his points are relevant here. He argues that three basic responses to the diversity of religious values in Britain have been suggested:

- to set up new independent Christian schools that are distinct from the existing church schools, and thus to withdraw from what is seen as an irredeemably secular maintained sector;
- to assume that the traditional values of England and Wales are Christian and to base education in the maintained sector on Christian perspectives, that is to Christianise the maintained sector;
- to promote values that offer absolute definitions of the good life based on rationality (Hirst) or humanisation (Grimmitt), and to seek a maintained sector where religious values are reduced in significance.

The first option has led to accusations of tribalism and indoctrination, though Cooling does not support these accusations and considers them engendered by 'ideological hostility'. The second option does not recognise that religion is a matter on which people may reasonably differ, and it may, in any case, lead to a contest between religio-political groups for the control of schools in the maintained sector. The third option may not be acceptable to religious believers who believe their ideal beliefs should form the framework of education.

As an alternative to these options Cooling suggests that we should see education as a *process* designed to fulfil the learning needs of people in a particular context. In this instance pupils are to be *prepared for their role as citizens in a democratic society* and it is the function of the government to be impartial amongst various religious groups, to hold the middle ground 'where various faiths can transact their business and engage in dialogue'. Teachers in this system must find their first commitment in their personal theological stance, and their second in supporting the pluralist principle, so that education and nurture complement each other. Thus Cooling attempts to develop an understanding of the secular realm that promotes fairness, while also respecting the integrity of the religions represented within British democracy.

Clearly Cooling's argument is relevant to all schools within the maintained sector, those receiving public money, and sees the preparation of future citizens as part of each school's remit. But where does this leave church schools? The logic of trust deeds and foundation documents is that pupils should be educated for or in faith. The logic of plural democracy is that pupils should be educated so that they may have a fair appreciation of the faith positions of other people. These two logics, when they converge in a church school in the maintained sector, are compatible: it is possible for church schools to teach with an eye both to their foundation and to the wider society of which they are part. Indeed, the foundation documents of Victorian church schools were written at a time when churches were taking a vital part in democratic debate. So, it makes sense to see church schools as preparing young people for democracy, since many Christian values are also democratic values.

Conveying information about religions

Another important part of the rationale for teaching religious education is the understanding that, regardless of its ultimate truth, there is a valuable body of knowledge *about* religions concerning the beliefs, practices and attitudes of believers. The content of religion is important on educational grounds, therefore, whatever a pupil's own belief system.

Acquiring information about religions also is important for future employment and social engagement. An understanding of the background beliefs of religious groups is essential for those whose jobs lead them to interact with the public. Without this understanding there is a danger of giving inadvertent offence. Even in ordinary social life, it is important to know that, on a particular day, a Jewish friend might be facing the demands of the Day of Atonement or a Muslim colleague might be undergoing the expectations of Ramadan.

Despite the fact that religious education has been part of the school curriculum for many years, there is still a widespread ignorance of religious belief and practice. It may be that an emphasis on moral rather than religious education has produced this result. Certainly, many undergraduates are unable to understand the religious allusions of literary texts written prior to the 1950s, and the majority of people are unable to understand the religious background to much of the daily news from the Middle East or former Yugoslavia. Thus, on *educational grounds*, pupils need information about religions in order to make sense of the contemporary world.

Delivering a progressive scheme of education

Teachers understand and apply the concept of progression in all aspects of the curriculum, but often leave this aspect out when it comes to religious education. The reasons for this are complex, and are related to the attitudes of adult believers to their own learning (see Hull, 1985). We identify three uses of the term progression:

- progression in understanding through intellectual maturity;
- progression from one religion to another;
- progression from one topic to another.

In primary schools in particular, religious education is often based around biblical work. Bible stories are often told with the understanding that they convey only one possible interpretation, a moral point, and having covered this point, no further learning is encouraged, and the same story, with the same point is re-iterated through to adulthood. This method does little justice to biblical stories, and even less to enhance the progression of pupils' understanding.

Sometimes progression is interpreted in terms of movement through religions, from the familiar to the unfamiliar. This has the disadvantage of presuming that the starting-point, Christianity, is familiar to children. It also gives the impression that the religion last studied is much more interesting and sophisticated than that tackled at an earlier age.

Teachers themselves need a level of understanding of religious traditions to enable them to teach progressively. For a variety of reasons (lack of initial training, no in-service work) this understanding is rarely present. Teachers need to approach their work in religious education in the same way they prepare background knowledge for any other subject of the curriculum. We give an example below to show what a progressive scheme (in the sense of progressing from topic to topic) is like. It builds on what has been taught in previous years and, at the same time, reserves the most difficult and abstract concepts for older pupils.

Progressive scheme for Christmas

Year 1 focuses on the birth of Jesus and recounts it through the biblical narrative. The importance of Jesus to visitors who travel so far and in unexpected ways to see him.

Year 2 focuses on the gifts given to Jesus and recounts the arrival of the Wise Men and the giving of gold, frankincense and myrrh. The whole concept of gifts, from God to us and from us to God, is illustrated.

Year 3 focuses on selected Christian practices and recounts the various traditions, especially those connected with the celebration of Christmas, that are held by Christians in different parts of Europe.

Year 4 focuses on selected Christian practices and recounts the various traditions, especially those connected with the celebration of Christmas, that are held by Christians in other parts of the world,.

Year 5 focuses on the angels in the Christmas narrative and recounts their speaking to Mary, to Joseph (in a dream) and to the shepherds. The concept of communication is illustrated and this allows questions to be asked about the way God communicates with us.

Year 6 focuses on the identity and powerlessness of Jesus as a baby. The concept of Incarnation is explored. The Wise Men worship the child Jesus and so illustrate the paradox of helpless Majesty, divine humility, God made flesh.

You will see that the scheme moves from the simple concept of birth to the much more theological complex concept of incarnation. The scheme, in other words, returns to the same events more than once and, on each occasion, draws from them concepts appropriate to the age of the pupils.

Developing appropriate skills

There are skills which pupils must practise to master any curriculum area in addition to skills which are peculiar to religious education. Skills are usually thought of as learnable competencies. For example, we might talk about 'football skills' in referring to the ability to dribble the ball, or 'reading skills' in referring to the ability to associate sounds and letters or sounds and words. The terminology relating to skills is not always exact and it is not always clear what should or should not be counted as a skill. Is driving a car a skill? Or is it an art? Is driving made up of sub-skills? If it is, how should these be related to each other?

We take the view that skills are discrete units of learning, usually without intellectual or interpretative dimensions. For example, we would not think that understanding Shakespeare or the bible are skills, but we would agree that typing is a skill. Many of the skills required in religious education are common to other text-based educational activities. And some are partly skills and partly abilities that are too big to fit inside our preferred usage of the term skill.

Here are some skills commonly used in religious education, though also needed in other parts of the curriculum:

- investigating information from a variety of media;
- listening to the views and practices of others;
- sharing or collaborating in group activities;
- evaluating thoughts and feelings;
- expressing personal views.

Here are some skills that are specific to religion:

- observing religious activities;
- describing religious activities;
- interpreting religious language and symbols;
- thinking in silence.

We appreciate that thinking in silence may be needed for literary or artistic appreciation but we take the view that it also has a specifically religious use. Reflecting in silence and thinking deeply without distraction is in danger of being lost by children who have spent no time on their own and who do not manage to escape the radio or television long enough to appreciate what might be experienced in silence.

Two recent writers on religious education have addressed its distinctiveness from other points of view. Neither of these writers thinks of particular *skills* associated with religious education, but they both express facets of the subject which lead to the development of skills. The first writer is Hammond (see also unit C of this module). He says religious education should aim to (Hammond *et al*, 1990, p 17):

> help pupils to learn to be aware of and to take seriously their own inner experience and their potential to be aware. Hence learning to respect the inner experience of other people... to help pupils be aware of the power of language and intention to structure our experience, but not by entering into religious practice in a 'confessional' sense

The second writer, Watson (1993, pp 54f), is concerned with the methods of religious education. While including work with symbols and metaphors for older pupils, she contends that imagination is vital in religious education for:

- getting on the wavelength of religious people;
- understanding religious language and other forms of expression;
- gaining knowledge in religion.

Activity B4 (optional)

Plan a brief scheme of work lasting for half a term on the subject of God, with a view to meeting the following aims. Pupils should be given opportunities to:

- express thoughtful personal responses to religious beliefs and questions;
- practise using religious language appropriately;
- reflect quietly, using different kinds of focus;
- ask questions which address some of the puzzling aspects of life.

B2 Religious education's distinctive contribution

Since religious education was omitted from the National Curriculum (for reasons given in unit A of this module) some teachers have regarded its place in the curriculum as semi-optional. Religious education is often the last subject to be awarded a policy document, and last on the list for resourcing. Despite the lack of priority it is sometimes given, religious education has its own distinctive place in the curriculum and its contribution cannot be covered by other curriculum subjects. In this section you will:

- reflect upon the purposes of education in religions;
- evaluate the contribution of religious education to the teaching of morality;
- identify skills unrepresented in other areas of the curriculum.

Education in religions

All cultures develop and change. This process maintains links with what has gone before and re-interprets experience in the light of new circumstances. The present generation is not the first to have faced questions about ultimate truth and meaning and we often derive the form of those questions from our western cultural heritage. A very large part of this heritage has been drawn from the intellectual side of Christianity, dealing with philosophical questions, but some of it has been drawn from expressions of passion and emotion in the arts. Therefore from the point of view of the sciences as well as the arts, the religious heritage of Europe is significant.

In addition to this emphasis on Christianity, we need also to take account of the other religious traditions that have been historically present in Europe and which have also had an effect in shaping our contemporary view of the world. Jews and Muslims have made vital contributions to European development. More recently Sikhs and Buddhists have done so too.

From the point of view of a church school which takes its Christian foundation seriously there is also the issue of our treatment of those who are different from ourselves. The strong tradition of hospitality and respect for 'strangers' should be evident in the curriculum of the school and should also be represented in religious education. This also holds true for pupils who do not profess a religious belief themselves: there is still a moral issue about learning more about people who embrace a different life-style. Although this might be applied to believers from a range of different world religions, it holds equally true for Christianity, which has many different denominations.

But there is an inevitable tension between the foundation of a school and openness to other faiths.

Activity B5

Read the chapter on 'The church school: commitment and openness' by Geoffrey Duncan, in L.J. Francis and D.W. Lankshear (eds) *Christian Perspectives on Church Schools*, Leominster, Gracewing. Then consider these two questions.

- What options does Duncan identify?
- What are their strengths and weaknesses?

Comment on activity B5

Duncan identifies three possible positions, namely commitment and neutrality, commitment and openness, and commitment and witness. He begins from the assumption that Britain is a plural society and considers the role of commitment in such a society. He argues that the tensions between commitment and openness are more prevalent than those between commitment and neutrality. He agrees with Brenda Watson, that 'true openness is paradoxically only possible on the basis of firm convictions' and that 'the opposite of firm commitment is not no commitment but a confusion of weakly-held or conditioned commitments'. Against this background, he believes church schools in the twenty-first century in Britain may have to prepare children to 'affirm and rejoice in difference' in a 'spirit of altruistic Christian service' so that Christian schools are Christian in ethos but not in dogma.

What Duncan might also have addressed is the issue of how ethos and dogma are related (see unit B of the module *History and Philosophy*).

Morality within a religious context

Activity B6 (optional)

For many primary teachers religious education is thought of as the main vehicle for moral education in the school. What would be your responses to the two following questions?

- If religious education is concerned with moral behaviour, how is this element to be assessed?
- If there is overwhelming agreement amongst Christians that commitment to the faith is no protection against wrongdoing, then why should the teaching of religious education make a difference to moral behaviour?

Comment on activity B6

These are some of the points you might have noted:

First, assessing pupils' *understanding* of moral issues, actions and their consequences, rights and responsibilities, may take place within the context of religious education. Moral behaviour, however, is dependent on many factors (including personality, situation and training) other than understanding.

Teachers can assess pupils for their moral understanding, insight and imagination, especially where this derives from moral dilemmas arising from religious teaching. Should the Buddhist eat meat if not to do so entails starving to death? Should the Jew commit suicide to save the life of others? Should the Christian allow euthanasia? Written work or discussion groups on hypothetical dilemmas are useful here.

Second, religious commitment has produced many saints, but also many sinners, and there is no guarantee that learning in religious education will affect behaviour positively. However, all religions are concerned with morality and it is the largest store of wisdom we have. Moral issues need to be addressed directly in education and religious education is one of the areas where this will happen, with considerable resources to draw from, in the way of teaching, examples and role models. Moreover, there is large-scale empirical evidence that belief in God by modern British teenagers *does* correlate with acceptance of moral strictures against crime (Francis and Kay, 1995).

Ainsworth and Brown (1995) develop the topic of moral education systematically and by interacting with SCAA and OFSTED documents. They point out that a school's ethos can be planned by ensuring that teaching and learning styles imply concern for pupils. Where teachers adapt to the individual needs of pupils, then the ethos of the school becomes real in the experience of pupils. The care that teachers say they feel for students is demonstrated in the quality of education offered. The same may be said about the pastoral system of the school. Moral education can be encouraged by providing young people with a moral framework in which to operate and by helping young people decide *what* is right and wrong, *why* they think so and *how* they should act. religious education syllabuses generally aim to help pupils evaluate religious and moral issues, and this evaluation becomes sharper when it is realised by pupils that religions teach distinct moral obligations.

B3   Religious education and other areas

There are obvious overlaps between some of the content of religious education and the content of other subject areas. This is of particular relevance to church schools, where the denominational character of the education that is offered may not always be evident in all areas of the curriculum. A Christian theology of education will seek to apply some of the insights gained in religious education to all areas of activity in the school.

In *The Effective Teaching of Religious Education,* Watson (1993, p 175-190) outlines three ways in which the curriculum as a whole affects religious education: in attitudes, assumptions and outcomes. Attitudes are promoted by teachers in all subjects, and they should be aware of what they are promoting. Assumptions about what is right or desirable underlie those attitudes, and the contents and methods employed produce outcomes which may be helpful or harmful.

Activity B7

In what ways might religious education contribute towards an understanding of:

- sex education;
- multicultural education;
- information technology.

Comment on activity B7

This is given separately in the sections below.

Sex education

You might have mentioned that, as part of the school's Christian commitment, it would need to set all sex education in a framework of relationships and responsibilities. Christians agree that God created men and women as sexual beings, who have the capacity to express their sexuality in life-giving ways. This should prevent the type of sex education that dwells only on personal problems. On the other hand, all gifts from God are capable of misuse, and when things go wrong in sexual relationships this can have devastating consequences. Nevertheless, Christians believe that disastrous situations (such as the ones the pupils may find their parents have got themselves into) are capable of forgiveness and redemption. The opportunity to start again after failure is always available.

Multicultural education

An important understanding of Christian faith is that all people are made in the image of God, and for this reason must be shown respect. One way of showing respect is to learn about those whose ways are strange to us. In this section you might have included the importance of providing information from different world religions to promote greater understanding and tolerance.

In an overwhelmingly secular culture it is important to point out that most societies, past and present, have taken religious belief very seriously, and any study of a multicultural nature will take this into account. Religious education can thus assist in enabling pupils to understand the basis for different cultural patterns, e.g. the vegetarianism of Hindus or the pacifism of Buddhists.

Information technology

Information technology is important for communication and information retrieval. In common with all tools it may be used in ways that are positive, or ways that are trivial, time-wasting or evil. Since many pupils have access to the internet and many more will have access soon, the importance of relationships, real and electronic, across the world might be stressed.

Religious education is open to the use of information technology both by accessing CD-ROM material, by computer simulations of historical epochs and by simple games based on religious events. For example, quest, journey or pilgrimage games allow the player to move on to the next stage by answering a question or making use of an item collected during a previous episode.

Working with the sciences

The debate between science and religion is worth spending some time on, since negative attitudes to religion as a consequence of a simplistic attitude toward science can prevent successful religious learning. Despite much work by scientists and theologians in the area at the interface between scientific and religious studies, there persists an attitude that the two ways of looking at the world are in fundamental conflict. Many teachers and their pupils place the findings of the sciences in the realm of that which is certain and proved. This attitude is dependent upon the following beliefs:

- information is gained from the five senses;
- truth is discovered by empirically testing information gained through the senses;
- such testing involves *reasoning*, using intellectual capacities to devise appropriate tests;
- verified (that is, tested) information situated in a rationally constructed conceptual framework *is* scientific knowledge, and this is the only worthwhile type of knowledge;
- since this knowledge may be repeatedly tested, it is in the public domain and therefore objective.

In contrast to science, religious beliefs are often seen in the following ways:

- religious truth is a matter of personal opinion; it is dependent on where you live, and whether you feel a need for the comfort which religion can bring;
- religious believers claim truth about God and the world through personal experience and through learning about the personal experiences of others;
- such personal experience is by definition subjective and cannot be tested or repeated to confirm its validity;
- experiences of God are influenced by the interpretative framework we bring to them;
- these religious experiences are private; it may be that we will give them up as science provides more and better explanations.

These summaries contain simplifications that need to be qualified before any progress can be made on thinking about the contribution that religious education may make to work on the sciences. We take the view that science and religion are in many respects similar as the following considerations show.

- Science and religion make predictions on the basis of hypotheses (or formal suppositions) and in both areas these hypotheses are tested through experience. In both areas hypotheses have to be amended, or changed altogether as a result of experience.

- Hypotheses are generated on the basis of large-scale worldviews but, because the hypotheses are modifiable in the light of testing, they do not claim to offer ultimate truth about the way the world is: it is the worldviews which do this.

- Science and religion are complementary areas. Religious ideas may affect the way scientists work by asking questions about the morality of their undertakings (in genetic engineering, for example), and in reminding scientists that there are other ways of approaching truth in human experience, such as through intuition, emotion, imagination and revelation. Scientists may help religious believers by pointing out the wonder of the natural world, and by preventing lazy and immature thinking in religious belief.

To learn more about the history of the relationship between the two disciplines a good introductory text is *A Guide to Science and Belief* by Poole (1994).

The separation between the two disciplines of science and religion has had an effect on teaching in both areas. Pauline Hoyle, Science Inspector in Islington (*Times Educational Supplement,* 12 January, 1996), claimed that social and moral perspectives have been lost in the latest version of the Science National Curriculum. There is a growing emphasis in classrooms on getting the 'right' answer. Pupils were coming to think there was only one answer to complex questions. In contrast, those who have made a study of the scientific enterprise draw attention to its limitations. Only a restricted range of questions can be tackled, and its findings are always provisional.

The difficulties of this attitude amongst teachers has been pointed out by Kevin McCarthy who introduces the notion of 'dualism', that is, of a world where there are fundamental pairs of categories like subject and object, mind and matter, and so on. Monism presents an alternative to dualism. The monistic view sees one category where dualism sees two. McCarthy (1994) writes:

> Schools are continuing to perpetuate a scientifically out-of-date dualism, a divided thinking which provides an inadequate and partial picture of the world. Real scientists, of course, have to perform experiments. They have to form hypotheses, which they then test in order to arrive at a theory. In order to satisfy AT1 in the Order for Science, children as young as seven are expected to carry out investigations along these lines, ideally designing the 'fair test' and controlling the variables themselves. A good example of this is an investigation of snails... this kind of detachment, the playing with animals in this way, is liable to engender the wrong relationship with Nature. It separates us from the world and implies an unpleasant domination and manipulation of living things, as if they were no more than machines to be tested. Descartes used to slice off the end of live dogs in order to feel the pulsing of the blood.

Is it really so alarmist to trace a similar mechanistic spirit at work in these latter day experiments?

Activity B8

In what ways might schools examine their teaching of the sciences, in order to avoid 'out of date dualism'? You might want to ensure that you consider social sciences as well as general science programmes and the use of such topics and specific sciences like biology and chemistry. You might want to ask yourself questions about the extent to which dualism is essential to science or how science manages to solve the problem it creates.

Comment on activity B8

You might have included:

- some work on the attempts by science to cope with the problems of dualism by making explicit the criteria it uses to ensure repeatable measurements;
- some work on appreciation of the aesthetic qualities of pattern and order within scientific understanding, in order to recognise beauty and elegance within the natural world;
- the importance of natural rhythms in making sense of the world, celebrated in the religious life at festival times;
- spiritual, moral, social and cultural perspectives in all science teaching;
- resistance to teaching science as 'disembodied knowledge'; it should be grounded in the work of scientists themselves, including their methodology and the provisional nature of their findings;
- teaching about revolutions in scientific and religious thinking, showing that intuition and inspiration, as well as careful and systematic methods, have played an important part in human understanding;
- encouraging pupils to form and evaluate their own hypotheses about the nature of the universe;
- examining the ways in which scientific and religious thought have complemented each other, e.g. Muslim advances in mathematics and scientific thinking;
- Christian understandings of stewardship and environmental science;
- using methodologies that complement the values taught in religious education, e.g. observing living things in their context, rather than in the classroom, where damage will occur.

Working with arts and humanities

When religious education is taught badly pupils are left disadvantaged in many areas of the curriculum. Those curriculum subjects that work with the past, such as history and English literature, have no baseline of religious understanding on which to draw. Pupils are left ignorant of the religious and moral convictions that motivated historical or literary figures.

Curriculum subjects that concentrate on the present, such as geography, have to contend with confusion about religious groups. Similarly the creative arts, music, art and drama, which have so often drawn their inspiration from religious themes, find that religious background must be taught before appreciation of the artist's intention may occur.

Since the skills that are needed within religious education may often be found in other curriculum areas, it makes sense for the teacher to identify these, and to recognise the possibilities for development across the whole of the spectrum of arts and humanities teaching.

B4 Other contributions to religious education

In the previous section you considered the role of religious education in making a contribution to the whole of the school curriculum. This section will deal with the support that other subject areas may give to religious education.

There are obvious generic skills and common fields of knowledge which are shared across a range of subjects, as well as transferable teaching and learning methods. However, these are not our main concern.

The formation of personal and communal identity is an important task for education, in partnership with parents and communities, and one in which religious education may play a major part. Exactly what kind of understanding of identity it would be appropriate to foster and how to begin to plan and implement policies that would achieve this aim are by no means clear. Nevertheless, it is expected that schools will make a major contribution here and will do so across the whole curriculum. In this section you will begin to consider some of the issues involved in this debate, including the role of multi-faith teaching in religious education, and the formation of Christian identity in a church school.

Links in knowledge, skills and understanding

Although the National Curriculum is implemented in discrete subjects, many primary schools still organise teaching and learning thematically. Teachers are therefore skilled in covering a variety of attainment targets and programmes of study using integrated topic work (see next section). Below are listed some Key Stage targets:

Key Stage one targets

- can give an account of some of the main beliefs of Christianity and one other world religion;
- shows an awareness of diversity in religious beliefs, practices and values;
- is able to use a range of resources;
- is able to identify and understand the meaning of some religious symbols;
- is able to reflect quietly for short periods;
- can use some religious language appropriately;
- expresses some thoughtful and imaginative personal responses;
- asks questions which engage with puzzling aspects of life;
- shows respect for the beliefs, practices and values of others;
- displays a sense of curiosity;
- responds with empathy to unfamiliar traditions;
- can relate moral aspects to personal situations.

Key Stage two targets

- can give an account of the main beliefs, practices and values of Christianity;
- can give an account of some of the main beliefs, practices and values of two other major world religions;
- can recognise similarities and differences in the religions studied;
- can indicate a knowledge of the various ways in which religious beliefs have been communicated, through a variety of media;
- can recognise that everyone has beliefs and values, which may differ;
- can respond, using evidence and argument;
- can explain the meaning of some religious concepts, using appropriate religious language;
- is able to reflect quietly and explain why this practice may be important to a believer;
- can recognise human qualities that are respected in faith communities;
- can give an account of some of their own beliefs and values;
- can address questions of meaning and purpose;
- can empathise with and show respect for religious traditions;
- can demonstrate the connection between belief and behaviour.

Activity B9

Use these examples above of end of Key Stage statements to identify some curriculum subjects which would complement work in religious education and give some examples of activities. Choose the Key Stage with which you are most familiar.

Comment on activity B9

Your own experience of schools, especially primary schools, will have enabled you to make connections. For example, historical work might enable pupils to understand diversity in religious beliefs and practices, the expression of thoughtful and imaginative responses would flow from language work, empathy might be encouraged in drama and dance, use of evidence and argument might arise from science work and the use of a range of resources would be compatible with information technology.

B5 Classroom issues for religious education

Organisation of religious education in the primary school may depend on more than a decision about the best way to teach the subject successfully. For instance, there may be a school policy to choose wide-ranging, cross-curricula themes against discrete subject blocks (or *vice versa).* The strengths and weaknesses inherent in each approach must be recognised and managed, and we discuss them briefly below.

Teaching discretely

Many schools have decided that they can fulfil their statutory duty to teach the National Curriculum and religious education most effectively by teaching each subject discretely, particularly in the junior years. Although this makes planning and progression much easier, it may not necessarily match the learning needs of pupils who might benefit by making links between subject areas.

An argument *for* teaching religious education discretely is to counteract a tendency to use other subjects to set the theme and shape of a topic, and to fit religious education in as an after-thought. The worst example of this type of planning is when the bible is trawled for key-words relating to the topic, and bible stories appropriated without regard for context or relationship to the programme of study. Teaching discretely ensures that a proper regard for progression can be maintained.

An argument *against* teaching discretely is that it can result in a fire-wall being erected around the subject, so that its relevance and significance to other ways of learning about the world are ignored. This does not equate with the experience of believers, who would regard their faith as embracing every part of their lives.

Bates (1992) highlights the difficulties of providing a coherent and progressive scheme of religious education, within a topic framework that may not necessarily lend itself to such subject matter. He commends a model derived from the work of Bruner, who advocated a spiral curriculum, in which key concepts are re-visited at increasing levels of complexity. He reviews a variety of methods, including implicit religious education (Goldman and Loukes) and depth themes (Grimmitt and Holm). The Christmas scheme offered earlier in this unit follows a broadly spiral theme, that is, the same topic is revisited several times, and a new and appropriate aspect of it is introduced.

Bates (1992) suggests that religious education taught thematically can only achieve success by ensuring that:

- the aims of religious education are respected by integrating it into whole school planning, rather than being left to individual teachers;
- themes and topics should be chosen giving due regard to religious education, as well as the other subjects involved, which might involve the inclusion from time to time of religious education-led topics in other subject areas;
- religious education should retain pattern and coherence by ensuring that the curriculum relates to the school's general programme of study.

Activity B10 (optional)

Using the programmes of study of your school as a starting point, and the year group of your choice, plan the religious education component of topics on Victorians and India, each topic to last for one half-term. Make a note of the difficulties involved in integration, and the gains that you feel you might achieve.

Comment on activity B10

We are not able to comment in detail on this activity because we have not specified a year group. The difficulties of integration often resolve themselves into issues of organisation and distinctiveness. The religious education component can be swallowed up in the history component unless care is taken to avoid this. Organisation requires detailed planning to preserve the balance of the curriculum and to make sure the resources of the area and of the school are fully exploited. You may find, for instance, that there are resources you had not thought of using (a Victorian church building; travellers' tales from India, for example) or resources that have been used in one way that can now be used in another (information on Victorian schooling showing how the Ten Commandments or the Lord's prayer were often displayed on the walls of schools).

B6 Religious education beyond the curriculum

The relationship between religious education, school worship, spiritual and moral development, and the ethos of the school is necessarily complex. One way of clarifying the relationship is to approach the practice of a single school through its documentation.

Activity B11 (optional)

Collect your school's policies on religious education, school worship, spiritual, moral and social development and the mission statement and aims of the school. Repeat the exercise with the documents of another school of a similar foundation.

List the aims of the five areas, as recorded in the documentation. Augment these, in the case of your own school, with your own experience.

Critically assess whether or not the aims of each document are clear and compatible with each other. Is there an understanding of the way in which these five areas both support each other and differ from each other? Are there mechanisms in place for monitoring the achievement of these aims?

Comment on activity B11

As a way of comment on this section we summarise the work of Webster (1993) who discusses 'spirituality' in a way that allows him to draw together the separate elements of a school. He defines spirituality as the quality of human experience involving the reflections teachers have of themselves, their understanding of the teaching relationship, the methodologies they evolve and their perception of children.

Christian spirituality finds that 'the personal experience of God' is at its heart, and this experience of a triune God may impose sharp questions on the practice and assumptions of church schools. In Webster's view Christian spirituality will manifest itself in admission policies welcoming non-Christians where the Christian community is strong, and planning a missionary strategy appropriate to a pluralist society where the community is weak. The recruitment of staff will take seriously the need for theological literacy, ecumenicism with other Christians and other faiths will be considered, and a commitment to equality and peace will be possible.

Part of the difficulty with the term 'spirituality' is that its meaning is diffuse and tends to be context-dependent. Although Webster helps in some ways by tying spirituality down to practical school policies, in another way he does not take us very much further forward since, as we have seen, SCAA tend to define spirituality rather differently (see comment on activity B1).

B7 Conclusion

This is the final section of the unit. By this stage you should be much better placed to make some informed decisions about the way religious education might be justified and organised within your school. As a result of the statutory basis of religious education, context is more important in this area than in any other on the school curriculum. For this reason the policy documents that define and guide religious education in schools are unique. In aided schools the governors have a responsibility to ensure that these are as good as possible, and the role of the headteacher and teachers is crucial in providing the best advice. In controlled schools both teachers and foundation governors have the responsibility of ensuring that the planning and organisation of religious education has taken due account of the Christian status of the school.

The most important predictors for success in your work are:

- to be sure of what you want to achieve;
- to be reasonably satisfied that your aims are realistic;
- that you have the resources you need to hand;
- that you have the structures for monitoring progress and recognising success.

Now you have reached the end of this unit you should be in a position to review aspects of your own practice and the practice of your school. You should move on to the next unit to find out more about the approaches to religious education, and their philosophical bases.

This unit has dealt with the subject from the point of view of the classroom teacher, and those responsible for the curriculum. The module on *Method in Religious Education* deals with a wider range of issues including the point of view of the pupil. Ultimately all these factors need to be considered together to produce religious education that is worthy of the name.

Readers

You will find helpful sections 3.3, 12.1, 12.2, 13.1, 13.2, 14.2 and 14.3 of L.J. Francis and A. Thatcher (eds) (1990), *Christian Perspectives for Education*, Leominster, Gracewing. You will find helpful section 4.1 of L.J. Francis and D.W. Lankshear (eds) (1993), *Christian Perspectives on Church Schools*, Gracewing.

Bibliography

Ainsworth, J. and Brown, A. (1995), *Moral Education*, London, The National Society.

Bastide, D. (ed.) (1992), *Good Practice in Primary Religious Education*, London, Falmer Press.

Bates, D. (1992), Developing RE in topic-based approaches to learning, in Bastide, D. (ed.), *Good Practice in Primary Religious Education: 4-11*, London, Falmer Press, pp 101-130.

Bradford, J. (1995), *Caring for the Whole Child: a holistic approach to spirituality,* London, Children's Society.

Brown, A. (1992), *The Multi-Faith Church School*, London, The National Society.

Burns, S. and Lamont, G. (1995), *Values and Visions,* London, Hodder and Stoughton.

Cooling, T. (1994), *A Christian Vision For State Education*, London, SPCK.

Duncan, G.S. (1993), The church school: commitment and openness, in L.J. Francis and D.W. Lankshear (eds), *Christian Perspectives on Church Schools*, Leominster, Gracewing, pp 116-127.

Francis, L.J. and Kay, W.K. (1995), *Teenage Religion and Values*, Leominster, Gracewing.

Hammond J., Hay, D., Moxon, J., Netto, B., Raban, K., Straughier, G. and Williams, C. (1990), *New Methods in RE Teaching*, Harlow, Oliver and Boyd.

Hull, J. (1985), *What Prevents Christian Adults from Learning?* London, SCM.

Hull, J.M. (1994), Christian theology and educational theory: can there be connections? in J. Astley and L.J. Francis (eds), *Critical Perspectives on Christian Education*, Leominster, Gracewing, pp 314-330.

Lankshear, D.W. (1992), *A Shared Vision: education in church schools,* London, The National Society.

Lankshear, D.W. (1992), *Looking For Quality in a Church School,* London, The National Society.

McCarthy, K. (1994), *Science, Nature and Human Spirit*, Oxford, Farmington Papers.

McLauglin, T., O'Keefe, J. and O'Keeffe, B. (eds) (1996), *The Contemporary Catholic School: context, identity and diversity*, London, Falmer Press.

National Society (1990), *The Curriculum: a Christian view*, London, The National Society.

Oldfield, W. and Davies, K. (1994), *Sun, Wind, Snow and Ice,* London, A. and C. Black .

Poole, M. (1994), *A Guide to Science and Belief,* Oxford, Lion Publishing.

Rudge, J. (1993),The experience of the religious educator, *RE Today,* 11 (1) , p 27.

SCAA (1995), *Spiritual and Moral Development* (discussion paper 3), London, SCAA.

SCAA (1996), *Education for Adult Life: the spiritual and moral development of young people* (discussion paper 6), London, SCAA.

Tahan, M. (1994), *The Man Who Counted,* Edinburgh, Canongate Press.

Thiessen, E.J. (1993), *Teaching For Commitment: liberal education, indoctrination and Christian nurture*, Leominster, Gracewing.

Watson, B. (ed.) (1990), *Priorities in Religious Education: a model for the 1990s and beyond*, London, Falmer Press.

Watson, B. (1993), *The Effective Teaching of Religious Education*, London, Longman.

Webster, D.H. (1993), Being aflame: spirituality in county and church schools, in Francis, L.J. and Lankshear, D.W. (eds), *Christian Perspectives on Church Schools,* Leominster, Gracewing, pp 130-140.

Philosophy of Religious Education

Unit C

Different approaches to religious education

Dr Mark Chater

Bishop Grosseteste University College

Lincoln

Contents

Introduction

Aims

After working through this unit you should be able to:

- understand the rationales for three major approaches to religious education;
- be critically aware of the continuing debate about the philosophy of religious education and its major approaches;
- develop a rationale for a professional approach to religious education suited to your own beliefs and context.

Overview

This unit will develop your historical and theoretical knowledge of changes and debates in religious education, and will introduce you to the essential theoretical and philosophical base upon which three approaches are built. It will also encourage you to make connections between these units and your own experiences and beliefs as an educator. The questions which you will be asking, and seeking answers to, include the following.

- What theological beliefs have influenced religious educators in the past?
- What philosophical movements have had an influence on religious education?
- What is the evidence of this influence in the various approaches to religious education now?
- Which theological and philosophical influences suit me personally?
- In what way are the ideas still changing and developing today, and how does this affect me as an educator?

C1 Three approaches to religious education

This section provides you with an outline of the three subsections dealing with different approaches to religious education. It is recommended that you take each subsection in turn, as there is a natural sequence to them. At the top of each subsection you will find further information about what it contains.

Confessional approach

This is a study of historical and contemporary issues relevant to *Christian* approaches to religious education

The word 'confessional' is used in relation to two contexts. It may mean the specifically Christian religious education practised within church contexts, for instance in preparation for confirmation, or in the religious education programmes of church schools. This approach is as ancient as Christianity itself and continues, with evolutions, to influence Christian educators in present-day schools. Its intention is to help Christians to grow in their faith.

It may also apply to the approach taken universally within the maintained sector in British religious education up until the 1960s. This approach was bible-based, assumed a mono-cultural Christian society and, usually, expected most of the population would recognise and attend major Christian festivals like Christmas and Easter. It was an approach used in church schools and county schools alike, as agreed syllabuses and examination courses from the 1930s onwards show. The intention, again, though perhaps less explicitly stated, was to help children grow in their faith (and the assumption, of course, was that they had a Christian faith in which to grow).

Although the confessionalism of the 1950s and 1960s has been important and influential in the gradual evolution of other types of religious education, it is now usually considered inappropriate for publicly funded education and is not the main focus of this unit. What is of more importance is the confessional Christian religious education, which has roots in the early church and is still influential on the efforts of church schools. This forms the main focus of the confessional section of the unit.

Phenomenological approach

This is a study of the philosophical roots of phenomenology and an evaluation of its quest for a scientific and objective approach to religions.

The section dealing with phenomenology will show how a world religions approach, influenced by Husserl and others, emerged through the work of Ninian Smart in the 1960s and 1970s. This approach provided a new, more objective, and therefore more academically respectable justification for a subject which had been discredited and weakened by the collapse of 1950s-style confessionalism. Smart's work transcended phenomenology in many ways, helping to give rise to the third approach.

Experiential approach

This is a study of the work of David Hay, John Hammond and others to find out about the philosophical assumptions behind this approach, including its critique of other approaches.

The experiential approach is both close to, and distinct from, phenomenology. It shares several theoretical foundations but emphasises different outcomes. Its emergence and popularity in the 1980s and 1990s has been attributed to its ability to address some weaknesses in phenomenology.

Contemporary issues facing the approaches

This is a brief study of the theories of faith development, the current interest in spiritual and moral development, and the realignment taking place among all three approaches to religious education.

The three approaches outlined here, and the critical issues facing them, form a coherent whole for this unit. It is important to establish the relationships between the three approaches. The three approaches are presented as distinct entities, but naturally enough they relate closely to each other and influence each other. The final section of the unit shows how contemporary thinkers are re-evaluating the relationships between the three.

C2 Confessional approach

This section will look at the origins of the Christian confessional approach to learning in religion. It will show you a range of sources in theological, philosophical and educational thought, all of which have contributed to the emergence of the confessional approach.

Activity C1

Read pages 7 to 18 of *The Philosophy of Christian Religious Education* by Jeff Astley (1994) and explain what the term 'Christian religious education' means. Do this in two ways:

- work out what Christian religious education is and then what it is not;
- compare terminology in Britain and the United States.

Comment on activity C1

Christian religious education is learning *of* Christianity; it is not just 'learning *about*' Christianity.   Christian religious education can include secular experiences, the profane even; it does not require the division of the world between the sacred and the profane.   Christian religious education can include other world religions; it is not designed to restrict enquiry.   Christian religious education is keen to enhance the development of critical and analytic skills; it is not a covert form of indoctrination.   Christian religious education is a lifelong process and involves the family and the church; it is not restricted to children and to school.

The problem of definition is confused by the different usage of terms in the United States and Britain.   In the United States, 'religious education' is usually seen as church-sponsored and church-orientated and leads to a wide variety of Christian outcomes in learners; as such it is similar to what in Britain is called 'Christian education' or 'Christian nurture'.   In the sense that these terms describe activities intended to aid formation in religion, they are in Britain described as 'confessional'.

In Britain 'religious education' refers to the non-confessional activity of studying religion in the classroom, though there is a qualification here in that church schools *do* see part of their task as nurturing the faith of children (and this *is* a confessional activity).

In Britain 'Christian education' is, on the whole, the term used for the confessional activity of teaching the Christian religion, and in Roman Catholic circles this is known as 'catechesis'.   Astley argues that the term 'Christian religious education' should be used for the 'churchly activity of evangelism, instruction and nurture'.

In summary, *religious education* is a non-confessional activity carried out in schools, although in some church schools a confessional element is added (Britain); or it is a confessional activity carried out by religious communities (USA).   *Christian education* is equivalent to the terms 'Christian nurture' or 'catechesis'; it may also refer to a Christian approach to, or philosophy of, the general curriculum (Britain); or it is the churchly activity of evangelism, instruction and nurture (USA).   As used by Jeff Astley *Christian religious education* is the churchly activity of evangelism, instruction and nurture.

The terminological differences arise partly because in the USA no religion is allowed in publicly funded schools.   The American Constitution divides church and state so strictly that any inclusion of religion in schools would be thought to breach this division.

Activity C2

Thomas Groome distinguishes not only between the general meaning of terms but also the processes they use. Read chapter 2 of *Christian Religious Education* by Groome (1980) and explain what the term 'Christian religious education' means. Do this in two ways:

- draw up two columns, one headed 'Christian religious education is...' and the other headed 'Christian religious education is not...';
- comment on the direction of Groome's remarks.

Comment on Activity C2

You may have arrived at a conclusions along these lines:

Christian religious education is...

- a deliberate attending focused on God's activity in our present;
- a deliberate attending focused on the story of the Christian faith community;
- promoting a quest for, and relationship with, the transcendent (God?);
- focused on the Christian vision (i.e. aimed at promoting the reign of God);
- a political activity in that, like all education, it intervenes in the lives of individuals and communities.

Christian religious education is not...

- distinct from what counts as education in other contexts;
- intended to indoctrinate children to obey an official church;
- disconnected from humanity's cultural heritage;
- disconnected from consciousness of relationships;
- purely a political activity intervening in the lives of individuals and communities.

Groome (1980) believes that religious education describes the 'general investigation of the religious dimension of life and the common human quest for the transcendent ground of being' (p 24) and Christian religious education, because it concerns love of one's neighbour, is opposed to a privatised spirituality that ignores political implications. Catechesis is a 'specifically instructional activity within the broader enterprise of Christian religious education' (p 27).

Rejecting the confessional approach in county schools

Within many country schools and in some voluntary schools any confessional approach began to be questioned and finally rejected as a consequence of seven factors (partially referred to in units A and B of the module *Church Schools: history and philosophy*). These factors occurred very closely together within the 1960s.

Theological questions

There was a theological revolution in Britain in the 1960s symbolised and catalysed by Robinson's (1963) book, *Honest to God*, that brought the ideas of Tillich, Bultmann and Bonhoeffer to wider notice and implicitly rejected traditional views of the authority of scripture and of the mission of Christ.

Social changes

There was a growing consensus that post-war Britain, from the late 1950s onward, became a plural or pluralist society, that is, one where a range of religious opinions were equally acceptable. This change was partly brought about by immigration to Britain from the commonwealth countries of Pakistan, India, Ceylon and the West Indies and the consequent appearance of non-Christian communities whose worship and lifestyle did not fit the pattern that had been tacitly accepted prior to that date. Such changes continued to be recognised and celebrated in official reports (for instance the *Swann Report* of 1985) which, in a minority recommendation, argued for the extension of the dual system principle to cover the Muslim community.

Educational changes

The introduction of comprehensive schools from 1965 onwards had an impact on the kinds of curricula children were able to follow. Previously children selected by educational ability who attended grammar schools were able to pass public examinations in religious knowledge with very little difficulty and were happy to add a further exam pass to their portfolio. The advent of mixed ability teaching and larger schools entailed the scrutinisation of established curricula, including those relating to religious education.

Psychological investigations

The work of Ronald Goldman (1964, 1965) and Ken Hyde (1965) questioned the usefulness of entirely bible-based religious education. Goldman considered that proper understanding of the bible required an ability to think abstractly, and that this ability was not possessed by the majority of primary school children, nor by many at secondary schools. Hyde considered that children failed to learn religious materials, especially those which were Christian in content, without the stimulus and support of church attendance. Since church attendance was generally low, learning was poor. The only way to remedy this situation was to alter curricula.

Philosophical considerations

Hirst (1972; 1974; 1976; 1981; for easy reference see Astley and Francis, 1994, chapter 6.1, and Francis and Thatcher, 1990, chapter 1.2) developed a critique of Christian education by showing, or attempting to show, the impossibility of specifically Christian fields of discourse, when these fields had been established by principles which had nothing to do with Christianity. A Christian form of mathematics was non-existent because mathematics is an autonomous body of knowledge. Since education involves the induction of pupils into autonomous bodies of knowledge, each with its own procedures, rules, history and concepts, it was illogical to speak of a Christian education in any meaningful sense. Alongside this kind of thought was a growing demand by secularists for a re-focusing of religious education. This case is illustrated by the Durham Report (1970, p 345) and the Plowden Report (1967, p 489f).

Methodological innovations

Before the National Curriculum the curricula followed in schools in the UK tended to be regionally flavoured and determined by the necessities of examination courses offered by national exam boards. There were also large-scale national curriculum projects developed by teachers and academics working together and these were taken up or not by local education authorities and schools without any legal or other coercion. Some of the Schools Council projects and working papers recommended new approaches to religion, and rejected the confessional approach as inappropriate to maintained school classrooms (e.g. Schools Council, 1971).

Individual projects

Those who wrote on religious education (e.g. Loukes, 1961, 1965; Grimmitt, 1973; and Holm, 1975) all recommended changes to, or the abandonment of, a confessional approach and devised schemes of work to fit the new educational scene and pluralist climate.

Theoretical foundations of the confessional approach

The confessional approach to religious education takes a particular faith as its starting point, guide and end-point; it refers itself to that faith at all times, operates within that faith community, and aims to help the learner see things from that community's point of view.

A confessional approach can take place in the context of any major world faith: there is Jewish education in the *Schul* at the Synagogue; there is Islamic education in the Qur'an class at the Mosque, and there is teaching involved in attending worship at a Sikh Gurdwara (temple). All religions may be said to engage in forms of confessional religious education, through instruction at the home or in the place of worship, through rituals and sometimes through formal schooling. However, this section will focus specifically on Christian confessional education as it takes place in religious education in voluntary-controlled or voluntary-aided schools, or in grant-maintained or independent schools with a clear denominational Christian identity.   At its fullest the confessional approach means:

- echoing, celebrating and imitating the faith, including the fostering of moral values and encouraging moral action;
- bringing a child up in a relationship of dependency on a faith, and initiating the child into fuller faith.

Ultimately Christian confessional education takes its rationale from the words of the New Testament, for instance in the words ascribed to Jesus at the conclusion of Matthew's Gospel (Matthew 28.18ff, Jerusalem Bible):

> All authority in heaven and on earth has been given to me. Go, therefore, make disciples of all the nations; baptise them in the name of the Father and of the Son and of the Holy Spirit, and teach them to observe all the commands I gave you. And know that I am with you always; yes, to the end of time.

This significant text contains several clues to the character and belief-world of early Christian confessional education. The basis of the whole enterprise is a belief in the risen Christ, who has conquered death and is present among his people in the form of his spirit (All authority has been given to me) and who commanded his followers to evangelise and teach, so the entire Christian educational effort through two millennia is based on this command (Go, therefore... and teach). Moreover, the early church practised baptism, and prepared people for it through a course of lessons which became known as catechesis; in this way, sacramental celebration was inter-woven with education, and remains so today in some aspects of confessional Christian education (baptise them) so that Christ, present among his people through his Spirit, rules over the church and blesses its efforts to propagate itself (I am with you always).

Activity C3

Think about your own experience of Christian confessional education, especially RE. To help you to perform this task, three stimulus questions appear below. Each question asks you to look at a different aspect of Christian education. Choose the question(s) which come closest to your own experience.

- Have you taught in a church school? If so, reflect on the ethos and values of church school education, including religious education. Was it different from what you would expect, or experience, in a maintained school?
- Have you assisted or run a study group, enquiry group or house group, whether with adults or children, as part of a church ? If so, reflect on the aims and educational methods used in this group, and the extent to which you feel people successfully achieved the goals which they wanted.
- Do you have children of your own whom you try to nurture in Christian faith? If so, reflect on the successes and frustrations you have had, the things which impede or threaten nurture, and the things which support it.

Try to write a short description of your work in Christian education, whatever it was or is. Use the following questions as a guideline.

- What role have you had in Christian education?
- What were you aiming to do in this role?
- How did you set about the work?
- Did you enjoy it? Give reasons.
- What assistance did you have?
- How did you and others identify success and failure in this role?
- Do you have any other reflections on your role in Christian education?

Comment on activity C3

In your answer, you have described and reflected on the roles, aims and experiences you had as a Christian educator. Since the purpose of the task is to look at your own experience, this course cannot presume to tell you what should be in your answer; instead, what appears below under three headings is a collection of comments and insights which may or may not match your own, and should stimulate you to further thinking.

Individuals who have experience of teaching in a church school may make the following kind of observations.

- My role was that of an auxiliary. I supported the teachers.
- I saw my aim as helping the parish and the families to bring them up as Christians.
- My main contribution was to show them the difference between right and wrong.
- I enjoyed it very much, because I could see how important it was.
- I didn't enjoy it, because of the constant frustrations of time, workload and lack of resources.
- We had plenty of assistance from the other teachers and from church workers.

- The church gave us very little official help.
- I felt that most of the time we were battling against forces of materialism, prejudice and violence, so I find it difficult to see how we were succeeding.
- For me, it is a mistake to look for signs of success; it takes years to see the fruits of what I am doing.

Individuals who have experience of assisting or running a group in a church context may make the following kind of observations.

- I led a bible study group in my house for three years.
- It was part of a parish programme to get people studying the bible more deeply.
- We were given a programme, but we were told we could depart from it if the group wanted to - frequently we did.
- It was a good experience at first, but later it began to go round in circles and that's when we got frustrated.
- We were given no help, no training, and no chance to report back. If we were doing it again, we would really need this kind of support.
- The main success was that we and others learned a lot. The main failure was that, if we had been better prepared and the sessions better structured, we and others would have learned a lot more.

Individuals who have experience of nurturing children in Christian faith may make the following kind of observations.

- It has to be more than just taking them to church.
- My experience has been joyful and successful. My children have grown up to be thoughtful, prayerful and dedicated. They do question things, but we always talk about it until everybody feels they have had their say.
- My experience has been hard. When my children were getting ready to leave primary school they started to question everything. It didn't matter what I said; I was always wrong in their eyes.
- The official church could help us more through courses on parenting and youth activities.
- Trying to nurture the children's faith has really opened me up. I think the most important thing is to give them an experience of unconditional love, combined with information about the church, regular worship, and the feeling that they are allowed to ask questions.

Thomas Groome's confessional approach

In his two major works to date, *Christian Religious Education* (1980) and *Sharing Faith* (1991), Groome has attempted to give both a theoretical and a practical description of his approach, which he calls 'shared Christian praxis', and which is loosely confessional.

For purposes of this unit Groome's chapter (5.1) in Astley and Francis (1994) will give you all you need for the tasks set here. However, it is important to note that the later work, *Sharing Faith*, develops his thinking on a theoretical level and also extends his method beyond education to other ministries in the church, including liturgy, pastoral counselling, and justice and peace. Although not necessary to this unit, the second book is substantial, important and rewarding. We base our explanation of Groome's method on this longer presentation. The shared Christian praxis approach follows this outline.

- Initial Step: briefly focusing pupils on content/theme.
- Step 1: identifying experience or prior knowledge of topic.
- Step 2: critical reflection on experience and knowledge.
- Step 3: access to the tradition and new knowledge.
- Step 4: critical reflection on the tradition and new knowledge.
- Step 5: towards decisions on action and study.

Initial step: focusing

The first step is to gain pupils' attention and focus on the content and experiences under discussion by using key phrases like:

- We're going to...
- Our topic is...
- We've all had the experience of...
- Many people are concerned about...
- There was once a person who...

This step is brief and concise, designed to be an opening movement. Therefore the teacher should aim to speak briefly at this stage.

Step 1: identifying experience

The next step enables pupils to identify and share with each other their knowledge and experience on a particular topic. Brainstorming sessions can be triggered by phrases like:

- Talk to your working partner about your experience of...
- Ask your partner or group what you think a word means...
- Write five lines on... and then share it with partner or group...
- What is your experience/understanding of...

This process is important, as it builds up working partnerships in the class and shows pupils clearly that they already have some insights on a topic and are therefore able to contribute and learn more. It instils confidence and self-esteem, as well as encouraging reflectiveness.

Step 2: critical reflection on experience

This is then followed by critical reflection on the information/experiences shared in step 1 above. Again, group work is presumed and the sort of questions asked are:

- Why did you use that word?
- Why do you think that happened to you?
- Does anyone else see it that way?

The teacher can also engage in dialogue with the group as they feed back the results of their work in step 1 and from this dialogue give small groups further questions or points to consider with each other. This phase, which can seem rather unstructured, is crucial for the development of critical and analytical skills. Real critical reflection prevents step 1 from becoming a mere talking shop.

Step 3: accessing the tradition

Following this time of discussion and exploration, there is teaching, or input, from the tutor. All kinds of media can be used at this point including lectures, information sheets, video/audio technology, board/flipchart/OHPs, textbooks and artefacts, as appropriate. This phase needs to be kept brief and interesting, staying with and developing the points made in the first three steps.

Step 4: critical reflection on the tradition

After this pupils evaluate the content presented or discovered in step 3. This involves taking ownership of religious concepts, clarifying, amending, accepting, rejecting. The groups are re-assembled and asked to discuss what they think and feel about the presentation of the new information they have heard or seen.

Some people have described this phase in an eating metaphor: it prevents the 'swallowing-whole' of material which is not understood and is then 'regurgitated' in later assessments. Instead, content should be broken down and digested. Or, in Freire's metaphor, this phase prevents the information-giving in step 3 from being mere 'banking' education, and instead turns the process into something dialogical and liberating. Pupils leading and participating in seminars should be encouraged to grapple with ideas, to ask questions, and to express informed opinions in a balanced and mature manner.

Step 5: decisions towards action

Here the method turns from reflective and input or teaching phases into an action phase. Depending on content, pupils will identify action outcomes from their critical reflection on the tradition. Pupils may wish to write a diary, discuss with their teacher how they want to respond to what they have heard and thought and to re-form discussion groups to evaluate their action plans. They may also wish to take decisions affecting their lifestyles and to support relevant campaigns or to visit churches.

This step is vital if the students are to take opportunities to learn *from* and *about* the content. The whole person, as thinker, feeler and doer, is engaged in learning at this point. Clearly this step leads students round again to step 1, in which experience and knowledge is again identified, this time at a deeper level.

Critical views of the confessional approach

We have already seen why the confessional approach was rejected in county schools. We now consider confessionalism more broadly. Criticisms may be divided into those which have been offered from within confessionalism itself, and those which have been offered from outside confessionalism.

Criticisms from within confessionalism

Reliance on catechisms and doctrines produces stilted religious education. This point of view, held by Richard Rummery (1975) and others, holds that catechisms and other credal statements of belief are an inappropriate basis for religious education with children. He believes this because catechisms are written in theological language which tries to summarise truths in a general sense, without examples and without falling into error; this type of language, it is argued, is particularly inaccessible for pupils and for many teachers.

Rummery's argument may be applied to any confessional or catechetical endeavour within contemporary Christian education, but he intended it to apply particularly to religious education in church schools. Comment on catechesis is found in Francis and Thatcher (1990), chapter 11.2.

As members of a plural society, Christians must take account of other faith traditions. Several Christian religious educators hold the view that confessional religious education must look sympathetically at other faiths. Gabriel Moran (1983) argues that this will increase a pupil's appreciation of her own faith. Several recent Roman Catholic religious education syllabuses have included other faiths (see, for instance, the primary *Veritas* programme, the primary *Here I Am* programme, and the secondary *Weaving The Web* programme). Also, the Church of England's report on religious education, *The*

Fourth R (Durham Report, 1970), recommended the study of world religions in Christian religious education.

Criticism from other educationalists

The method is basically indoctrinatory.   One of the issues often raised in connection with confessionalism, or the confessional teaching of children, is that of indoctrination. If children are taught entirely from a faith perspective, isn't this indoctrinatory?

The argument is as follows: the starting-point of this view is that education in a liberal western democracy must aim for the development of the rational autonomy of each individual. Any process which attempts to tell learners what to think cannot be described as education at all. To educate pupils with an expectation or an assumption about their faith-commitment is to remove a vital element of their autonomy. Therefore confessional religious education is indoctrinatory. This charge may be sharpened by defining indoctrination as an attempt to ensure that learners come to believe certain predefined things. Thus indoctrination is defined by its *aim*.

But, since such aims are difficult to pin down and may co-exist with other legitimate aims, it is also possible to define indoctrination by its *methods*. Any method involving the uncritical learning of faith-based information may be called indoctrinatory. But, again, since very young children must learn uncritically because they have no ability to criticise rationally, indoctrination may be defined by its *content*. In this instance indoctrination may be literally taken as the inculcation of doctrines.

Recently, Theissen (1993) has dismissed the whole charge of indoctrination as incoherent or as inevitable. It is either incoherent because it includes types of learning which are generally agreed to be desirable (for instance children learn the road safety code without knowing why they should obey it) or because it is impossible to start in the process of learning without taking information on trust from others. There are basic truths or basic conditions that must be grasped or fulfilled as a precondition to any learning taking place.

Alternatively, it may be argued that much of the information given about the desirability of democratic ideals and of social consensus functions in a way analogous to religious doctrine. Thus critics, often secular critics, who attack religious education on the grounds that it is indoctrinatory are likely to be guilty of the same thing. The debate is unresolved, partly because its protagonists tend to take extreme positions. You are referred to Astley and Francis (1994) and the four important essays there in chapter 8.

There is a tension between formation in Christian faith and open, critical education. This view is a nuanced version of the third, above. In one form or another, it has been expressed by leading non-confessional religious educators such as Michael Grimmitt, Brenda Watson, Alex Rodger, and John Hull. Hull argues that while there can be consistency between the two for much of the time, there are underlying differences; and that, when it comes to a choice, Christianity will always choose formative goals over rational ones. 'No one can serve two masters.'

Activity C4

You have now read about the main criticisms of the confessional approach. In this task, you will be asked to apply the criticisms to your own planning, and see if they are appropriate.

- To what extent are these criticisms fair and accurate when applied to your experience as a practitioner of Christian religious education?
- To what extent, in your view, might they be fair and accurate of Christian religious education generally?

Comment on activity C4:

You may have thought that the legal and institutional context of religious education is crucial to its style and delivery. You may consider that what is appropriate in an aided school (see unit A) is quite different from what is appropriate in a controlled school or a county school. Confessionalism of some kind has a place within a church school, either on legal or historical grounds, or because parents who choose to send their children to church schools do so in the knowledge that a distinctive and faith-based approach to religious education may be chosen.

Whether this religious education is stilted or not depends on the expertise of the teacher, the resources available and other issues. Stiltedness may occur in non-confessional religious education, that is, there may be a formality and lack of imaginativeness in any kind of religious education if the teacher is uninspired.

The matter of indoctrination is much harder to pin down. We take the view that indoctrination occurs when pupils are not able to, or encouraged to, use their own powers of reason to evaluate religious claims. Provided that pupils are given classroom time to discuss and are presented with counter arguments to religious claims, it may be said that they are not being indoctrinated. In other words, indoctrination is a matter of balance across a range of lessons and over a period of time. This is one view. Your own experience, however, may lead you to different conclusions, and we cannot comment on all the possible permutations of circumstance here.

C3 Phenomenological approach

This section will look at the origins of the phenomenological approach to learning in religion. It will show you a range of sources in philosophical and educational thought, all of which have contributed to the emergence of phenomenology as an approach or method in studying religion.

Theoretical foundations of phenomenology

As an approach to the teaching of religious education in schools, phenomenology emerged in the late 1960s and was popular in the 1970s. But its theoretical roots lie further back.

The word *phenomenology* focuses on religious *phenomena*, i.e. items associated with religion. The phenomena might be tangible, such as a prayer wheel, a holy book, a temple, a cross; or intangible, such as a prayer, a belief, a hope, a prejudice. The approach to these phenomena is to study them neutrally and without presuppositions.

As a method, phenomenology is usually traced back to the work of the German philosopher Edmund Husserl (1859-1938). Several of his books (*Ideas*, 1931; *Phenomenology and the Crisis of Philosophy*, 1965; *The Idea of Phenomenology*, 1964) outline and use the technique of objective study of religions and philosophy. It is important to note that Husserl and those who followed him conceived this approach within, and for, higher education, not schools.

Husserl's ideas themselves owe much to previous philosophers. The European Enlightenment was a movement of thought in the eighteenth century; it is associated with free open enquiry giving full rein to the rational human mind. The new intellectual freedom born of the Enlightenment was in contrast to the perceived dogmatism of the middle ages and the religious warring of the sixteenth and seventeenth centuries. Therefore the Enlightenment saw the emergence of a new, more human-centred way of understanding and approaching religion: this was the study of religions as expressions of the *human* quest for meaning, in contrast to the more traditional study of theology as *revealed truth*.

Several other thinkers adopted Husserl's objective approach, among them Gerardus van der Leeuw (1890-1950) and Mircea Eliade (b. 1907). Van der Leeuw described religions as natural human interpretations of a central reality, that of power. Eliade identifies religious consciousness as a constituent element of the human make-up.

Some thinkers within the Christian tradition also used phenomenology as a method. The most famous example is Rudolf Otto (1860-1937) whose book *The Idea of the Holy* (1923) analysed the way human beings apprehend the numinous or spiritual. Also important is Jacques Maritain (1882-1973) who argued that humanity has built into it a primordial intuition of being, an awareness of mystery. Both thinkers, Roman Catholics, accepted the intellectual integrity of the phenomenological method, which they believed would lead them naturally to divine truth.

Husserl argued that phenomenology contains an *eidetic* (or vivid mental image) dimension. The basic method of phenomenology as a whole arises from Husserl's contention that 'all consciousness is intentional', that when we think we think *of* something, when we are frightened we are frightened *of* something, and so on. And so, while we are conscious, we are not perceiving purely and simply but are influenced by what he called the 'intentional structure' of each phenomenon. When we perceive a cube, its intentional structure ensures we are aware of those parts of the cube that cannot be seen from a particular position.

According to Husserl a so-called phenomenological description consists of two parts: of the experiencing and of the thing experienced. And those things experienced also consist of two parts: of particulars (this particular triangle or person) or of universals (the idea of triangularity or personhood).

In order to perceive the universal directly we must remove, or bracket out, the existing world and any part of it and redirect our attention to the phenomena of consciousness. After this we must bracket out particulars so that the universal can be directly intuited. By this process, Husserl maintained that we have access to the 'essential forms constraining physical existence'.

The term coined early on for this mental act of setting aside assumptions was *epoche*, meaning distancing or bracketing. For an explanation of this term, let a founding phenomenologist, Gerardus van der Leeuw (1938, p 646) speak for himself:

> The term *epoche* is a technical expression employed in current phenomenology by Husserl and other philosophers. It implies that no judgement is expressed concerning the objective world, which is thus placed 'between brackets' as it were. All phenomena, therefore, are considered solely as they are presented to the mind, without any further aspects such as their real existence, or their value, being taken into account; in this way the observer restricts himself to

pure description systematically pursued, himself adopting the attitude of complete intellectual suspense, or of abstention from all judgement, regarding these controversial topics.

This technique of 'bracketing out' is most simply described as a mental procedure for objectivity. People often refer to 'bracketing out' assumptions; but a careful reading of the above text shows that it is the objective phenomena themselves which are placed 'in brackets', in order to protect them from the assumptions of the external world.

Clearly, Husserl is *not* an easy thinker to grasp but his notion that it is possible to get to the reality of existence by removing everything that clouds our access to it has an appeal. It is parallel to some forms of religious meditation.

In the context of religious studies the phenomenological methods claim to give us an ability to remove particular examples of religion, in order to be able to see universal forms. The eidetic reduction assumes that universal forms lie behind all religious phenomena, giving them unity. For instance, Christian worship might be studied in its specifics - prayers, eucharistic rituals, hymns - but the specifics should be set aside by the student in order to apprehend worship itself.

More controversially, Husserl believed that the student of religion must also leave his or her own self behind, transcending the individual ego in order to apprehend religious phenomena with the maximum purity.

Phenomenology is not a united tradition, and not all of its exponents have had equal influence on British school-age religious education. The main influence was through the work of Ninian Smart which argued for a neutral, open study of religions, coupled with an empathetic understanding. This neutral, open study with its willingness to try to set aside prejudice is a simplified form of the complex philosophical approach advocated by Husserl.

Activity C5

Read again the quotation from Van der Leeuw (above) in which he explains the concept of *epoche* in the phenomenological approach. Note down what you think are his most important phrases; then try to express them briefly in your own words.

What is your own experience of a totally objective approach to the study of religion, or other subjects such as philosophy, history, literature or politics? Given the content you were studying, was this approach successful for you? Did pupils/students appreciate it?

Comment on activity C5

In your response to the first question you should have mentioned the following central points about the concept of *epoche* :

- it is a technical term used in phenomenology;
- it aims at the suspension of judgements about phenomena;
- it is designed to ensure that the student sees religious phenomena as they really are, and describes them accurately as they appear;
- it is effective when all external considerations are suspended.

You may have found that it was impossible to be 'totally objective' since you were never sure when you had eliminated absolutely all subjective elements. You may find the whole idea of trying to 'bracket out' parts of your thought processes quite self-contradictory since the processes must bracket themselves out. On the other hand, you may find that you are aware of your prejudices and idiosyncrasies and that, with an effort, you can put them aside to allow you to perceive much more purely.

Smart's adaptation of the phenomenological method

The most celebrated user and developer of phenomenology in Britain is Ninian Smart. His work not only developed the method at an academic level but also made it available to school-based religious education. Smart's main contribution, his theory of religious dimensions, will be studied in the next section.

Smart is not a phenomenologist in the same sense as Husserl, van der Leeuw, Eliade and others. For him, the method involved not only looking at external phenomena but also the inner life of a religion. The student was faced with the challenge of penetrating the heart and mind of the believer. This, for Smart, was a scientific but also an empathetic process. Empathy here means the ability to feel what other people feel, to identify with them in their feelings.

Smart's development of phenomenology made it accessible to school-based religious education. Smart's thinking shaped two landmark documents: *Religious Education in Secondary Schools*, working paper 36 from the Schools Council (1971), which advocated a phenomenological approach, and the *Birmingham Agreed Syllabus* of 1975, with its inclusion of Communism and Humanism as life-stances to be studied by secondary pupils.

The Schools Council paper dealt with secondary religious education and argued for a phenomenology-based approach which Smart, Rummery and others had evolved at Lancaster University. It is to be noted again that an approach designed in and for higher education was being offered for use in schools.   This was to form the basis of some of the criticisms of the phenomenological approach. The Schools Council working paper 36 advocated and popularised a world-religions approach which strongly emphasised qualities of critical judgement, openness and respect.

Smart's theory of the dimensions contributed to the Schools Council paper and to the subsequent wide-scale adoption of world-religions syllabuses.   The dimensions do not, strictly speaking, belong only to phenomenology; one of them, the experiential dimension, lends itself strongly to the experiential approach which will be discussed in the next section.   Nevertheless, the dimensions were influential in the devising of textbooks and agreed syllabuses in the decade or more immediately following the publication of the Schools Council working paper.

Smart's dimensions of religion

Ninian Smart devised a structure for understanding religions.   Instead of attempting definitions of particular religions, Smart developed the idea (begun by others) of defining *what makes a religion a religion* as distinct from, say, a philosophical or political movement, or a tribal culture.   His definition of religion involved seven dimensions (see below).   The first six dimensions were explained in his *Secular Education and the Logic of Religion* (1968).   The dimensions were explained again, and the seventh (the material) dimension added, in a later work, *The World's Religions* (1989).   Smart's dimensions appear below, with our matching examples.

- *Doctrinal*: formal beliefs and teachings; e.g. the Christian creed, the Muslim belief in the oneness of God, the Hindu belief in reincarnation.
- *Mythological*: stories and myths (historical or not), sacred books, oral traditions; e.g. scriptures in Buddhism, stories of the ten Gurus in Sikhism, the bible and lives of the saints in Christianity.
- *Ethical*: the expectations on a believer to adopt a moral lifestyle; e.g. in relation to food, marriage and sexuality, use of money, violence, case law and commandments.
- *Ritual*: actions with meanings, usually focusing on worship; e.g. diva lamps in the Hindu service of Puja, prayer five times a day for Muslims, wearing of Tefillin for Jews.
- *Experiential*: the inward or emotional dimension of religion; e.g. the feelings of a Muslim on pilgrimage to Mecca, the devotion shown by a Christian receiving communion, the grief of bereavement at a funeral, the experience of the mystic in meditation.
- *Social*: the organised aspect of religions; e.g. a Hindu political party, a school attached to a synagogue, a parochial church council.

- *Material*: tangible objects with religious significance; e.g., the river Ganges, the wailing wall in Jerusalem, the Ka'aba in Mecca, St Peter's Basilica for Roman Catholics, Canterbury for Anglicans.

Activity C6

Imagine yourself at a Christian wedding by recalling a wedding you have attended. Now draw up a list of all the examples you can identify of each of Smart's seven dimensions of religion listed above.

Comment on activity C6

Your list will be organised around the following headings:

- doctrinal;
- mythological;
- ethical;
- ritual;
- experiential;
- social;
- material.

Critical views of the phenomenological approach

Smart's phenomenology, and phenomenology in general, has sometimes been unfairly criticised for an obsession with objectivity; but in fact most phenomenologists, whether of the nineteenth or the twentieth century, have recognised the limitations of objectivity as an approach to religion. The phenomenological approach of 'pure' neutrality has received much criticism, both as an approach for adults, and especially when used as an approach in the classroom. The criticisms usually rest on two points.

The first point is that such an approach is impossible to achieve. It is argued that school-age pupils, particularly in the primary stage, will find it difficult or impossible to make the conscious move of setting aside their own assumptions, backgrounds, beliefs and other habits of mind in order to concentrate purely on religious phenomena as they present themselves; that this act of 'de-centering' is simply beyond the powers of most children, especially those in what Piaget describes as ego-centric stages of thinking. The further acts of eidetic reasoning (setting aside specifics in order to perceive universal types or forms of the phenomena) will be even harder for children to achieve, involving the levels of abstract thought which it does. Husserl's third and most controversial element, that of setting aside one's own self, is highly contested as very much beyond the powers of most pupils.

The second point is that even if it were possible, it would be undesirable. It is argued that, even were pupils to succeed in their attempt to 'de-centre' and to approach phenomena objectively, this type of learning would yield little of use or relevance to them and would be a dry, demotivating exercise. Some argue that this approach can do positive damage in that it may reduce religious study to a study of social anthropology; and that studying religious phenomena with no provision for personal relevance may induce boredom, cynicism or racism into the minds of students.

Further criticisms of the phenomenological approach are offered by Chris Arthur (1990) in chapters 10 and 12 of his book *Biting the Bullet* and by Brenda Watson (1993) in chapter 4 of her book *The Effective Teaching of Religious Education.*

C4 Experiential approach

This section will look at the origins of the experiential approach to learning in religion. It will show you a range of sources in philosophy, theology and the human sciences, all of which contributed to the emergence of the experiential approach.

Theoretical foundations of the experiential approach

The experiential approach grew gradually out of the phenomenological approach which we have already studied. While some would argue that it has now become a fully-fledged and separate approach, most will agree that it still shares many of the same methods and assumptions as its phenomenological forebear. This section will show how many of its theoretical roots are shared. In particular, the two approaches share:

- a general assumption that religion is an expression of human existence, rather than a message or revelation from the divine to humanity;
- a desire to explain and categorise religion as exactly as possible.

However, differences also exist between the two approaches. While phenomenology traces its philosophical roots back to Husserl and the rationalism of nineteenth-century Germany, the experiential approach by contrast traces its roots to the USA at the turn of the century.

William James, brother of the novelist Henry and a product of Harvard Medical School, pursued a career as an academic psychologist. In the years 1901-2 he was invited to give the prestigious Gifford Lectures at Edinburgh University, and he chose the subject of 'The varieties of religious experience: a study in human nature'. These acclaimed lectures became the classic book *The Varieties of Religious Experience* (1902 and reprinted many times).

James' approach was in some ways similar to that of the phenomenologists. His scientific powers of observation were as keen as theirs; his desire to classify, to understand, to describe accurately and to analyse was as great. However, where phenomenology typically focused on *external* religious phenomena such as a rite, an artefact, a taboo, James shifted the focus to the *internal*. He was more interested in that which individuals experienced within, and he usually identified the inner experience, not the outward manifestation, as being the source.

This approach, then, was more interested in the religion that went on inside a person than outside. The differences between phenomenology and the experiential approach might be characterised as follows. While the phenomenological approach interprets religion as outward, the experiential approach interprets religion as inward. While the phenomenological approach focuses on observable phenomena, the experiential approach focuses on individual feelings.

Since William James, other writers have used a similar approach. Perhaps foremost among these is Rudolf Otto (1923), whose book *The Idea of the Holy* is both an academic and a spiritual classic. Otto identifies the holy, sacred or numinous as a reality encountered by human beings. By 'holy' he does not mean comparatively or absolutely good, but rather the wholly other, the ineffable, supernatural, transcendent reality which is a category of human experience and interpretation.

Although Otto saw himself as a phenomenologist (and indeed received a letter of praise from Husserl on the publication of his book), Otto made two important points which were implicitly critical of phenomenology:

- a God who can be understood ceases to be God (see Otto, 1923, p 25);
- while any approach to religion must take into account the rational element, it must not disregard the numinous or non-rational; if the non-rational is disregarded, this will impoverish religion (see Otto, 1923, p 109).

These two points were to become central to the experiential approach in theory and as practised in schools.

Activity C7

To experience the 'flavour' of the experiential approach, particularly its method and its written style, read *The Varieties of Religious Experience* by James (1902). What are the main points made by James in chapter 1?

Comment on activity C7

James, in making psychological investigations, says he is bound to confine himself to religious feelings and impulses 'recorded in the literature produced by articulate and self-conscious men'. He acknowledges the distinction between 'religious propensities' and their 'philosophic significance' and says that his lectures will deal with religious phenomena from the existential point of view, from the point of view of what immediately precedes them, from their context, so far as it can be known, in the mind of the experiencer.

He goes on to consider that those with 'religious genius' tend to be mentally unusual and quotes part of the journal of George Fox, the Quaker. Fox's behaviour is strange: he takes off his shoes and walks through the city of Lichfield saying, 'Woe to the bloody city of Lichfield'; and believes he has done so in memory of the slaughter of Christians there during the reign of the Roman emperor Diocletian. Fox's behaviour might be dismissed as pathological, as the raving of a mentally ill person; but on the other hand, if such religious experiences are dismissed in this way, it is equally possible to dismiss the dismissals as the result of mental illness. In other words, an attempt to reduce spiritual experience to physical causes is unhelpful and in no way enables a judgement to be made about the value of the spiritual experience. The only way to judge experiences is by their 'fruits', by their effects, rather than by their 'roots', by their causes. Quotations from Jonathan Edwards and Saint Teresa underline this conclusion.

Existentialism: a foundation of the experiential approach

The experiential approach to explaining and describing religion has been influenced by philosophy and theology. Existentialist philosophers in the twentieth century include Martin Heidegger (1889-1976) and Jean-Paul Sartre (1905-1980). They both shaped existentialism into a way of doing philosophy in the midst of concrete, historical human situations, focusing on human actions and choices.

Existentialists argue that whereas other living things, like plants or animals, express their essence through the unfolding of their natures (an acorn becomes an oak tree; a dog runs around and barks), human beings have no essence except that which they express through choices. I am what I choose to be. And, in choosing, I am free. In Sartre's development of existentialism my freedom is my essence and, if I allow myself to be constrained by ordinary morality or by everyday concepts, I am thereby imprisoned. What matters is authentic living, choosing according to principles that must not be justified, and so avoiding the trap of becoming a 'being-for-others', a being whose choices are illusory and thus an unfree being (Copleston, 1994; Scruton, 1994).

Liberal Protestant theologians such as Paul Tillich (1886-1965) were influenced strongly by existentialism. Tillich came to see religion in terms of human experience because human experience automatically raises questions about the supernatural. In his theology, divine things are seen as rather like extensions of natural things; God is 'divine being', and faith is 'ultimate concern'. In his work the terms of traditional theology are translated into terms compatible with existentialist thinking.

Rudolf Bultmann (1884-1976), another Protestant theologian, allowed existentialism to influence his thinking. His interest was in re-expressing the biblical and early Christian message in existentialist terms, stripping away biblical 'myth' in order to arrive at the central message or Word which is spoken to every individual in his or her own situation, so allowing authentic choices.

Existentialism has provided an important philosophical and theological underpinning for the experiential approach because of its method of starting with human experience, rather than with systems or divine givens. This starting point sets the exact pattern for the way in which experiential religious education begins with, and develops, the experience of the child.

Religious Experience Research Centre

This section introduces a contemporary project which is attempting to gather statistics on religious experience in Britain.

The Religious Experience Research Centre (formerly known as the Religious Experience Research Unit or the Alister Hardy Research Centre) investigates and publishes on reports of religious experience in Britain. It was founded in 1969 by Sir Alister Hardy, sometime Professor of Zoology and Comparative Anatomy at Oxford. He advocated the use of social science techniques to investigate the nature and frequency of religious experience.

David Hay (1982) published some of the centre's findings in his book *Exploring Inner Space*. Approximately 36 per cent of respondents reported having had religious experience of some sort, and this number rose as people became older, though many of the most valued religious experiences had taken place in childhood. The term 'religious experience' included:

- a sense of God's presence and closeness;
- answered prayer;
- a presence, not named;
- a sense of harmony or profound joy in nature;
- a sense of the presence of the dead;
- a premonition;
- a meaningful pattern of events;
- a conversion.

A majority of the reported experiences were private, powerful and intense and usually gave meaning and peace. They were often felt by non-religious people in the church-going or committed sense. All experiences were unsought.

Another researcher at the centre claimed that such experiences are recurrent, that they happen to us all intermittently, and that they seemingly atrophied or became forgotten in some people (Robinson, 1977, pp 147-8).

If we are to believe these research findings, it is highly likely that some pupils we have taught have also had similar experiences. What is your knowledge or awareness of this? What is the implication for the way we teach religious education?

Critical views of the experiential approach

The experiential approach has been influential in British religious education. In part, this has been attributed to a reaction away from phenomenology and a search for personal relevance in religious education processes. Arguably, this approach has also fed into government thinking on spiritual and moral development, as expressed in the discussion paper, *Spiritual and Moral Development* presented by the School Curriculum and Assessment Authority (SCAA, 1995).

The discussion paper by SCAA (1995) emphasised the importance of spiritual and moral development, and argued that this responsibility ought to be carried by the entire school community, not by one curricular subject. Among the elements of spiritual development identified are several which link in with affective (i.e. to do with emotions) and experiential learning, such as awe and wonder, awareness of transcendence, opportunities for quiet reflection, and awareness of ultimate questions. According to SCAA (1995), this aspect of the school's work should be visible in religious education and collective worship, but it should also be shared by the whole curriculum and by the ethos of the school, whether a church school or a secular school.

This emphasis is built into several local agreed syllabuses, which feature attainment outcomes such as expressing meaning, relationships, ultimate questions, or personal understanding. Those sort of outcomes differ markedly from more cognitively-based ones such as beliefs and values or celebrations. The former tend to emphasise the personal search of the individual, exploring emotional, affective and relational areas which are sometimes known as right-brain activity; the latter tend to emphasise the informational, factual areas of religious education, sometimes known as left-brain activity. There can be a tension between the two.

Because of this tension, experiential religious education has been criticised on several points. Grimmitt's (1987) and Watson's (1993) reservations about the approach may be grouped as five main points.

First, the approach sits uneasily with more phenomenological methods. Pupils may miss out on opportunities to make connections because of the very different styles of learning involved in the two methods.

Second, there is a lack of clarity and rigour in the definition of religious experience as part of human experience.

Third, teaching based on religious experiences may simply replace a phenomenological 'hermeneutic of suspicion' with a confessional 'hermeneutic of faith'. This may re-introduce a faith-nurture approach to religious education and thus be a covert form of indoctrination, educationally illegitimate. It may even be open to manipulation by the teacher and to a covert return to confessionalism.

Fourth, if the experiential approach leads to the deliberate seeking of religious states of mind such as awe, love, joy, and encouraging pupils to associate these states with particular religious beliefs, then it is no longer education but indoctrination.

Fifth, the experiential approach might lead to a stress on the individual rather than on faith communities or traditions; to the spiritual more than the religious, the inward more than the outward.

Response to criticisms

Many of these criticisms are answered in the book *New Methods in RE Teaching: an experiential approach* by Hammond *et al* (1990) which popularised the experiential approach. It is hard to offer a summary of the debate and you would be wise to think about the extent to which the writers successfully rebut Grimmitt's criticisms.   In particular, look out for the following points:

- that a religious education process based entirely on fact-giving will become dry and irrelevant to the pupil's needs;
- that experiential work is not the same as indoctrination because the aims are different, and the context in which it takes place will be carefully arranged by the teacher so that any improper leading of pupils is avoided;
- that pupils enjoy experiential activities and benefit from them.

Review and evaluation of the experiential approach

The three approaches you have studied have been the confessional, phenomenological and experiential.   Each of them has its own distinctive philosophical or theological roots.   Up until recently, they were all seen as being three separate approaches to religious education, or three separate models, which could be in dialogue with each other but which were fundamentally apart from each other, forcing the practitioner to choose between models.

Recently, however, it has been suggested that the models might realign or even converge with each other.   This means that the models themselves evolve, and that the distance between them is reduced.   It may mean that some new model emerges, which subsumes what is seen as good in all the previous models.   One example of this realignment of thinking is to be found in Watson (1993).

Activity C8 (optional)

Read chapter four in *The Effective Teaching of Religious Education* by Watson (1993). Make notes on her argument for a new model. Look at the positive and negative points which she makes about the models and assess whether a new model based on features of the old ones might be sensibly constructed.

Comment on activity C8

Watson brings an original mind to bear on religious education. She discusses the confessional and phenomenological models and also a model she has invented called the 'highest common factor' model. Her view of the confessional model is that it has redeeming features. For instance, it shows how religion is related to modern society and, indeed, to a global understanding of the world. In this model religion is seen to be relevant and capable of being educationally open. On the other hand, confessional religion presumes truth-claims that cannot be publicly demonstrated and this can easily lead to a narrowing of intellectual perspectives.

The phenomenological model likewise has positive and negative features. It attempts to leave the integrity of pupils intact and to educate about religion in a way that goes beyond the merely informative. Yet, it ignores the shape of religions by trying to squeeze them into manageable units (doctrinal, ethical, mythological, and so on) which distort and over-simplify them. The richness of religion can be lost and a hidden message about the impossibility of fair evaluation of various religious positions is inevitably conveyed.

The highest common factor model is implicitly adopted by those unhappy with the confessional model who have sought to escape from the dilemmas it poses 'by subtracting from the equation of religious education all that is controversial and likely to cause trouble' (p 41). Highest common factor religious education tends to melt into moral education or into PSE (personal and social education), a tendency that has recently been considerably reinforced by the popularity of the experiential approach to religious education. Yet the highest common factor model lacks conceptual rigour. Paradoxically, on the surface this model is profound, but deep down it is superficial.

Watson's criticisms of the models seem to be fair enough. After all, different models would not have arisen if one or other had commanded universal agreement. The models have arisen in reaction to each other and for this reason the strengths of one tend to compensate for the weaknesses of another. But this sharpens the question about the possibility of convergence between the models. Are they so conceptually distinct that they cannot combine? Or are they in terms of aims or teaching methods sufficiently similar to allow them to be knitted together? Watson proposes that 'Essentialist RE' concentrates on 'what is essential from several points of view, with regard to breadth, depth, relevance and time' (p 48). She suggests that this form of religious education 'is brave enough to opt for doing a little well'. It accepts the 'rootedness' of confessionalism, the moral education of the highest common factor model, the tolerance and openness of the phenomenological model and the teaching style that 'homes in what is of central importance and relevance to each pupil' (p 50).

There is much value in what Watson proposes. It remains to be seen whether, in practice, her Essentialist religious education will attract followers.

Readers

You will find helpful sections 5.1, 6.1, 8.1, and 8.2 of J. Astley and L.J. Francis (eds) (1994), *Critical Perspectives on Christian Education*, Leominster, Gracewing. You will also find helpful section 9.1 of L.J. Francis and A. Thatcher (eds) (1990), *Christian Perspectives for Education*, Leominster, Gracewing.

Bibliography

Arthur, C.J. (1990), *Biting the Bullet: some personal reflections on religious education,* Edinburgh, St Andrew Press.

Astley, J. (1994), *The Philosophy of Christian Religious Education,* Birmingham, Alabama, Religious Education Press.

Bettis, J. (ed.) (1969), *Phenomenology of Religion*, London, SCM.

Copleston, F. (1994), *A History of Philosophy* (volume 9), London, Doubleday (first published 1977).

Durham Report (1970), *The Fourth R*, London, The National Society and SPCK.

Eliade, M. (1991), *The Eliade Guide to World Religions*, San Francisco, Harper.

Goldman R.J. (1964), *Religious Thinking from Childhood to Adolescence*, London, Routledge and Kegan Paul.

Goldman R.J. (1965), *Readiness for Religion*, London, Routledge and Kegan Paul.

Grimmitt, M. (1973), *What Can I Do in RE?* Great Wakering, McCrimmon.

Grimmitt, M. (1987), *Religious Education and Human Development*, Great Wakering, McCrimmon.

Groome, T.H. (1980), *Christian Religious Education*, San Francisco, Harper and Row.

Groome, T.H. (1991), *Sharing Faith*, San Francisco, HarperCollins.

Hammond, J., Hay, D., Moxon, J., Netto, B., Raban, K., Straugheir, G. and Williams, C. (1990), *New Methods in RE Teaching: an experiential approach*, Harlow, Oliver and Boyd.

Hay, D. (1982), *Exploring Inner Space*, Harmondsworth, Penguin.

Hirst, P.H. (1972), Christian education: a contradiction in terms? *Learning for Living*, 11, 4, 6-11.

Hirst, P.H. (1974), *Knowledge and the Curriculum*, London, Routledge and Kegan Paul.

Hirst, P.H. (1976), Religious beliefs and educational principles, *Learning for Living*, 15, 155-157.

Hirst, P.H. (1981), Education, catechesis and the church school, *British Journal of Religious Education*, 3, 85-93.

Holm, J.L. (1975), *Teaching Religion in School: a practical approach*, London, Oxford University Press.

Husserl, E. (1929), Phenomenology, *Encyclopaedia Britannica* (fourteenth edition).

Husserl, E. (1931), *Ideas: general introduction to pure phenomenology*, London, Allen and Unwin.

Husserl, E. (1964), *The Idea of Phenomenology*, The Hague, Nijhoff.

Husserl, E. (1965), *Phenomenology and the Crisis of Philosophy: philosophy as a rigorous science, and philosophy and the crisis of European man*, New York, Harper and Row.

Hyde K.E. (1965), *Religious Learning in Adolescence* (University of Birmingham, Institute of Education, Educational Monograph number 7), London, Oliver and Boyd.

Jackson, R. and Starkings, D. (1990), *The Junior RE Handbook*, Cheltenham, Thornes.

James, W. (1902), *The Varieties of Religious Experience*, Glasgow, Collins.

Leeuw, G. van der (1938), *Religion in Essence and Manifestation: a study in phenomenology*, London, Allen and Unwin.

Loukes, H. (1961), *Teenage Religion*, London, SCM.

Loukes, H. (1965), *New Ground in Christian Education*, London, SCM.

MacQuarrie, J. (1963), *Twentieth Century Religious Thought*, London, SCM.

Moran, G. (1983), *Religious Education Development: images for the future*, Minneapolis, Winston.

Otto, R. (1923), *The Idea of the Holy*, Oxford, Oxford University Press.

Plowden Report (1967), *Children and their Primary Schools*, London, HMSO.

Read, G., Rudge, J. and Howarth, R.B. (1986), *How Do I Teach RE?* London, Mary Glasgow Publications.

Robinson, E. (1977), *The Original Vision: a study of the religious experience of childhood*, Oxford, Religious Experience Research Unit.

Robinson, J. (1963), *Honest to God*, London, SCM.

Rummery, R.M. (1975), Catechesis and religious education, in N. Smart and D. Horder (eds), *New Movements in Religious Education*, London, Temple Smith, pp 149-162.

SCAA (1995), *Spiritual and Moral Development* (discussion paper 3), London, SCAA.

Schools Council (1971), *Religious Education in Secondary Schools* (working paper 36), London, Evans Brothers and Methuen Educational.

Scruton, R. (1994), *Modern Philosophy: an introduction and survey*, London, Sinclair-Stevenson.

Smart, N. (1968), *Secular Education and the Logic of Religion*, London, Faber.

Smart, N. (1989), *The World's Religions*, Cambridge, Cambridge University Press.

Snook, I.A. (1972), *Indoctrination and Education*, London, Routledge and Kegan Paul.

Swann Report (1985), *Education for All*, London, HMSO.

Theissen, E. (1993), *Teaching for Commitment*, Montreal, McGill-Queen's University Press.

Watson, B. (1993), *The Effective Teaching of Religious Education*, London, Longman.

Westerhoff, J. (1981), *A Faithful Church: issues in the history of catechesis*, Connecticut, Morehouse-Barlow.

Method in Religious Education

Method in Religious Education

Unit A

Critical analysis of different approaches to religious education

Dr Mark Chater

Bishop Grosseteste University College

Lincoln

Contents

Introduction

Aims

After working through this unit you should be able to understand:

- the methods used in religious education;
- the strengths and weaknesses of these methods in theory and in practice;
- which are most effective and appropriate in the professional context of church schools;
- which methods are best suited to you personally.

This unit, unlike many others, is very closely related to another unit in the programme and refers back to it frequently. We have made the assumption that you will be working through the present unit after having completed unit C of the module *Philosophy of Religious Education*. Nevertheless, in case this is not so, we have attempted to make the text of the present unit intelligible without prior reading.

Overview

This unit outlines different methodological approaches to religious education. It is recommended that you take each section in turn, as there is a natural sequence to them. The first three subsections deal with three major 'visions' of religious education which were discussed in unit C of the module *Philosophy of Religious Education*; here, you will look at these three approaches in detail, and gain practical experience of them. The next subsection (on artifacts) is shorter, but no less important in dealing with essential aspects of understanding good quality religious education.

The *confessional approach* (teaching for commitment) explores and uses *Weaving the Web* or *Here I Am* and the work of Thomas H. Groome. The *phenomenological approach* explores the approach and resources developed by the Westhill Project, and finds out about critiques of phenomenology. The *experiential approach* (education with a spiritual emphasis) studies the work of John Hammond and his colleagues. Finally, the approach using *religious artifacts* (hands-on experience of religion) reviews and offers practical experience with the use of artifacts in the classroom.

A1 Confessional approach

This section refreshes your memory about the theoretical foundations of the confessional approach and the criticisms made of it. We will then show you examples of the confessional approach in practice and invite you to evaluate them. In order to make this evaluation as effective as possible, you should try this approach out in the classroom. If this is not possible, then you will have to work through the materials here either on the basis of the observation of lessons or on the basis of the comments included here and the books referred to during discussion.

In order to complete this section and its tasks, you will need, if possible, access to one of the following books and resources: *Here I Am* by Byrne and Malone (1992), and *Weaving the Web* by Lohan and McClure, (1988).

The confessional approach to religious education is usually employed uncontroversially within the Christian community, either in the family or in the parish. It is concerned with raising and forming the young in faith, within a particular tradition, be it Catholic, Anglican or another tradition. For this reason the confessional approach does not find a place within the modern county school.

In unit C of the module *Philosophy of Religious Education*, the theological and philosophical background to religious education and Christian religious education were discussed. Confessionalism is based on the dominical commands within the New Testament and was supported by the social and religious consensus that existed in Britain until the 1960s. One of the most influential forms of the confessional approach has been developed by Thomas H. Groome and we discuss this below. Nevertheless, there have been criticisms of confessional religious education, however it is delivered. The most persistent criticisms concern the aims of education and their apparent incompatibility with confessional aims. Confessional religious education has been accused of being indoctrinatory, though there is a lively debate on how fair or accurate this characterisation is.

Groome's method as a guide to planning

In this section, you will look at one example of planning a theme using Groome's shared praxis approach. Then you will be asked to devise a similar plan yourself, using the same approach.

We will use the five steps of shared praxis to outline an approach to the subject of worship since this is a subject close to the heart of confessionalism. The approach requires you to work with a group and we envisage a group of children in a classroom going through the steps laid out below. If you do not have access to a group of children, then an adult group would also be feasible.

1. Naming present action

This involves sharing information about the pupils' present practice by tactfully finding out: Who goes to church? Who do you go with? Which church do you attend? How do you worship there? This work could be done by talking in pairs and feeding back.

2. The participants' stories and visions

This step involves the beginnings of critical reflection on the pupils' present action. Questions discussed in the group might be: Why do you go to church? What do you get out of it? What feelings do you have when you are there? What form does your worship take - prayer, singing? Why do you feel happy/bored? What is the most important thing about your church?

3. The Christian community's story and vision

This step aims to offer pupils a Christian theology of worship, appropriate to their level. This might be done by listening to a visitor talking about why he or she worships; or by watching a video, reading books/resources, or taking part in a service, or a combination of these.

4. Dialectical hermeneutic: the Christian story and participants' stories

Pupils will engage with the speaker/video/resource/worshipping community, through conversation and questioning, in order to assimilate the parts which they feel are appropriate. Much of this engagement will begin with phrases like, 'I liked the hymns...', 'Why did the minister say "Peace be with you....?"', 'If God is so big, why does God need our praise?...', 'In my church they don't carry a cross in. What does this mean?...'

5. Dialectical hermeneutic: the Christian vision and participants' visions

This step follows on from the fourth and allows pupils to work out for themselves new ways of belief and action in response to the learning experience. For instance, pupils may respond by saying, 'Now I understand what the readings are for, I'll listen more carefully'; 'I'd like to start going to church again'; 'I'd prefer a church where they have a children's group'; etc. This will lead out into pupils' lives in terms of celebration and action. Sometimes diary-writing, final statements in a round, or a concluding celebration are appropriate ways of taking this step.

Activity A1

Now try preparing your own theme using the same five steps suggested by Groome's shared praxis approach. Begin by identifying and writing down the five steps, with their names, so that you are clear about the structure. You may wish to choose a theme from the following list:

- baptism;
- caring for the environment;
- forgiveness;
- Jesus heals sick people;
- journeys - Abraham's journey.

Comment on activity A1

You should have found it relatively easy to follow the five steps we have illustrated. Groome's terminology can be slightly off-putting, but the tasks it describes are quite simple to perform.

Examples of confessional material and approaches

In this section, you have the opportunity to browse thoughtfully in some pupil textbooks which offer a confessional or Christian approach. This will be a useful preparation for your own planning and teaching.

You should try to look at one of the following series: *Here I Am* by Byrne and Malone (1992) or *Weaving the Web* by Lohan and McClure (1988). Choose the series which suits your phase of education. If you cannot get access to these resources, or feel they are not appropriate, choose another textbook dealing with Christianity. Do so in consultation with your tutor.

Activity A2

Make notes on some lessons in the resource you have chosen.

- What is distinctively confessional about the activity?
- Is prayer or worship involved?
- Is it expected that children will respond in a believing, accepting way to the material?
- What themes, topics and content have you seen?
- What is the resource aiming at?
- Which activities regularly recur (e.g. prayer, community action outside school, investigation, assembly or collective worship, links with home)?

What improvements could you suggest on the activities, especially bearing in mind the approach of Thomas H. Groome?

Comment on activity A2

We will comment on *Here I Am* (which is designed by Roman Catholics with Roman Catholic schools in mind). The entire scheme is built on three basic Christian categories: *redemption*, *creation* and *incarnation*, but these three categories are also respectively conceptualised as *purpose*, *life* and *dignity* so that they may be interpreted by those of other Christian traditions and other faiths.

Each basic category is itself explored by three themes. So, for example, redemption/purpose is explored by reconciliation/inter-relating, by the universal church/the world and by Pentecost/serving. In addition each theme is explored through four topics and each topic is developed through five levels from nursery to years five and six.

When individual lessons are examined, they follow a four 'rs' scheme: recognise, reflect, respect and relate. With reference to years three and four the first topic in reconciliation/inter-relating is that of *choices* and it deals with moral choices, especially those leading to relationships. The second topic deals with *change*, especially how people can change for the better or worse. The third topic deals with *freedom and responsibility*, showing how the two are connected. The fourth topic deals with building bridges as a sign of *reconciliation*. The topics are explored using biblical materials, stories from other faiths and with universal experience.

You may have noticed that the confessional nature of the course is implicit, to do with structure, rather than explicit, to do with evangelism. Moreover, since there are so many topics, and since they are all related to universal experience, even the confessional implications may be by-passed if necessary. The activities that regularly occur are those found in most humanities subjects. There are no ritual activities built into the course.

Thomas H. Groome's approach might run into problems with young children since they would have difficulty in explaining why they carried out certain activities. Moreover, Groome tends to elicit from participants their reflection on an action instead of introducing them to a new action. Yet, Groome does ask participants to reflect and it is this aspect of the method that is likely to add a further stage to the sorts of topics carried out by *Here I Am*. The content of the topics would not be changed by invoking Groome's perspective.

Activity A3 (optional)

Select one or two lessons (or lesson topics) from the *Here I Am* series or the *Weaving the Web* series, or from some other resource chosen in consultation with your tutor. If you are going to teach these lessons yourself, make sure the lessons are ones you feel comfortable about teaching, in terms of your knowledge and your usual approach.

When you have selected these lessons, study any advice which is given to the teacher in the resource you are using. Then devise your own set of aims and objectives for the activities, giving attention to the following advice.

- Plan lessons of whatever length best fits your usual practice and the needs of the pupils. If appropriate, plan more than two lessons. Feel free to adapt the approaches suggested in the book until they are something you feel comfortable with.
- Use the sequence suggested by the resource; use it flexibly in your plan. But remember that one of the distinctive hallmarks of the confessional approach is its link to worship and its focus on attitudes and action.
- Teach the two or more lessons, feeling free to proceed with your usual working methods.
- Evaluate the lessons on the basis of their success in delivering the aims and objectives you identified.

When you have taught the lessons, pay careful attention to your own professional experience and feelings as you evaluate them.

Comment on activity A3

The following points are designed to help you to measure the success of the lessons *in terms of the confessional approach*, rather than in terms of resources, pupil management or other criteria.

- Did my planning and delivery achieve the aims and objectives I had set?
- Was the activity successful in reflecting Christian belief and practice?
- Did my planning and delivery succeed in bringing pupils closer to a knowledge and appreciation of the Christian message and the church?

You could sum up by listing the criticisms you have made of your lessons in confessional terms. Compare them with the criticisms made of the approach, identified in unit C of the module *Philosophy of Religious Education*. You could finish by writing a paragraph analysing how you have either fallen into, or avoided, the traditional weaknesses of the confessional approach.

A2 Phenomenological approach

This section refreshes your memory about the theoretical foundations of phenomenology and the criticisms made of it. We will then show you examples of the phenomenological approach in practice, and invite you to evaluate them. In order to make this evaluation as effective as possible, you should try this approach out in the classroom. If this is not possible, then you will have to work through the materials here either on the basis of the observation of lessons or on the basis of the comments included here and the books referred to during discussion.

In order to complete this section and its tasks, you will need access to the following books and resources: *How Do I Teach RE?* by Read, Rudge and Howarth (1986) and *The Effective Teaching of RE* by Watson (1993). The phenomenological or world religions approach to religious education is based upon the attempt to help the child to understand religious commitment *from inside*, without any assumptions about the child's belief-world.

In unit C of the module *Philosophy of Religious Education*, the theological and philosophical background to phenomenology and its application within religious education were discussed. The method is based on the work of Edmund Husserl (1929) and involves bracketing out presuppositions about what is presented before the mind. It was taken up by Ninian Smart (1968, 1989) who analysed religion into seven main dimensions that could be the focus of work in the classroom. Smart's dimensions are as follows:

- *Practical and ritual:* this dimension is important in faiths of a strongly sacramental kind and in religions that have well developed liturgies.
- *Experiential and emotional:* this dimension is identified with the feelings of awe, calm peace, love, hope, gratitude and so on, that the religion generates. Smart instances the prophetic experiences of the prophet Isaiah (Isaiah 6) and the vision given to Arjuna in the Hindu Song of the Lord (*Bhagavadgita*).
- *Narrative or mythic:* this dimension is the 'story side of religion', its tales of saints and heroes, and the life of its founder or leading figures.
- *Doctrinal and philosophical:* this dimension is the developed teaching of the religion. Smart instances the incarnation in Christianity and the philosophical vision of the world found in Buddhism.
- *Legal and ethical:* this dimension applies the narrative and doctrinal aspects of the religion to daily life. The commandments of Judaism or the *shari'a* of Islam are examples here.
- *Social and institutional:* this dimension applies to the community or group of people who join together to live a religion. There may be all kinds of

institutional and organisational features of a religion that are unique to it and without which it could not function.

- *Material:* this dimension refers to the buildings, works of art and other creations that are the product of social and institutional life. Smart instances the statues of Hinduism and the icons of Eastern Orthodox Christianity.

Smart wanted pupils to enter imaginatively and sympathetically into the experience of religious believers. But the approach has been criticised in the areas suggested by the following two questions.

- Is complete objectivity possible?
- Is objectivity desirable?

The dimensions of religion as a guide to planning

If a pupil is to receive a balanced religious education, it must be one in which all facets or dimensions of religion are represented. For instance, if a child only learns about religious festivals (ritual dimension), religion will perhaps be trivialised and made to seem fun all the time. Or if a child only learns about beliefs (doctrinal dimension), religion may seem very dull, distant and abstract.

Some phenomenologists believe that a teacher can plan a balanced curriculum in religious education by using the dimensions as a checklist. If all dimensions are reasonably represented over a period of years, it can be assumed that most facets of religion are being covered. However, it is arguable that not all dimensions are suitable for the whole age range.

Activity A4

Against each of the following phases of education, identify dimensions of religion which you feel to be appropriate, and those you feel to be inappropriate:

- infants;
- early juniors;
- middle juniors;
- top juniors;
- early secondary;
- middle secondary;
- sixth form.

Comment on activity A4

You may have decided that for infants and early juniors, an approach focusing on the doctrinal would be inappropriate and, for middle to upper secondary pupils, the mythological dimension (stories) may seem babyish. On the other hand, it seems odd to study a religion at any age if the behaviour of participants is left unexplained. What is the point of knowing about baptism, for instance, if the doctrinal elements of baptism are omitted? Baptism becomes a meaningless custom, and the same could be said of almost any religious rite in any religious tradition.

The experiential aspect of religion might be more suitable for older pupils since they would be able to distinguish different kinds of experience, and their own from that of others, more easily. Younger children, who tend to confuse fantasy and reality, might be misled by attempts to invoke the experiential. The ethical aspect of religion would probably be most suitable for older pupils, though younger children can certainly distinguish kindness from unkindness.

Tangible objects with a religious significance, especially if they are rivers, temples or mountains, are unlikely to be appreciated by young children whose knowledge of geography is limited.

You may have thought of other factors. You may also have considered that the construction of a religious curriculum that covers every dimension of every religion is likely to be complicated and possibly counter-productive. Is coverage of different places of worship really helpful when mythological and ritual dimensions are omitted? In other words, how realistic is it to separate the dimensions from each other?

The Westhill Project as an example of phenomenology

The Westhill Project is a series of pupil textbooks, photopacks and a teacher's handbook designed to cover a range of religions through all four Key Stages from age 5 to 16. The materials are produced to a high standard and have adapted phenomenological principles in a number of ways to suit the needs of primary and secondary pupils. The project began publishing in 1986 through Mary Glasgow Publications, but more recent materials are published under the Thornes imprint.

Read, Rudge and Howarth (1986) refer, in the handbook of the Westhill Project, to one main aim and seven principles of religious education. The principal aim of religious education, they say, is:

> to help children mature in relation to their own patterns of belief and behaviour through exploring religious beliefs and practices and related human experiences.

This aim, you will notice, is broad and very specifically related to the intention that children should be helped to maturity. The broadness of the approach is indicated by its inclusion of 'related human experiences' along with 'religious beliefs and practices' and is further signalled by the notion of 'exploring'. Here is no checklist of dimensions or prescription saying which beliefs should be explored or how they should be addressed.

Following this aim, seven principles are enunciated, some of which relate to children, others of which relate to teachers and yet others to the role of religious education. These principles are that:

- children need to develop their own beliefs and values;
- religious education has an important contribution to make to the personal and social development of children;
- the role of the religious education teacher is that of educator;
- religious education ought to be related to the ages and abilities of children;
- religious education helps children explore a range of religious beliefs and practices;
- religious education contributes to multicultural education;
- religious education does not make assumptions about the personal commitments of teachers or children.

The thrust of these principles is against confessionalism and in favour of a rationale for religious education that shows how it supports other areas of the curriculum (multicultural education and personal and social education) and, at the same time, enables children to work out their own beliefs. There is a sense, then, in which the value of religious education, for the Westhill Project, is partly *instrumental*, that is, to achieve other ends than simply to be educated about religion. If we take an analogy, we might say that mathematics education was to help children understand mathematics regardless of its usefulness to science, technology, accountancy or the general business of living. Read, Rudge and Howarth fight shy of building their principles on the boldest and simplest justification of religious education: that it educates children in a worthwhile field of knowledge.

As a consequence of the aim, Read *et al* outline three main areas of content in religious education: traditional belief systems, shared human experience and individual patterns of belief. They consider that these belief systems are exemplified in personal life, family life, public life and community life and are observed in symbols, stories and people. Likewise shared human experiences are exemplified in the same areas which, in this case, are observed by looking at answers to the crucial question, 'What does it mean to be human?' Finally, individual patterns of belief are also exemplified in the same areas, though 'the way in which individual patterns of belief emerge in the classroom, and become material for exploration, is entirely informal and *ad hoc*' (p 25).

The informal and *ad hoc* nature of the emergence of individual patterns of belief is intended to stop adults imposing their religious concepts on children, a praiseworthy aim but one likely to make curriculum planning difficult. Religious concepts are intended to emerge from the kinds of questions children ask about matters of importance, but this intention does not preclude *some* sort of guidance about recognised theological conceptual systems.

Two sets of concepts are identified. The first set of concepts includes concepts within traditional belief systems like 'salvation', 'God', 'faith' and 'spirituality' that belong to all religious or non-religious systems and, above this, are concepts specific to particular religions. The second set of concepts is found within human experience and relates to matters of 'authority', 'destiny', 'meaning' and 'value'.

These concepts should be acquired by skills of investigation and enquiry. 'One of the best ways of helping children to explore them is to present them with situations where they encounter what they are studying first hand' (p 30), and by this the authors mean that children should meet members of faith communities. Such a programme of religious education will have the additional benefit of making children more tolerant and empathic, and lead to reflection and evaluation (p 31).

Activity A5

Reflect on the ways in which the Westhill Project has adapted the traditional phenomenological approach, and ideally, look at Read, Rudge and Howarth (1986) for yourself. For instance, has it:

- set itself aims and principles new to phenomenology?
- introduced new areas of content?
- accepted the acquisition of certain attitudes as legitimate?
- answered some of the criticisms of phenomenology previously made?

Select, for this task, a combination of photopacks and pupil textbooks from the Westhill Project. Ensure that the materials cover more than one religion and are appropriate for the level and phase in which you normally teach. If you are an infant teacher, you could select the *Muslims* photopack and the textbooks *Islam 1* and *Christianity 1*. When you have selected these lessons, study any advice which is given to the teacher in the resource you are using and then evaluate the lessons.

Westhill identifies two types of planning for religious education: the *systems* approach and the *life themes* approach (see teacher's handbook pp 39-46). These correspond to what Michael Grimmitt called the dimensional and the existential approaches in his book *What can I do in RE?* (see Grimmitt, 1978, chapters 5 and 6). How are these approaches different?

Comment on activity A5

When you have delivered the teaching sessions, pay careful attention to your own professional experience and feelings as you evaluate them. The following questions are designed to help you to measure the success of the lessons *in terms of the phenomenological/Westhill approach*, rather than in terms of resources, pupil management or other criteria. Use the questions as a stimulus in your written evaluation.

First, did my planning and delivery facilitate the children's acquisition of a range of concepts, skills and attitudes? Did I name the concepts, skills and attitudes delivered, evaluate the degree of success in doing so, and point to evidence of this in the pupils' work?

Second, was my planning and delivery objective? Was my role an educational one? Did it help them to explore a range of religious beliefs and concepts in an open way? Did I avoid making assumptions about personal commitments?

Third, did my planning and delivery contribute to the children's personal development in moral, spiritual and social areas? Were my lessons appropriate for their age and stage?

You could sum up by listing the criticisms you have made of your lessons in phenomenological terms. Compare them with the criticisms made of the approach, identified in unit C of the module *Philosophy of Religious Education*.

You could finish by writing a paragraph analysing how you have either fallen into, or avoided, the traditional weaknesses of the phenomenological approach.

The two approaches identified by Westhill may be explained as follows. The first, the *Systems* (dimensional) approach, delivers a lesson which looks explicitly at a religion or an element of a religion, e.g. a lesson on Christianity or on worship in a Mosque, or on the story of Divali. The second, the *Life themes* (existential) approach, delivers a lesson which looks at human issues and questions, and through them discovers something about religious beliefs and practices. For example, a lesson on caring may lead to an understanding of the Muslim practice of almsgiving, or a lesson on suffering may lead to an appreciation of the Four Noble Truths of Buddhism.

Examples of the two approaches are given in the teacher's book, pp 43 and 44. You might have found it worked more easily if you had reversed the order, and taught a life-themes lesson first, looking at pupils' experience. This could then lead on to a systems lesson in which a relevant religious belief or practice is explored.

A3 Experiential approach

This section refreshes your memory about the theoretical foundations of the experiential approach and the criticisms made of it. We will then show you examples of the experiential approach in practice, and invite you to evaluate them. In order to make this evaluation as effective as possible, you should try this approach out in the classroom. If this is not possible, then you will have to work through the materials here either on the basis of the observation of lessons or on the basis of the comments included here and the books referred to during discussion.

In order to complete this section and its tasks, you will need access to one or more of the following books and resources: *Eggshells and Thunderbolts* (especially part 2 of the video, starting 28 minutes into the tape) by Lazenby (1993), *New Methods in RE Teaching: an experiential approach* by Hammond, Hay, Moxon, Netto, Raban, Straugheir and Williams (1990), or *The Effective Teaching of RE* by Watson (1993).

The experiential approach to religious education seeks to let religion appeal to children, not only through their heads, but also through their hearts. It is an approach which does not satisfy itself with teaching about the religions, but wishes to allow children to develop their own religiosity. The word affective is sometimes applied to this approach, since children's emotions are engaged, together with their senses, in a total encounter with issues, people or ideas in religion.

In unit C of the module *Philosophy of Religious Education*, the theological and philosophical background to the experiential approach was discussed. The origin of the approach lies partly in discovering that religious experience in modern western society is much more widespread than had been previously thought.

But the approach has been criticised in the areas suggested by the following questions.

- Does it sit easily with other forms of education?
- Is its rationale clear and rigorous?

- Is it a 'stalking horse' for an inappropriate return to confessionalism?
- Is it too individualistic?

These questions will serve to remind you of the rationale of this approach to religious education, and to review the critical arguments about its validity.

Children's religious experience as a guide to planning

Building on the work of David Hay and others in the field of research into religious experience, we now turn to the topic of using children's religious experience as a basis for planning and implementing religious education.

The evidence accumulated by surveys suggests that religious experiences often take place in childhood and are more likely to be reported on by women, especially, in Britain, by middle-class church-going women. The experiences, though they may be directly related to a religious function (like going to church) are also to be found through the natural world and are usually positive, life-enhancing and characteristically convey a sense of being at one with life or God or nature. Kay and Francis (1996) give a detailed summary of research in this area.

The prevalence of women among those reporting religious experiences has suggested that women are more sensitive to spiritual life than men or that they are more willing to talk about their experiences than men. It should not surprise teachers if girls are slightly more forthcoming on this subject than boys.

Lessons that describe religious experience, often by using poetry or music, may be fitted into schemes of work so that, for instance, a study of world wide Christianity might offer a chance to listen to a brief extract of the Russian Orthodox Easter Liturgy. Similarly Jewish music, especially that sung in celebration at the end of a festival, brings Judaism to life.

Activity A6

Use the experiential approach to help you plan a course of religious education. Make a note of the kind of difficulties that this approach runs into, especially bearing in mind the professional and ethical problems that can arise with this approach. Consider some of the general implications of this approach for syllabus construction.

Comment on activity A6

We have to be careful here. We are not talking about:

- asking children to share experiences of a religious kind;
- encouraging children to seek mystical experiences;
- teachers or other adults sharing their innermost experiences.

Any of these three expectations would be both unprofessional and counter to the spirit of experiential religious education. Such expectations therefore have nothing to do with this approach.

What is the approach then? An experiential approach builds on a theory that human beings, including children, do have experiences which may be called religious. These will range from the simple to the extraordinary, the commonplace to the profound. Such a theory, if accepted, encourages the teacher to be open, and in particular to adopt styles of learning which will foster acceptance of experiences.

Your plan should include experiences associated with religion, perhaps using art or music as a stimulus, and should be suitable to the age, abilities and backgrounds of pupils. We suspect that the considerations which drive syllabus construction are related to the cognitive development of children. For this reason experientialism may be a means by which religious concepts are illustrated or opened up rather than a method for structuring a syllabus. Beyond this we cannot comment in detail.

Some examples of experiential approaches

In this section, you should try to look at a range of classroom ideas for the experiential approach, make notes on their aims and procedure, and critically reflect on what these approaches achieve for the pupils.

First, notice that Hammond and his colleagues want people to learn to value personal experience and to extend awareness of it. They begin by helping pupils to become aware of simple sensory experience. They recommend taking a radio and using it to demonstrate how 'difficult it is to tune in to one station when there is a lot of interference'.

Pupils are asked to find a waveband where two stations are transmitting simultaneously or to move from one station to another through a patch of interference. During this process they are asked to listen to the sound of the radio and to be aware of their own thoughts; to think what makes it difficult to understand what is being transmitted; to spend a minute or two talking about this experience with someone else; and then, after turning the radio off, being still, closing eyes and listening to all the sounds outside the room, and then to all the sounds inside the room, then to the sounds of their own bodies and being aware of just one sound. From the exercise of listening to natural sounds pupils are asked to think about the clearest sounds they heard and to talk with a partner about this experience.

Later pupils progress to imagining themselves to be something, perhaps a car or a piece of fruit or another object. Then pupils are asked to compare with each other the kinds of things they have imagined themselves to be. The purpose of this stage is to allow pupils to begin to embody awareness, and by this means to realise that experience differs from person to person, from body to body. After this pupils develop skills of empathy through the recognition of different perspectives. Awareness is framed and, finally, extended by reflecting on the meaning of experience (Hammond *et al*, 1990, p 22).

Some people may feel unsure about trying the experiential approach because it seems so vague. We hope that when you have seen some examples of the approach, you will feel that you understand its purpose. It is important to understand the purpose before trying it out in the classroom.

Activity A7 (optional)

This activity is about experiential approaches in practice in the classroom. You will need either to teach a lesson of this kind yourself or to observe someone else doing so. Then evaluate the lesson(s).

Whichever of the books listed at the start of the section you use, take notes on an experiential activity you chose. In particular, note the role of the teacher, the atmosphere which is necessary, and the resources which would be needed. Make a note of any improvements or alterations which occur to you.

Plan lessons of whatever length best fits your usual practice and the needs of the pupils. If appropriate, plan more than two lessons. Feel free to adapt the approaches suggested in the book until they are something you feel comfortable with. Don't be too anxious if there is no explicit religious content in your planned activities.

Use the following questions to stimulate your critical thinking on each of the lessons you have seen or given.

- What does it offer the children?
- What is the teacher aiming to do?

Try to write down a set of aims for the activities you offered or observed.

- Is each example justifiable educationally?
- Are the activities open to criticism of the kind that we saw in the last unit?

Comment on activity A7

You should have ensured that the lessons/activities selected:

- are ones that you feel would be appropriate for the pupils;
- are appropriate for the level and phase in which you normally teach.

You should have evaluated the lessons on the basis of their:

- success in delivering the aims and objectives you identified;
- relevance to pupils;
- success in opening up issues and facilitating free exchange of views, new and old;
- different experiences or ways of seeing things, sense of excitement.

The following questions are designed to help you to measure the success of the lessons *in terms of the affective or experiential approach*, rather than in terms of resources, pupil management or other criteria; use the questions as a stimulus in your written evaluation.

First, did the planning and delivery achieve the aims and objectives that had been set? Evaluate the degree of success in doing so, and point to evidence of this in the pupils' work.

Second, was the activity relevant to pupils' emotional, social and other experience of life?

Third, was the planning and delivery successful in opening up issues, facilitating free exchange of views, offering new and different experiences or ways of seeing things, and generating a sense of excitement?

Sum up by listing the criticisms you have made of your lessons in experiential terms. Compare them with the criticisms made of the approach, identified in unit C of the module *Philosophy of Religious Education*.

A4 Working with religious artifacts

This section will discuss the use of religious artifacts. The use of artifacts does not, of itself, constitute a fully-fledged approach to religious education. This is because artifacts can be used with any approach, though the use to which the artifacts are put may be slightly different in each context.

In order to complete this section and its tasks, you will need access to the following books: *Investigating Artifacts in RE* by Howard (1996) and *Religion and the Arts in Education: dimensions of spirituality* by Starkings (1993).

Artifacts: problems and possibilities

'Artifacts' is the (perhaps slightly artificial) word used to define all those objects of significance which are used in the daily life or worship of a faith community. One member of a faith community remarked:

> They may be 'artefacts' to the teacher, but to us they're everyday things which have a special, holy significance

Examples of artifacts from Judaism include:

- the Menorah (seven-branched candelabra, symbolising the six days of creation and the day of rest, which is lit at the start of the Sabbath)
- Tefillin (scrolls of the law kept in a box and wrapped around the non-dominant arm with a leather strap).

Examples of artifacts from Sikhism include:

- the Kirpan (the sword or dagger worn by Sikh men as a symbol of resisting evil and injustice);
- the Guru Granth Sahib (the holy book containing the sayings of the first 'Guru' or teacher).

Examples of artifacts from Christianity include:

- the paten (plate for holding wafer of bread which is blessed at communion or mass);
- Easter card (sends greetings at the Easter festival, reminding people of the good news of Christ's victory over death).

This gives you an idea of what artifacts are, how rich they are in meaning for the believer, and how that can be used for explaining and understanding the beliefs and practices of a religion.

Activity A8

Can you identify the following artifacts and explain their significance briefly?

Each artifact is named and its religion is given. Try to write a description (i.e. what it is), followed by an explanation of its meaning for the believer. The examples get harder as you go along.

- Rosary beads (*Christianity*)
- Prayer-shawl (*Judaism*)
- Prayer-mat (*Islam*)
- Puja tray (*Hinduism*)
- Prayer-wheel (*Buddhism*)

Comment on activity A8

From Christianity: rosary beads look like a necklace. They are simple beads in groups of ten on a string. The rosary is used as a focus for prayer and meditation in the Catholic tradition. The prayers associated with it are the 'Our Father' and the 'Hail Mary'. The prayers can be counted by using the beads.

From Judaism: a prayer-shawl is a blue and white shawl with tassels at each corner. The shawl is worn during prayer. The colours of the sea and sky, it reminds the Jew that God holds the four corners of the earth, and the sky, in his hands. Blue and white are also the colours of the flag of the state of Israel.

From Islam: a prayer-mat is a rug, large enough for one person to kneel on, usually decorated with scenes from Mecca. The Muslim's duty to pray standing, prostrating himself, and kneeling, at five fixed times of the day, is fundamental to Islam. The prayer mat gives him a sacred space in which to pray, wherever he may find himself, and ensures that physical discomfort will not put him off his prayers.

From Hinduism: a Puja tray is a metal dish containing a variety of jars and sprinklers. Puja, the household or temple-based worship service, involves giving an offering to the gods - usually flowers, water and bread. The Puja tray is used for carrying the offerings and for holding the jars filled with water.

From Buddhism: a Prayer-wheel is a cylindrical container with a long handle coming from one end; the container holds tiny scrolls fitted in to a wheel. When shaken the wheel revolves rapidly. The scrolls are prayers. When the wheel revolves, the scrolls move so rapidly that the prayers are 'said' hundreds or thousands of times. Many temples have a large prayer wheel which may run by wind or electricity.

Use of artifacts in schools

Questions are sometimes asked about whether it is right to use artifacts in a classroom for purposes for which they are not designed and in a context to which they do not belong. With regard to the possibility that use of artifacts in religious education might offend the faith community, we take the following view: obviously all artifacts should be treated with respect, but there are only a very few available objects which are held to be so sacred in themselves, as objects, that handling them in the classroom might cause any offence; and even then, simple precautions should avoid offence. The following examples should be kept in mind.

In Islam, the Holy Qur'an (the sacred book), when in Arabic, is considered to be the actual, literal words of God. It should be kept carefully wrapped and placed on the highest shelf of the room. The user should wash hands before opening or touching it. The Qur'an in English, and the Qur'an stand, are not subject to these restrictions, although they should be treated respectfully.

In Christianity, the bread and wine when consecrated (i.e. after the priest or minister has spoken the words which invoke God's spirit and give the bread and wine the significance of being the body and blood of Christ) should only be used in the context of eucharistic worship. Altar bread and wine before consecration, and the paten and chalice which hold them, are not subject to these restrictions, although they should be treated respectfully.

In Judaism, the scrolls of Torah (Law of God), whether in the synagogue or in a mezuzah or tefillin, are sacred, although the container is not sacred. People may touch the container, but should where possible avoid touching the scroll itself. Readers use a *yad* (pointer). Other items in Judaism, such as the Passover *Seder* dish, *menorah*, and *havdallah* (end-of-sabbath candle), may be touched and used. The holiness is in the significance, not in the object itself.

Sometimes teachers ask whether acting-out rituals in the classroom will cause offence. Several teachers have staged 'pretend' baptisms, or have role-played a Passover meal or a Sikh wedding. These are usually acceptable, so long as it is quite clear in the teacher's mind, and made explicit to the pupils and parents, that this is not a *real* baptism or Passover meal or wedding.

An artifacts approach in the classroom can yield very good religious education. Specifically, it can:

- engage the pupils' interest in an object which may be beautiful, intricate and unusual;
- generate questions (what is it? why is it....? how is it used?);
- lead to further knowledge;
- encourage positive attitudes to worship in general, and to the particular faith.

A5 Conclusion

It s appropriate that you use the notes and other tasks you have built up during this unit; they may be of use to you in the future when you work in or with a school. As you conclude this unit, you may wish to ask yourself the very general question, 'What makes good religious education?' and the answer, we hope, will utilise aspects of the approaches we have considered in this unit.

Readers

You may wish to look at sections 5.1, 8.1, and 8.2 of J. Astley and L.J. Francis (eds) (1994), *Critical Perspectives on Christian Education*, Leominster, Gracewing. You will find helpful section 10.1 of L.J. Francis and A. Thatcher (eds) (1990), *Christian Perspectives for Education*, Leominster, Gracewing.

Bibliography

Bastide, D. (ed.) (1987), *Religious Education 5-12*, London, Falmer Press.

Bastide, D. (ed.) (1992), *Good Practice in Primary RE,* London, Falmer Press.

Byrne, A. and Malone, C. (1992), *Here I Am: a religious education programme for primary schools*, London, HarperCollins.

Grimmitt, M. (1978), *What can I do in RE?* (second edition), London, Mayhew-McCrimmon.

Groome, T.H. (1991), *Sharing Faith: the way of shared praxis*, San Francisco, Harper.

Hammond J., Hay D., Moxon J., Netto B., Raban K., Straugheir G. and Williams C. (1990), *New Methods in RE Teaching: an experiential approach*, Harlow, Oliver and Boyd.

Howard, C. (1996), *Investigating Artifacts in RE*, Norwich, Chansitor Publications.

Husserl, E. (1929), Phenomenology, *Encyclopaedia Britannica* (fourteenth edition).

Jackson, R. and Starkings, D. (1990), *The Junior RE Handbook*, Cheltenham, Thornes.

Kay, W.K. and Francis, L.J., (1996), *Drift from the Churches*, Cardiff, University of Wales Press.

Lazenby, D. (1993), *Eggshells and Thunderbolts: religious education and Christianity in the classroom*, London, BBC Educational and Culham College Institute.

Lohan, R. and McClure, M. (1988), *Weaving the Web: a modular programme of religious education*, London, Collins (a teacher's book and six pupil books).

Read, G., Rudge, J. and Howarth, R.B. (1986), *How Do I Teach RE?* London, Mary Glasgow Publications.

Smart, N. (1968), *Secular Education and the Logic of Religion*, London, Faber.

Smart, N (1989), *The World's Religions*, Cambridge, Cambridge University Press.

Starkings, D. (ed.) (1993), *Religion and the Arts in Education: dimensions of spirituality*, London, Hodder and Stoughton.

Sutcliffe, J. (ed.) (1984), *A Dictionary of Religious Education*, London, SCM.

Watson, B. (1993), *The Effective Teaching of RE*, London, Longman.

Method in Religious Education

Unit B

Creative religious education

Gaynor Pollard
University College
Chester

Contents

Introduction

Aims

After working through this unit you should be able to:

- analyse and critically evaluate the contribution that creative approaches may make to the teaching of religious education;
- show an awareness of the contribution the creative arts might make to the teaching of religious education;
- demonstrate how the use of a variety of media may enhance the teaching of religious education;
- identify suitable contexts for the use of affective methodologies;
- apply insights about creative religious education to your own professional practice.

Overview

During your study of this unit you will consider creative methods of teaching religious education which make the subject come alive for pupils. You will have opportunities to consider a variety of methods and to reflect on appropriate opportunities for their use. Religious language and concepts are rich in meaning, but their complexity can be daunting to teachers wishing to introduce new ideas and unfamiliar terms to young children. Creative religious education deliberately sets out to present the language and concepts of religions in ways that will capture the imagination of pupils.

Some of the methods that you will study are easily incorporated into your day-to-day teaching. Others are more ambitious, and may need a great deal of preparation and prove to be expensive. It may be that visits to faith communities and their places of worship will only be possible once during a pupil's school years.

If you are not a teacher, then you would be helped by gaining access to a school where you can observe religious education lessons. You may find that a school would be quite grateful for this extra help, but if you find difficulty you might like to contact your local Diocesan Director of Education, who may be able to make some suggestions. But even this may not be possible for you and, if this is the case, you should read this unit imaginatively so as to gain an understanding of the basic concepts it involves.

B1 What is 'creativity'?

We normally use this word in a positive sense to describe people or work that is imaginative, passionate, unusual, innovative or ingenious. But the word 'creative' can also be defined in regard to the arts since the artistic process is almost synonymous with the creative process. These two senses of the word 'creative' may separate in the practice of education. This is because the arts can be pressed into service in the classroom unimaginatively. Genuinely creative religious education will only take place where both senses of the word apply: where there is imaginativeness *and* where the creative arts are employed.

Certainly what should be avoided is the typical instance that occurs in many classrooms with the instruction to 'draw a picture' following the instruction to 'write the story in your own words'.

Even when genuine creativity is achieved, however, there may be difficulties with the overall notion because it may seem to lack academic rigour. This is because it is difficult to judge something that is original. How can old criteria apply to a new product? Yet, since the National Curriculum emphasises thoroughness, differentiation and coherence and these qualities *can* be delivered to the classroom by genuinely creative methods, the problem of academic rigours in reference to creativity ought to be met without undue difficulty.

Theological ideas

Christian theology has always taken creativity seriously. One of the most powerful understandings of God is as creator of all that exists. As God is thought of as creator, so human beings are regarded as made in the image of God, and therefore participate in God's activities as co-creators. Since no human endeavours are regarded as outside God's concern, every creative activity contributes to this understanding. Nevertheless, some Christians are uneasy about including manufactured items as examples of creativity. At a service of thanksgiving for the motor car in Coventry Cathedral in 1996, protesters made this point. Some were concerned with the celebration of a machine that has caused so much destruction to human lives and to the environment, but others were unhappy about connecting God the creator with human artefacts. For these people God was concerned with the natural beauty of the world rather than the ingenuity of human creations.

Matthew Fox, an American Dominican priest, has attempted to shift the central concerns of Christian theology. He has argued that we must not think of human beings only in the context of original sin, fallenness and redemption, but also as receivers of an original blessing from God, given at creation, which is recoverable without the notion of sacrifice or forgiveness. He has called this way of thinking 'creation theology', and many Christians have been active in finding new ways to express their creativity in the light of this positive understanding of themselves and the world. (More details of Fox's theology are given in unit C of the module *Church Schools: history and philosophy*.)

But Christians have always used a variety of methods to express their beliefs and their prayers. Sometimes this has been in art and music, sometimes in architecture or crafts. Some have enacted their beliefs by addressing social injustices. Traditionally Christians and Jews have relied on the Holy Spirit for creativity, and this reliance stems from an understanding of the Holy Spirit's role at the beginning of the book of Genesis ('hovering over the waters', Genesis 1.2) fructifying the lifeless world and in such accounts as the building of the tabernacle in the wilderness where we are told that the main craftsman engaged in the task was 'filled with the Holy Spirit, with skill, ability and knowledge in all kinds of crafts' (Exodus 31.2).

Thus, whether or not Fox's attempt to shift theology away from redemption is successful, there are resources within traditional Christian theological understandings to allow for innovation, invention and artistic expression. For example, the poet John Milton, writing his epic poem *Paradise Lost*, begins with an invocation to the Holy Spirit and a request for inspiration and wisdom.

When we apply these theological considerations to the practicalities of teaching and to the tasks of education, we discover teachers may present classwork in extremely creative ways without managing to engage pupils in thinking or performing creatively. Pupils are used to taking the role of passive observer in front of the television set and quite happily agree to be entertained by a teacher attempting a star turn! The teacher therefore needs to involve the powers of discovery and imagination possessed by *pupils*. In order to do this it is best to plan for the actions pupils will be asked to take part in. Planning methods can use active verbs to describe the opportunities that will be available to pupils.

Activity B1

Using these words as a starting point, plan some activities for a class that is studying the topic of 'Christian worship'. Plan for the age-group of your choice, and explain how these activities might enable children to *encounter* Christian worship and *respond* to it.

| Observe . . . | Listen to . . . | Taste . . . |
| Visit . . . | Touch . . . | Enact . . . |

Find out by . . .	Sing . . .	Dramatise . .
Write . . .	Paint . . .	Reflect . . .
Question . . .	Discuss . . .	Make . . .

Comment on activity B1

All these activities require children to be active, sometimes on their own and sometimes in groups. They allow new experiences to be assimilated and they allow for a variety of experiences using most of the five senses.

Some of these activities are most suited to encountering Christian worship in all its many forms. Observing or visiting would allow children to see or take part in a service. Other activities, like making things, painting, writing, reflecting, would allow children to respond to worship.

B2 Creative arts and religious education

In many schools religious education is linked with the humanities subjects, history and geography. They do share much in common, including an emphasis on language and literacy skills. However, religious education could equally draw support and ideas from the creative arts. Religious traditions have never limited their expression to the written word. It is interesting to see just how important physical movement is in the majority of services of worship. In Christian worship people stand up, sit down, kneel, bow, dance and make ritual movements. Buddhists pay particular attention to breathing and chanting. Hindus use traditional dances at festival times and Muslims use a particularly active form of prayer. It makes sense for teachers of religious education to take notice of these ways of expressing religious devotion and regard the creative arts as authentic ways of responding to religious thoughts. It could be argued that religious education has a particular role to play in emphasising these modes of expression. Hay and Hammond (1992) point out:

> In this respect it contrasts radically with much that passes for education in other areas of the school curriculum, where the emphasis is on the use of the intellect to the neglect of the whole person

As in most areas of religious education, relating the creative arts to teaching methodology is not without difficulties. Using dance, art, music or drama to explore religious concepts produces powerful reactions. Many have found a positive inspirational experience through these media, and religious expressions of these kinds rank amongst the greatest cultural treasures of the world, secular or sacred. It is precisely at this interface between the secular and the sacred that controversy may arise. Muslims do not regard dance or art as suitable media for expressing religious truth, and many Christians are offended by ornate decorations or vestments. Teachers must be sensitive and conscientious in fitting the subject content of the lesson with the method in order that offence does not occur.

Watson (1993b) points out that religion can be seen as a dimension of the arts or the arts can be seen as a dimension of religion. In one sense, to create artistically is to mimic the creative power of God (at least in the three Semitic religions), and for this reason artistic creation may be thought of as inherently religious. Yet, art can also be used to exploit, advertise and aggrandise religion, in a word to *abuse* religion. This double function explains why religions, at particular times in their history, are ambivalent towards the arts; the fear is that 'representation may become idolatry'. In one era Christianity expressed iconoclastic fervour or Puritan simplicity and in another it nurtured the genius of Michaelangelo; it has destroyed art and fostered art. It has also debased art by encouraging doggerel and sentimental tunes as media of worship.

In essence, though, it is arguable that art and religion are organically connected. Through them human beings reach out for meaning and beauty; through them awe and wonder are fostered; through them the inner life of human beings is read and its integrity brought into the open.

Watson contends that religious education cannot be related to the arts through either the phenomenological or the experiential approaches; the former places them alongside each other and the latter conflates them. What is needed is an *essentialist* model that allows the arts and religion to 'enhance, deepen, and challenge each other to their mutual benefit'.

Dance

To express religious feelings and insights through dance has a long and distinguished tradition. Children often dance with a great deal of commitment and enthusiasm. Waddup (1992) has pointed out that circle or sacred dancing was part of religious practice before the formalisation of worship, and that much medieval music was played in order to accompany celebratory and respectful dances.

Dance may be used in creative religious education in three basic ways:

- telling stories;
- specialist dances, e.g. Israeli or Indian dances;
- improvising on the relationship between the emotions and the imagination.

The National Curriculum targets for dance refer to performance, composition and appreciation. Each of these may be employed in the exploration of the three areas outlined above. In four important aspects of dance, those of action, dynamics, space and relationships, the emphasis for religious education work will be on relationships, that is, on how the pupil related to the issues explored through the medium. The skills of dance should be taught prior to relating them to a specific subject, as it is important that pupils realise that creative methods are not a licence for sloppy work.

Lealman (1993) gives an account of the connection between the drum-dances and traditional sculpture of the Innuit and an apprehension of an underlying mystery. Drum-dances were traditionally used in order to ask the shaman for something, perhaps for information that could not be worked out by rational means. This signifies, the beginning of new possibilities of being. She considers whether the traditional Innuit approach to creativity has anything to offer western education, and argues that young people today need a medium for protest against the 'Dominant X', consumer values, and the world's pain. She stresses the importance of waiting and receptivity (which are the components of creativity) that are needed to balance an over-rational curriculum.

Drama

Drama is a powerful tool for learning. It provides pupils with a safe and structured environment in which they can explore religious education in an affective way. The capacity of religious traditions for providing absorbing material has not been lost on popular film makers who have consistently used religious themes for their work. Although drama, as a teaching method, may be used to great effect, it demands meticulous planning and a willingness to combine it with a variety of other teaching methods, as issues arise.

Fleming (1992) suggests that drama can provide direct experience, enabling pupils to understand concepts, examine issues, solve problems, pose and answer questions and engage with the content of religious education. She works with the parable of the Good Samaritan and shows how to create an atmosphere which is intellectually, emotionally, socially and spiritually rigorous. She develops the idea of pair work, where pupils can examine power relations through different physical positions, enabling them to work with abstract ideas.

Alcock (1993) traces the link between drama and religion in western tradition, starting from the Theatre of Dionysus in Athens in the fifth century BCE, through the medieval mystery plays of England, to using drama as a teaching method today.   He discusses the work of Theatre-in-Education or TIE, a cross-curricular enterprise that, it is generally agreed, has the potential to stimulate receptivity to attitude change, particularly in relation to religious themes.   His discussion is at a theoretical level rather than a practical one, and so goes beyond the daily necessities of classroom religious education.

Activity B2

Either, plan and teach a lesson using the medium of dance, to explore that section of the story of Joseph where he is abandoned by his brothers. If you are inexperienced in teaching you might ask a dance and drama specialist to help you.

Or, teach the story of the Good Samaritan. Prepare a dramatic piece around these events and use the insights of Kate Fleming, mentioned above, to help you.

Evaluate the lesson.

Comment on activity B2

Your choice of activity will probably have caused you to think carefully about the difference between drama and dance. You may have decided that, whereas drama goes naturally with speaking and poetry, dance goes naturally with music. You may have decided that the ability of music to invoke emotion makes dance especially suitable for conveying simple, pure and direct human conflict or longing whereas drama is more suited to ideas, everyday life and narrative.

On the other hand you may also have made your choice on the basis of the facilities available to you. Drama needs entrances and exits and rudimentary scenery. Dance needs wide spaces and specialist footwear.

The question of the success or otherwise of a lesson must be set against the aims of the lesson and the abilities of the class with whom you are working. At the very least children should have learnt something from the lesson, where learning is broadly interpreted as becoming able to do or know something new. Perhaps they gained insights that were difficult to express in words. Perhaps they came to understand the power of human emotions, the ease within which individuals can be overcome by collective evil. If you were careful in your teaching, you will have made sure that the pupils did not simply learn that violence (selling Joseph; beating up a lone traveller) works. You will have shown that there is a remedy for suffering.

Pictorial art

In the Spring 1996 edition of the Christian Education Movement's journal *RE Today* there is an account by Howarth of a *Seder* meal, re-enacted at a primary school. The teacher had devised a series of activities to enable the pupils to engage with the festival, and to learn more of the Jewish people through the preparation for the festival. Some of the activities are listed below:

- decorating individual *Seder* dishes, allowing personalised 'place settings';
- making a *Hagadah* (order of service) for the children's own use at the meal;
- making individual *matzah* covers with Jewish symbols;
- making *kippot* (skull caps);
- arranging flowers for the table.

You will notice that the pupils were asked to use their own imaginations to complete tasks leading to their own celebration. Using the medium of art to copy the outlines of artefacts would mean that the pupils would have been assessed on their ability to reproduce visual images, quite a low-level task. By asking them to use their imaginations and personalising the activities, the teacher provided opportunities for engagement in a way that would enhance the pupils' understanding of the festival, and also allow them to relate the activities to their own lives.

Pictorial art may be used to capture the colour and vitality of religious traditions and to engage with some of the artefacts that are precious to believers. It can also be used to capture the moment of truth or tension in a story, formalise the expression of religious emotion and meditate upon and contextualise religious symbols.

Yeomans (1993) attempts to distinguish between sacred, religious and spiritual art. He defines the three categories in these ways: sacred art involves a special degree of sanctity, usually bound up with devotion and worship; religious art embodies narrative, a teaching function as well as spiritual meanings and values; spiritual art covers a broad spectrum of human feeling without necessarily being connected to, or bound by, a religious creed. He gives an overview of some artistic movements that inform a consideration of spiritual art, with particular reference to the early modernist period.

Activity B3

Using the story of the burning bush in Exodus chapter 3, explore the idea of God as fire. Find examples of artistic work on the passage, or related experiences and emotions from Yeoman's three areas of sacred, religious and spiritual to act as starting points. Working in groups, ask the pupils to produce a piece of art work that depicts God as fire.

Ask each group to work with different materials, including shiny paper, paint and a series of photographs of fires. When evaluating the work of each group, take particular note of their conversations as they produced the work. Would you say that this method of teaching was successful?

Comment on activity B3

The difficulty inherent in this activity is that of disentangling religious insight from artistic ability. There may be pupils who are clever at design or sensitive to the use of colour who are unimaginative and unwilling to entertain the existence of a spiritual dimension. There may be other pupils in exactly the reverse position: imaginative, sensitive to all the implications of God as a purifying, moving, mysterious fire, but unable to express these in an artistic way. The lesson will probably be a success if it is able to stimulate children to consider all the properties of fire, both singly and together, and to relate these to attributes of God as conveyed in the Exodus account.

Music

Response to God has always been enshrined in music. Pupils are familiar with their own participation in musical response during the act of worship in their school. Work on religious response through music might begin with a consideration of the hymns with which the pupils already have a familiarity. This will involve such questions as: who wrote this and why? What does the writer think God is like? How does the music show how the composer is feeling? How do you feel when you sing these hymns? From the territory of the familiar, pupils may be introduced to the music and chants from across a range of traditions, showing how these are used by worshippers, or in story-telling. They can examine the role of music in calling people to worship, with church bells, the Muslim *Call to Prayer* and the use of the bell in a Hindu *Puja Ceremony*. They can examine different musical traditions, in gospel music or Cathedral choirs. Alongside the formal use of music in worship, pupils could choose from a range of reflective music to achieve personal stillness, and consider how music is used in film and television to achieve the expression of emotion.

Green (1993) explores the way in which music relates to religious education by fostering the expressive and imaginative elements of religion. He quotes T. S. Eliot's observation that there is 'a fringe of indefinite extent' beyond the nameable and classifiable emotions of our conscious lives which only music can touch. Green's initial considerations are, however, severely practical and rooted in the need to make sure children think the work they do is fun. He recalls working on a class story with Noah and lots of animals and attempts to reproduce simple tunes for each animal. He also points out that a pastiche of, for instance, Indian music can aid the interpretation of a story from Indian religion.

Activity B4 (optional)

Desert Island Discs: choose five pieces of music that you would take away with you. Reflect on the reasons for your choices, on the emotions that these pieces of music evoke in you, and their connection with your life story. Then choose a portion of one of the Psalms that most closely connects with your reflections, and work out a simple score with a portion of the Psalm, and instruments that are to hand. You may now be in a better position to use music with a class!

Comment on activity B4

This is such a personal activity that we can offer no comment.

B3 Teaching through story

Hammond *et al* (1990, p 224) write about story:

> It is the ability of a story to convey vividly and with power, a particular incident or topic which makes it an essential element in values education.... Stories take us into the lives of the characters and through them we face dilemmas, weigh up alternatives and feel the consequences of an ill-considered or noble act.

Most teachers would agree that stories can hold the attention of pupils in a way that no other medium can achieve. The use of story in religious education nevertheless needs a strong rationale, since entertainment is not the primary consideration. Arthur (1988) has offered three reasons for the inclusion of story in the curriculum of religious education:

- it is a medium which encourages empathy;
- it possesses a unique cognitive potential which adds new dimensions to understanding;
- it is ideally suited to dealing with descriptively elusive material.

Arthur also identifies two pitfalls:

- since stories are often identified as material for the very young, there is a possibility that they will not be taken seriously;
- there is a widespread inability to recognise that a story may still be valuable, even if it is not true in the straightforward documentary sense.

Story is often best used when pupils are encouraged in astute questioning. To forestall the inevitable 'Is it true?' they should be encouraged instead to reflect on the questions: where are the truths in this story? Is there anything in this story that is true in your life?

Using examples from work based around children's stories, King (1992) emphasises the importance of choosing stories that enable pupils to gain a religious perspective on life. She claims that pupils have an innate capacity for awe and wonder which may be tapped by using this medium. She advocates the use of small group work to allow pupils to follow their own agenda, rather than the teacher's agenda.

Stories from the world religions

Story is an essential element within all religions. The written traditions themselves are very rich. They are the first point of contact for the nurture of young believers in all traditions, and also provide a means of opening up what might appear strange and alien to pupils in school.

One of the key points to appreciate in the examination of any story is the context in which it arose or, to put this another way, the reason why the story was first told and then written down. Some stories are explanatory, *aetiological* is the technical term, and account for customs or objects whose purpose seems impossible to explain. Howarth (1996) examines creation stories in this light, but the difficulty of this exercise is that, at this distance, we can only guess what the real original purpose of the story was. We may think the Genesis story was told to combat Babylonian polytheism, or to account for the variety of animal species and their inability to interbreed, or to explain the role of human beings in relation to the rest of the earth. But we do not know for sure what was in the mind of the first writer of the story and it is this that makes literary analysis an inexact discipline.

Parables make a virtue out of the multiple meanings they may generate. The Parable of the Prodigal Son may tell us about God, the father in the story, or about repentance (the younger son), or about jealousy (the older son), or about family relationships, or all three of these things. It is not designed to have a single, once and for all meaning, but can translate into different cultures and into different languages and still convey important religious truths. It is usually good practice to examine the meaning a story would have had for its original hearers, but that meaning, so far as we can ascertain it, does not exhaust the story's hermeneutical possibilities.

These two kinds of stories, creation stories and parables, illustrate the need to attempt to place stories in categories before using them with children. This might seem an exercise that detracts from the children's own open and free encounter with the story, but it should not be seen in this way since children themselves very early in their lives distinguish between fairy stories and space stories, between TV soaps and cartoons, between stories of things that happen to their friends and stories they read in books. In order to be faithful to the religion being taught it is helpful to attempt to categorise the story as the religion itself categorises it, rather than to impose an interpretative structure that comes from outside the religion. Religious people are rightly annoyed when a story which comes from their tradition and culture and which they have for centuries interpreted in one way is reclassified by a teacher from another culture who does not accept the tenets of their religion.

Fortunately, most religions do distinguish between teaching stories and historical accounts and this allows teachers to deal with one or other kind without doing violence to the religious tradition or to the religious traditions, if several are taught in fairly close succession.

In practical terms it is always best to begin this process by concentrating on the demands of the syllabus and to select stories that will support broad curricula aims and objectives, rather than beginning with a good story, without regard for the coherence of the pupils' learning. If you are going to select biblical material, then you would be wise to choose material that:

- supports the teaching of the religious education syllabus;
- is suitable for the developmental age of the pupils;
- will catch the interest and enthusiasm of the pupils;
- will support a deeper understanding of Christianity or Judaism.

When teaching stories from the bible it is of paramount importance to ensure that the context and general background of the story are understood. Good introductory handbooks are usually sufficiently informative.

Watson (1993a) examines some possible attitudes for teaching about and from the bible, including treating it 'like any other book'. She looks at possible interpretations of biblical material, including a spectrum of Jewish opinion. She summarises these main purposes for work on the bible in religious education:

- to help pupils appreciate what a religious response to the bible involves and how it can support faith in a basic way;

- to help pupils appreciate how, for both Jews and Christians, the bible is regarded with reverence and plays a significant part in public worship and private devotion;
- to give some knowledge of the techniques of historical and literary analysis as applied to biblical material, by enabling pupils to practise these techniques in a simple way themselves, and in so doing become better informed;
- to enable pupils to think theologically in relation to the text, in order to discover whether or not religious faith is reasonable, and to stimulate authentic thinking about it.

A more subtle set of questions about narratives is posed by Gooderham (1994). He sets out to explore the relationship between religious education and narrative texts written for children and young people, and the use of such texts in spiritual and moral development. He begins with an historical retrospect, and goes on to distinguish types of literary theory that would be useful in understanding how narrative texts might influence pupils. He gives an account of the distinction between texts which emphasise communication between different ages and different groups, and those which are written in order to call into question historical and cultural mediation. As a result of the work of the literary theorists it is acknowledged that the recovery of pasts and other cultures and an openness to possible futures may not be separated. He compares the terms 'participation' and 'distanciation' with the more familiar 'commitment' and 'openness'. Gooderham asks the question whether both understanding and critical distance may be taught to children of any age through narrative texts. He advocates the use of texts both as mediators of tradition and vehicles for opening up questions and future possibilities.

As a general rule pupils may be introduced to a variety of sacred texts by starting with short selected passages. In the examination of the way these texts are revered, pupils may come to an understanding of the importance of them in the lives of believers. Thus the treatment of the Guru Granth Sahib in a gurudwara or the Torah scrolls in the synagogue ark or the bible on a church lectern all signal the importance of these texts to the worshipping community.

Activity B5

Researching in a children's library, try to identify texts that:

- steer pupils towards a certain worldview, without encouraging the possibility of questioning;
- contain the two elements of participation and distanciation.

Do you think that the context of the church school should make a difference to Gooderham's argument?

Comment on activity B5

You may have found this activity more difficult than you thought at first. This is because the worldview implicit within a text is embedded so deeply that there are no obvious criteria for distinguishing between elements within a story that are just there as a piece of imaginative furniture and other features that push children towards a worldview. A ghost story, for example, only makes sense if there are ghosts and so it could be said that such a story pushes children towards a worldview where ghosts exist. Against this, it could be argued that a ghost story is like a fairy story that has its own conventions and style and that all it presses children into is a worldview that contains different cultural viewpoints. So the difficulty is to decide whether ghosts support a worldview or are arbitrarily placed in a story simply to make the plot move forwards.

Gooderham's argument has relevance to a church school in the sense that church schools should be willing to examine the Christian faith as well as to teach it and celebrate it.

B4 Using different media

More than most curriculum subjects, religion touches the totality of human life and, for this reason, is accessible to transmission by a wide variety of teaching media. All the media listed below might be used in a religious education lesson:

- cassette recorder;
- camera;
- cassettes;
- school grounds;
- design tools;
- atlases;
- video camera;
- video tapes;
- musical instruments;
- local area;
- food technology;
- calligraphy.

What nearly all these teaching media encourage is an *experience* of religion, a visit to a mosque, a video recording of a temple, and so on, and this encouragement fits well with experiential and phenomenological methods of teaching religion outlined in the module *Philosophy of Religious Education*. At the same time they have another implication: they show that it is possible to start teaching religion from the present day (a visit to a place of worship[1]) and relate this worship to the ancient sacred texts or to start at the ancient sacred texts and move forward to the present day. Text-based lessons may tend to be historical in perspective; experience-based lessons may tend to be more contemporary, though it is important to stress that this is not a hard and fast law and that texts can be experienced and that video material, for instance, can convey the size and shape of buildings in ancient times. Virtual reality representations of architectural structures enable us to walk inside the pyramids, for example, or to see Stonehenge as it originally looked.

Consequently syllabus construction for religious education becomes flexible once a range of media is utilised. As long as pupils can understand the rationale behind the use of various media the danger of an unstructured or disconnected set of learning experiences is avoided.

B5 Visits and visitors

Despite dire warnings of the secularisation of society, religious communities continue to play an important part in the contemporary world. Video and audio presentations of religion are valuable, but they remain a substitute for an encounter with a real place of worship or religious people who can answer the questions religion raises in the minds of pupils.

The pupils themselves may have no personal experience of faith, but they nevertheless should have the opportunity to meet believers face to face and to experience visits to places of worship. Many church schools make good use of their excellent links with local churches, and it may be a familiar experience for pupils to have contact with clergy, congregations and the churches themselves. Although these experiences are indispensable, pupils should also have opportunities to visit and be visited by a range of faith communities.

Muller (1994) encourages teachers to regard a visit to a cathedral as an opportunity to study it in its totality, in order that its nature as a spiritual building be understood. He suggests that an approach which concentrates on history alone will produce the attitude 'one destroys in order to dissect', and gives some practical examples of how a holistic programme might be achieved:

---

[1] All church schools are religious foundations. This may seem self-evident, but it is often a neglected part of the religious education curriculum. Many who work at church schools do so within the context of personal Christian faith. The school will often have close connections with its local church. This context enables creative work based on the school and the (church) community. This could include research on the history of the school, gleaned from sources such as the School Mission Statement and log-book, the local church, the diocesan office or local record office. It could also include making use of the staff of the school, in terms of asking some of them to share their experiences with the pupils.

The cathedral stands as a place where one confronts humanity and where humanity confronts God. In the light of recent comments from the Secretary of State for Education regarding the need to address spirituality, it is fair to say that no other building is quite so dedicated to spirituality as a cathedral.

Visiting faith communities

Although finance is a real issue in many schools, there is a strong argument for placing religious education on a par with history and geography in its need for field-trips. Most church schools will find that visits to the local Anglican church are a regular feature of the life of the school, but pupils need a more varied experience to inform their learning in religious education.

Homan (1993) recognises religious buildings as being rich and stimulating religious resources, but regrets that school visits often take place at a time when the worshipping community is absent. He makes a distinction between first-hand and second-hand learning, or direct and indirect learning during a visit. Direct learning is characterised by involvement, where the pupil experience may be similar to that of the believing worshipper. Indirect learning is characterised by detachment, and involves the pupils in observational learning. As soon as pupils enter a religious building they are encroaching on sacred space, which might be marked by the removal or donning of clothing or shoes, or other rituals. Homan takes the matter of 'boundary maintenance' seriously, asking what ritual behaviour might be appropriate for pupils on a visit. He favours the definition drawn from the work of Hammond and Hay (1990), where the pupil visitor is likened to the reader, who enters a novel without being part of it.

If you were to prepare a visit to a mosque, for instance, you would need to:

- write a letter to parents, explaining clearly the educational purposes of the visit;
- work out your own plan for the visit, taking into account Holman's warnings about the tension between experiencing and observing;
- write a letter to the Muslim community, explaining your needs and asking for specific help;
- devise a means of assessing whether the visit has achieved the learning objectives you planned.

Visitors to the classroom

Many teachers are rightly nervous of embarking on teaching in areas where they have little knowledge and no personal experience. One way of overcoming this difficulty is to arrange for faith visitors to visit the school. In this way the study comes alive for the pupils because it is grounded in a relationship, and an account of somebody's life, rather than in an abstract concept, 'Christianity' or 'Buddhism'. Many faith groups can provide visitors who are skilled in communicating with pupils and present their faith in a clear and exciting way. When a fee is involved schools might join together to bear the cost and to share the experience, perhaps across a year group.

As an example of how you might go about integrating a visitor's contribution into a scheme of work, for example, on Hindu worship at home, you might first show pupils a video on the topic and begin work on the story of Rama and Sita. The Hindu visitor would then be invited to the classroom and the following points would be explained:

- the aims of this unit of work;
- any knowledge and understanding that the children have already gained;
- the aims of the visit itself;
- a request that the visitor bring suitable items to show the children;
- the planned follow-up work after the visitor's departure.

Religious education and computers

The best of Internet or CD-ROM sources of information on religion are designed to be interactive so that pupils may do their own research at the screen. Not only does this enable pupils to become active learners, it also releases teachers from the tyranny of believing that they need to know every detail of a religious practice or belief before they can embark on teaching. Although the resource base in religious education is presently rather thin, there is every indication that the use of information technology as a teaching tool will become increasingly important, and this development will have huge implications for religious education as well as other areas of the curriculum.

Using the internet

Since technology moves so rapidly there is little point in providing Internet addresses for research. However there are areas with which you can begin:

- *Internet search engines:* all service providers give access to the facility to make searches for information, which will include multi-media information.
- *School exchange programmes:* there are several sites that enable pupils to connect with other countries in order to exchange messages by e-mail. This is an appropriate resource when studying religions, including Christianity, where young people may ask questions directly to believers in other countries, or of other cultures to their own.

- *Access to religious sites:* instead of learning from books or video pupils may log directly into sites such as the Vatican or the Archbishop of Canterbury's homepage.
- *Dedicated educational providers:* schools may buy into the services of a provider who runs pages dedicated to education. Many of these include areas for religious education, with links to other parts of the World Wide Web.

Activity B6

Spend some time with the information technology co-ordinator at your school (if you hold this position, contact your local advisory staff instead). Work out a development plan for the use of information technology in religious education over a period of three years. If you are able, try to cost the plan in terms of equipment and staff training.

Comment on activity B6

You would need to survey the whole field of information technology to assess what would be the most suitable point of entry for your school. You might consider that it would be best to have one computer linked up to the Internet and several with CD-ROMs or *vice versa*. You would need to decide what type of information technology would fit your school's religious education syllabus and its information technology syllabus and whether a match between the two could be found.

Once you had decided on the equipment necessary to deliver a particular syllabus, you would also have to decide whether modifications to the syllabus should be made in the light of the possibilities inherent in the capabilities of information technology. You would then need to work out a series of phases by which information technology and any syllabus changes would be introduced to the school, and any training requirements for staff would have to be fitted at the correct point in the phasing.

You would also need to decide which age group ought to employ information technology in religious education. Would it be best to offer it to younger children, or would older ones appreciate the new resources more? At each point in the process, you would need to review the appropriate Key Stage targets for information technology and religious education to ensure the resources fitted the developmental sequence implied.

We cannot comment on costing since prices fluctuate.

B6 Affective religious education

Although religious education has an academic base and concerns itself with knowledge and understanding, it also lays stress on *engagement*. Although the results of this engagement cannot be anticipated, this aim opens up the possibility that learning will affect the pupil, not just in terms of thinking but also in the areas of the emotions and personal development. In the book *Don't Just Do Something: sit there*, Mary Stone (1992) outlines some of the processes involved in using the methodologies of stilling, relaxation and visualisation in order to promote spiritual development in pupils. She lists the skills and capacities that pupils need to develop (p 6):

- being physically still, yet alert;
- being mentally still while being able to concentrate on the present moment;
- the ability to use all one's senses;
- an awareness of and enjoyment in using one's imaginative potential;
- quiet reflection during a lesson;
- individual self-confidence in expressing inner thoughts in a variety of ways;
- an inner peace;
- an appreciation that we arrive at some of our deepest insights through stillness and silence, whatever our religious convictions;
- an appreciation that silence can be a means of communication.

Religious education and the imagination

To speak about the metaphysical is to stretch language to breaking-point. In asking pupils to express opinions about the spiritual dimension and divine realities, teachers are asking pupils to step outside their usual empirical framework and to engage with those areas that are outside our day-to-day descriptive powers. In order to do this pupils need to have a vivid and active imagination. Teachers working in this area need to have a heightened awareness of the vulnerability of the pupils who undertake affective experiences in the classroom.

Watson (1993a) draws attention to the difference between a personal religious experience and the membership of a religious tradition. She sees four weaknesses in the experiential approach:

- it can be taught in a way that only touches upon the major religious traditions, with the possible exceptions of Buddhism and Hinduism;
- although the pupils seem to be enjoying freedom in their thinking, guiding by the teacher may influence them deeply and unpredictably; many experiential methods seem to favour the abandonment of the rational sense and an acceptance of subjective values;

- pupils may become confused between the activities of introspection and meditation, that is, self-centredness and centredness;
- the expectation that pupils will approach the work with an open mind is well-nigh impossible because everyone interprets in the light of what is already known and expected.

Activity B7

Using three examples of teaching methodologies drawn from *New Methods in RE Teaching* by Hammond *et al* (1990), critique these activities using Watson's (1993a) criticisms in the points above. Are you convinced by her objections?

Three possible exercises:

- (p 105) If I was a ... (a selection of objects, toy car, toy animal, piece of fruit etc.). Pupils are asked to choose one of the objects. If I was a car, what kind of car would I be? Let children share and compare their answers. What made individuals choose the way they did? How did they feel about their choices?
- (p 113) Working in pairs couples demonstrate how they walk and then try to experience their partner's way of walking.
- (p 118) Children are asked to concentrate on an object in the room (for instance, a soft shoe), and to try to become it. They should think of three qualities that it possesses. After this, they should introduce themselves to a partner using these qualities. How far can the partner identify the qualities?

Comment on activity B7

None of the exercises given by Hammond *et al* touch upon religious traditions. They are entirely secular and mundane. There is an enormous difference between imagining you are a shoe and imagining that you are about to engage in a ritual act, say, of sacrifice or a rite that involves human pain and mutilation. According to Piagetian psychology, one of the first things babies learn is where their own bodies end and where the rest of the world begins. In early childhood the confusion between fantasy and reality is often the basis for games but little is known about the effects of asking adults to encourage this confusion. Little is also known about the psychological effects of fostering fantasy and it seems reasonable to ask that further research should be done to clarify what the long-term effects might be, especially since some forms of mental illness are identifiable precisely by the delusions that are characteristic of them. Paranoia often manifests itself by a fear of persecution and schizophrenia by the hearing of voices. Children in danger of developing these kinds of mental illness would probably be badly damaged by using imaginative techniques, even though the ones given in the exercises here appear to be harmless enough. You may have reason to disagree with these comments and, if so, you should ensure your argument is soundly based on evidence.

Religious education and the emotions

Hammond *et al* (1990, p 10) point out:

> It is very easy to take an interest in religions because of their colourful customs, the beauty of their architecture, ceremonies or art forms, because of their doctrinal and ethical beliefs, or even because of the political power they exert. But if we fail to grasp that all of these things have grown up as a response to the experience of a sacred dimension to reality, we can have no understanding of the religious believer.

Working with affective (that is, feeling-based) methodologies means abandoning the position of the outside observer and attempting to enter into the experience of the believer in order to gain an empathetic understanding. It means engaging the emotions so that results and outcomes are not entirely predictable. This involves the teacher in risk-taking and responsibility, and the possibilities for emotional abuse will always be present. These dangers may be minimised by meticulous and rational planning that builds in a determination to be sensitive to possible pupil reactions and a time for evaluation.

Affective methodologies cannot be used successfully without establishing a suitable atmosphere in the classroom, and a calm manner in the pupils. A variety of techniques are available to us through religious traditions to help with the problem of slowing down in a world which values frantic activity. Some of these techniques entail:

- enjoying silence, starting with short periods and building up to five minutes;
- learning how to relax, by tensing and relaxing limbs, visualising a relaxing cat;
- clearing the mind, watch your thoughts as if they are appearing on a computer screen, then press the break key;
- paying attention to breathing and bodily sensations.

Hammond *et al* (1990, p 219) point out:

> Guided imagery as a means to open the door on our spiritual natures has a long and honoured tradition amongst the major world religions   Most cultures throughout history have employed fantasy as the traditional place where human beings transcend themselves and communicate with what they understand to be the ultimate.

Guided imagery is a means of developing a story within the pupils' imagination. A script is used as a basis, giving a chain of events through which the pupils are led, allowing them to build up their own picture of the details in their minds. Usually they then reflect on and evaluate what they have been guided through to draw out any possible understanding of others' circumstances, as a means of developing empathy.

To give an example of the kind of instructions that are given for this sort of work, here is an excerpt on the story of Jairus' daughter from the Diocese of Chester *Religious Education Guidelines* (1996):

> You are Jairus, and your 12 year old daughter is very ill. Walk along as if you are Jairus, trying to get through the crowds to Jesus. Hurry! Your daughter could die! You have found Jesus and he has agreed to come. Start to lead him to your house. You must wait while he heals a woman and she thanks him. One of your servants comes and tells you that your daughter has died. Show by your face and body how you feel. Jesus says: Only believe and she will be well. Show what you think by the expression on your face. You lead Jesus back to your house where all your neighbours are crying out loud. Jesus tells you to send them home. Show how you do this and then greet your wife. Inside your house you see your daughter lying on her bed. Go up to her and show me what you do. You watch Jesus holding her hand and suddenly she sits up. What do you do? How do you feel? What do you say?

Guided imaginative journeys offer a teaching method that requires almost no resources, an opportunity to come close to religious events or phenomena and a quite different kind of activity from that used in other curriculum areas. But concerns about the method have been expressed by various writers, including Thatcher (1993), who has argued that the whole notion of inwardness is misplaced in the sense that it differentiates between outward and inward parts of the human being when the human being should be seen as a whole without two quite separate modes of being.

B7 Special educational needs

The Special Educational Needs Code of Practice (James, 1995) requires Individual Education Plans to be used in order to plan, implement and review pupils' work. Brown (1996) suggests that this will include:

- the delivery of carefully structured teaching approaches;
- providing imaginative learning experiences which arouse and sustain the children's interest;
- supporting the learning that takes place in religious education in other curriculum areas.

As an example of how the topic of baptism might be planned she suggests the following sensory learning experiences:

- carefully look at the baptism clothes and notice how tiny they are;
- explore the shape of the cross with your fingers;
- watch the curving beauty of the candle flame;
- look at the greeting cards and notice the pictures on them; find any symbols which match the pictures on the card;
- look at the glass jug of water; move close to the jug and notice how clean the water looks;
- pick some pink or blue summer flowers and put them in a vase; smell the flowers;
- carefully open the prayer book and find the baptism service; put the ribbon marker at the first page of the service;
- share a cake decorated with icing.

B8 Creativity in the classroom

In aiming for truly creative religious education in the theological and educational senses explored at the beginning of this unit, there will inevitably be a tension between planning and spontaneity. Certainly, some of the most creative and rewarding work will occur at unexpected and unplanned moments, and it is a wise teacher who knows when to abandon carefully planned activities in order to respond to unexpected inspiration.

In Hammond *et al* (1990) Straugheir, a secondary teacher, reflects on the effect of changing her classroom furniture arrangement on learning. Pupils reacted favourably to carpets, posters, notice-boards, heating and space. Circle time also proved valuable in acquiring a sense of privacy. Pupils appreciated freedom to choose some aspects of their physical environment.

Few teachers have much room to manoeuvre by changing their environments but, by skilful use of the geography of a classroom, space can facilitate relaxation, artistic activities, a partnership in exploring the spiritual dimension between the teacher and pupils and space to reflect privately.

Assessing, recording and reporting

Assessment should always aid teaching and bear a direct relationship to it and no distinctions should be made between formal or experiential teaching methods. A variety of assessment methods should be used. These might include oral work (perhaps interviews), practical work (things made by pupils), written work (of an open-ended and creative kind) and teacher observation of pupils' contributions to discussion groups. Variety is the key to good assessment since this ensures a thorough sampling of pupil attainments possible.

Watson (1993a) addresses the question of whether assessment in religious education is a desirable thing, and notes that there are arguments both ways: religion and spirituality might be destroyed if they were interfered with by assessment; on the other hand, there are elements within any teaching system, and within the teaching of religion, which are assessable. For instance, assessment might be based usefully on the following four areas:

- *knowledge* of basic factual information about religions;
- *understanding* of the ways religious beliefs are expressed;
- *evaluation* of whether skills appropriate to religious education are being developed and whether there is an appreciation of the controversial nature of religion and the need to make informed judgements about it;
- *personal* in the sense of looking for appreciation, motivation, participation in the subject matter to hand.

B9 Conclusion

Now you have reached the end of this unit you should be in a position to review whether you have met the learning outcomes of this unit.

Readers

There are chapters in J. Astley and L.J. Francis (eds) (1994), *Critical Perspectives on Christian Education*, Leominster, Gracewing, which provide insights into religious education in the classroom.

Bibliography

Alcock, J. (1993), Spirituality, religious education and the dramatic arts: occasions of comfort and celebration, in D. Starkings (ed.), *Religion and the Arts in Education*, London, Hodder and Stoughton, pp 169-178.

Arthur, C.J. (1988), Some arguments for the use of stories in religious education, *British Journal of Religious Education*, 10, 122-127.

Bastide, D. (1992), *Good Practice in Primary Religious Education 4-11*, London, Falmer Press .

Brown, A. (1992), *The Multi-Faith Church School*, London, The National Society.

Brown, E. (1996), *Religious Education For All*, London, David Fulton.

Fleming, K. (1992), Drama as a teaching strategy in primary RE, in D. Bastide (ed.), *Good Practice in Primary Religious Education 4-11*, London, Falmer Press, pp 164-171.

Gooderham, D. (1994), Participation and distanciation: contemporary children's and adolescent literature in religious education, *British Journal of Religious Education*, 16, 164-173.

Green, R. (1993), Explorations in music and religion, in D. Starkings (ed.), *Religion and the Arts in Education*, London, Hodder and Stoughton. pp 159-168.

Hammond J., Hay D., Moxon J., Netto B., Raban K., Straugheir G. and Williams C. (1990), *New Methods in RE Teaching: an experiential approach*, Harlow, Oliver and Boyd.

Hay, D. and Hammond, D. (1992), 'When you pray, go to your private room' A reply to Adrian Thatcher, *British Journal of Religious Education*, 14, 145-150.

Homan, R. (1993), Visiting religious buildings, *British Journal of Religious Education* 16, 7-13.

Howarth, R.B. (1996), Creation stories: how do they influence lifestyles today? *RE Today*, 13, 12-13.

James, F. (1995), *The Special Needs Code of Practice*, London, Primary File Publishing.

King, C. (1992), The place of story in RE, in D. Bastide (ed.), *Good Practice in Primary Religious Education 4-11*, London, Falmer Press, pp 143-163.

Lankshear, D.W. (1992), *Looking For Quality in a Church School*, London, The National Society.

Lealman, B. (1993), Drum, whalebone and dominant X: a model for creativity, in D. Starkings (ed.) *Religion and the Arts in Education*, London, Hodder and Stoughton, pp 55-66.

Muller, A. (1994), Cathedrals through the whole curriculum: a contribution to spirituality, *British Journal of Religious Education*, 6, 82-89.

Starkings, D. (ed.) (1993), *Religion and the Arts in Education*, London, Hodder and Stoughton.

Stone, M. (1992), *Don't Just Do Something: sit there*, Lancaster, St Martin's College.

Thatcher, A. (1993), Spirituality without inwardness, *Scottish Journal of Theology*, 46, 213-228.

Waddup, H. (1992), Planning RE across an infant school, in D. Bastide (ed.), *Good Practice in Primary Religious Education 4-11*, London, Falmer Press, pp 24-46.

Watson, B. (1993a), *The Effective Teaching of Religious Education*, London, Longman.

Watson, B. (1993b), The arts as a dimension of religion, in D. Starkings (ed.), *Religion and the Arts in Education*, London, Hodder and Stoughton, pp 95-105.

Yeomans, R. (1993), Religious art and spiritual art: spiritual values and early modernist painting, in D. Starkings (ed.), *Religion and the Arts in Education*, London, Hodder and Stoughton, pp 70-82.

Method in Religious Education

Unit C

Action research

Dr William K. Kay

Trinity College

Carmarthen

Contents

Introduction

Aims

After working through this unit you should be able to:

- improve the quality of your own teaching or administration;
- evaluate important pieces of research carried out in the past;
- put your own beliefs and practices into a wider context;
- appreciate the impact of educational research on the historical development of education;
- describe some of the main forms of educational research;
- carry out action research relating to religious education;
- prepare for the elective module on educational research.

Overview

Our intention in this unit is to help you relate what you do as a teacher to educational research. This unit fits in with the earlier units in this module in the sense that various methodologies of religious education have been developed or tested using forms of educational research.

There is a constant search for better methods of teaching children and young people. There is a constant search for better methods of understanding the way children and young people learn. There is also a constant search for better methods of education, methods which are suited to the changing needs of society and the changing priorities of government policy. Educational research is one of the main tools by which this series of searches is carried out.

The main focus of this unit is upon one specific form of research, that is, 'action research'. But we are going to approach action research through a brief tour of other forms of research. This is because action research uses the findings or methods of other forms of research. As we shall see, one of the things that distinguishes action research is that it is *action* research: it is research carried out by people taking part in what they are researching. And it usually carries with it the aim of bringing about a change of policy or procedure or, in a word, action.

C1 What is educational research?

Educational research fits within the broad framework of research in general. Research in general fits within two other frameworks, the framework of science and the framework of epistemology (or the philosophy of knowledge). These are complicated subjects with histories reaching back to the classical speculations of the early Greeks. They have been part of western civilisation since its beginnings.

Research in more modern times, since the regular collecting of information for the purposes of planning and administration, has been regularised and supported both by government agencies and within academic departments of higher education.

Yet, for all its complexity and history, research is also, in some ways, simple. The simplicity arises from the goals of research. First, it is designed to find out what is 'really the case' or 'what really happened' or 'what would happen if...'. In other words, it is designed to obtain secure information about the past, the present or the future. Second, it is designed to enable rational decisions to be made on the basis of secure information.

Basic research is part of the normal behaviour of intelligent human beings. When we make enquiries about a train timetable or check the prices of food we are, in a sense, doing simple research. We are collecting information in order to make rational decisions. Train timetables tell us (in theory!) what is going to happen in the future so that we can plan accordingly. Today's food prices give us the best value for our meal tonight. Because there are all kinds of situations in which we might have to make decisions and, equally, because there are all kinds of information on which we might wish to base our decisions, there are many kinds of research.

Activity C1

Imagine that you are going for a job interview. What information do you want from the school before you are prepared to consider taking the post?

Imagine that you are going to buy a pair of shoes. What information do you want before you make the purchase?

Imagine you are interested in going to visit the house where your grandparents used to live when they were first married. What information do you need before you make the visit?

Look at the three types of information you have collected. In what ways are they similar? In what ways are they different?

Comment on activity C1

Here are some of the points you might have written down.

First, for the job interview, you might be interested in the job description, the catchment area of the school, the size of the school, the religious basis of the school (is it voluntary aided or controlled?), the policies and prospectus of the school, the last OFSTED report on the school, the pay scale you would be placed on, your prospects for promotion, the friendliness of staff and pupils and the ease or difficulty of your journey to work.

Second, for the pair of shoes, you might be interested in the colour, style, make and price of the shoes, but especially whether they were comfortable.

Third, for your grandparents' house, you would want to find exactly where the property was. The streets or roads nearby might have been changed. The property itself might have been altered. Perhaps you would need to find documentation about your grandparents (a wedding certificate, a will, a photograph or letter) to show you where they used to live. You might need to consult the local planning department if there had been considerable redevelopment in the area. Once you had found exactly where it was, you would need to contact the present owner to ask permission to look inside the property.

How do these types of information differ? In the main, the information about the school is to do with the present and the future, while the information to do with your grandparents is to do with the past.

Yet one of the main distinctions occurs because some of the information is objective and some is subjective and/or private. The information to do with the school is largely public and objective information (the policies and prospectuses, for instance) but also private and subjective. Are the staff friendly to you? Do you like the headteacher? The information to do with your grandparents might also be partly private (letters, for instance) and public (from the planning department). Again, the information about the shoes is partly public (their price or make) and partly private (their level of comfort). What we notice, then, is that some of the information is public and objective and some of it is personal and subjective.

Methods of research

In this unit we consider the use of surveys, case studies, correlational research, quasi-experimental research, ethnographic research, interviews, personal constructs or action research. Because we devote a whole elective module to the subject of research methods our coverage here is introductory.

Each method has its own strengths and weaknesses, and we shall draw attention to these. Each method is more or less suited to gathering certain kinds of information, and we shall also draw attention to this.

C2 Surveys

Surveys are intended to find out about particular populations, where the word 'population' is used in a slightly technical sense. It refers to a defined group of people. We can talk about the population of 14 year old girls or the population of homeowners. The survey might focus on fairly precise information like eating and smoking habits, earnings or how many hours of television children of a certain age watch each week, but it can also be used to collect less tangible information like opinions, beliefs or attitudes. In practice, any characteristic of a particular population may be surveyed and, obviously, a survey of people's weight is going to be carried out slightly differently from a survey of favourite television programmes. The first will use some type of weighing machine and an agreed unit of measurement (kilograms or stones and pounds) and the second will require asking questions which probably entail grading programmes in terms of preference.

Surveys very frequently make use of questionnaires though, in the example above, if we wanted to know about the weight of children, it would probably be better to arrange for them to be weighed by a teacher or researcher. Children could not be relied on to know their own weights as accurately. Whenever surveys making use of questionnaires are employed, however, they must be designed so that the questions are completely unambiguous and easy to understand. When people give answers to these questions, they can do so either 'open endedly' in their own words or by means of a set of possible responses which have been defined in advance and which cover every option. For instance, if you ask, 'do you like maths', it would not be sufficient only to offer the responses 'yes' or 'no' since children might like some aspects of maths and dislike others or like maths only when it is taught by some teachers.

It is normal when using surveys to approach a sample of the population which is being targeted. So, if you are interested in how well ten year old boys in England understand ecology, it is more or less impossible to speak to all of them. By the time you have got round to them all the children who are ten are now aged eleven! So, one has to approach a sample of ten year olds. The important thing here is to make sure that the sample is representative, that is, it truly has the characteristics of the target population. The main way in which this is done is by approaching a random selection of the target population. The theory here is that unusual aspects of the population will cancel each other out through the process of random selection. It might be, for example, that boys who live in the countryside are much more interested in the environment than boys who live in towns. A random selection would include both kinds of boy and would allow a generalisation to be made from the sample to the whole target population.

The trouble with a survey is that there are certain questions beyond its range. It cannot deal with information which is unknown to the respondent. There are lots of factors involved in education of which children are unaware. Their parents or teachers may be able to supply some of this information, but a survey of pupils would be of no use. In addition, and more crucially in some instances, surveys have difficulty in pinpointing interactions between people: between children in the classroom, between children and teachers, between children and parents. Interactions can only be assessed by collecting information from all the parties involved.

As we shall see, action research attempts to deal holistically with a classroom. It attempts to show how the class, teacher, school all relate to each other.

Activity C2

Imagine that you were carrying out a research project about food in school. As part of this, and using a questionnaire, what questions would you need to ask to find out what children thought about school meals?

Try to work out the phrasing of the questions you would ask about school meals and the pre-set responses you would offer children.

Comment on activity C2

Your assessment of school meals takes place within a larger project about food in school. You might wish to consider links between food offered at dinner time and food children had learnt about as part of their classroom work. You might wish to find out what food children enjoy eating. Alternatively, you might be interested in what children know about the nutritional value of various kinds of food.

Your questions should be clear and easy to understand. It is better to ask a lot of short questions than to try to find everything out in one long and complicated question. The answers you offer should cover the full range of possibilities. This prevents children being forced to choose an answer that does not express their thoughts as satisfactorily as they would like.

For instance, you might ask, 'Do you eat all of your school dinner?' and offer the responses, 'always', 'usually', 'only occasionally' and 'never'. For further clarification, you might follow this up by dividing the first course from the pudding. So you might ask, 'Do you nearly always eat your first course?' and offer the responses, 'yes', 'usually', 'only occasionally' and 'never' and then ask the same question about pudding and offer the same responses. Notice that by asking a question or set of questions about what children usually do, you can establish a baseline. You can then go on to construct questions about which foods they enjoy. Do they like vegetables? Are they keen on chocolate pudding, do they hate custard, and so on?

C3 Case studies

Observation schedules are often part of the case study approach. Here an observer makes a detailed record of behaviour during a set time span. For instance, an observer can chart how often a teacher asks a question to the class, how often a teacher uses the blackboard, how often a teacher reads aloud, how often a teacher gives instruction, how often a teacher praises students, how often a teacher works with a group or an individual or the class as a whole. The schedule builds up a profile of the activities of a teacher and allows an analysis of his or her typical teaching style. The method is painstaking and laborious, but it is largely objective and can be applied in many kinds of situation.

Case studies also often make use of participant observation. In other words, one of the participants in a particular activity is also an observer. This sort of research is less easy to apply to the classroom but it has been used to monitor congregational behaviour in church. The observer attends a church service and participates in the service, but his or her real intention is to make a record of what goes on for later analysis. It is clear that the participant observer is really carrying out two roles at once. The strength of this method is that the observer is fully involved in the interactions he or she is recording. The weakness of the method is exactly the same. It is very difficult to observe and participate simultaneously. Moreover it is often the case that, where other people know that a participant is also an observer, they will treat him or her differently.

Nevertheless case studies are extremely useful. They have the additional advantage of making use of a wide range of information in addition to the observation of participants. For example, a case study of two schools would draw upon as much documentation relating to the schools as possible. Inspection of schools is, in effect, a form of case study. The inspection team reads the school's prospectuses, policy documents, records and minutes of PTFA meetings and staff meetings and adds to these observation of staff interactions within the staff room and staff interaction with children and parents in the appropriate settings. From all this information an attempt is made to assess the value and effectiveness of the education being offered.

The real weakness of this approach, however, is that it is very difficult to decide whether generalisations can be made from individual case studies to other situations. Can we really suggest that school A in a little Scottish village is going to be similar to school B situated in a little Welsh village? We simply do not know. So the strength of the survey method is that it allows generalisations to be made. The weakness of the case study method is that it cannot permit generalisations. If we tried to generalise from case studies we would have to assume what we were attempting to find out: namely that schools we studied were similar to the schools we did not study. The only way we could show the similarity would be by carrying out case studies on each school or making use of information which had been gained by other means, for instance, by surveys.

C4 Correlational research

This kind of research depends on the possibility of showing how strongly variables relate to each other. Variables are measurements, like height and weight, which vary. You will have noticed that taller people tend to be heavier, but that this is not always the case since there are short heavy people and tall light people. In general height and weight seem connected. But how strong is this connection? A correlation coefficient gives the answer to this question.

The correlation coefficient is a number between +1 and -1. Perfect positive correlation is +1 and perfect negative correlation is -1. No correlation at all works out as 0. What this means is that, if a correlation approaching +1 is found, then the two sets of figures increase together: height and weight increase together. Conversely, if the correlation approaches -1, then as one number becomes larger the other one becomes smaller. The size of the correlation between height and weight indicates the strength of the relationship and the positiveness or negativeness of the correlation indicates whether weight increases with height, as we suppose it does, or whether it decreases with height.

Correlational research in education examines the relationships between features of the educational process which can be measured. Do levels on maths achievement correlate with levels on English achievement? Or do levels on maths achievement correlate more strongly with levels of achievement on information technology? How strongly does attitude toward Christianity correlate with church attendance or social class or age? Is attitude toward Christianity correlated with success in GCSE religious studies?

The advantage of this kind of research is that, when it makes use of statistics which are routinely collected for the purposes of administration, no real interruption within the educational process need be made. Exam results and school size, or exam results and age, for instance, can be correlated and general and wide-ranging findings can be reached.

This kind of research has the added advantage of being able to show the strength of a relationship. Other kinds may show that a relationship exists, or that where one feature of a situation is found, another is not far away (where there is truancy, there may be drug abuse), but correlations show quite precisely just how strong this connection is. Moreover, there is another advantage of correlational research: it can be combined with information provided by surveys.

The weakness of this kind of research is that it is possible that two variables may relate to each other, but only relate because of a third and, if the third is not identified, then the relationship may appear to be stronger than it is. For instance, height and weight in children are also related to age. As children grow older, they also grow taller. As they grow taller, they grow heavier. But even when they do not grow taller, they still grow heavier (especially after puberty). In order to obtain a full picture, it is necessary to take the 'intervening' variable of age into account.

C5 Quasi-experimental research

Most of us learn what experiments are in science lessons at school. We are presented with water, alcohol and milk and have to find out which one of these substances has the highest boiling point. It is very simple. Heat is applied. The liquids are observed and, when they start to bubble, you take the temperature. The experiment consists in treating three different substances in the same way and observing differences in outcome.

This is the essence of one form of experimental research. All kinds of problems and situations can be tested in this way. For instance, you might take two groups of children and offer them different mathematics curricula and test them at the end of the process. Which group does better? It is the same principle as is involved in boiling water, alcohol and milk. Before we start we need to make sure that the things we are testing are in the same state. In the case of the children, we need to make sure that both groups operate at equal standards of mathematics before they take the two different curricula. If we do not make certain of this we may misunderstand our outcomes. If we were interested in how fast water, alcohol and milk heated up, we would have to make sure that they started at the same temperature.

But research design can become complicated when we are testing for two effects which may interact with each other. Suppose we are testing our two mathematical curricula and also at the same time using different teaching techniques. Perhaps teaching technique A makes use of lots of equipment: tape measures, abacuses, calculators, weighing machines and technique B makes use only of chalk and talk. Now we have to make sure that the benefits of one curriculum over the other are not confounded by the teaching techniques employed. We would have to teach both curricula using both teaching methods and then make comparisons between the four outcomes.

The strength of the quasi-experimental approach is that it conforms most closely to the classic scientific model. Its weakness in education, and in the social sciences, is that it requires a manipulation of situations which may not be ethical. Is it fair to expose children to an experimental mathematics curriculum which may set back their understanding of maths? Those involved in the experiment become 'guinea pigs' whether they like it or not.

In practice, there are occasions when an experimental situation has been set up as a result of regional variations in educational provision. Middle schools may exist in some areas but not others. The syllabuses of one examination board are different from those of another and children in the same school may opt for one or both. Children from the same kind of churchgoing background may go to denominational schools or ordinary maintained schools. In each of these instances comparisons can be made which are akin to those achieved by a pure experimental design.

C6 Ethnographic research

This method arose during the study of particular tribes and peoples. The ethnographer was an anthropologist attempting to describe and understand a whole culture. In educational terms, ethnography is especially concerned with the meaning of situations for participants. How do children understand the rituals and power structures of education? The good ethnographer is concerned to observe rather than to prove a theory. The information collected is in the form of field notes, and these will include observations of the physical setting of education as well as its more symbolic interactions. The physical setting will include details of the classroom, dress of the teacher and pupils, and the symbolic interactions will include details of whether the pupils have to stand up when the teacher enters the room or whether the teacher's desk is on a dais, and so on. The symbolism of education may be less evident in the classroom and more evident in assemblies or on special occasions.

Ethnographic research will use interviews and may tape record classroom sessions or conversations between pupils in the playground. It will attempt a complete description of the school environment, both physical and social, and will generally avoid mathematical analysis or any other data than that which is in a verbal form.

The strengths of the ethnographic method are in the fullness of the descriptions it provides, and its weakness lies in its subjectivity. Everything is seen through the researcher's eye and ultimately everything is interpreted by him or her. There is no guarantee that another ethnographer would have described the culture identically and understood it the same way.

C7 Interviews

Interviews are very flexible. The interviewer can explore a particular line of enquiry in response to the answers he or she is being given. Interviews may also generate a great deal of personal information which might be difficult to obtain through other methods. But, equally, the interview may be an ordeal for the person who is being questioned. They may dislike the interviewer. They may answer in monosyllables. They might be much happier to fill in an anonymous form than to provide face-to-face information about themselves to a stranger. The weakness of the interview, then, is that there is an unknown interaction between the interviewer and the interviewee. The strength of the interview method is that it can provide, in a non-threatening situation, a huge amount of relevant personal information.

One of the ways in which interviews are set up for the purposes of research is to adopt an 'interview schedule'. Here there are various headings which the interviewer wishes to cover. Does the child enjoy religious education? Does the child attend a church? Does the child know any bible stories? Does the child have brothers and sisters? Does the child pray? Under these headings the interviewer can explore in more detail. What particularly in religious education does the child enjoy? What particularly does the child dislike? Why is this so? This information, if sensitively collected, is valuable. We could gain an insight into the minds of children. A survey has more difficulty in obtaining this sort of fine grain information. A case study works with larger units (the class, the school, and so on) but rarely with the individual child. The interview, moreover, is particularly valuable with very young children who have difficulty in reading or concentrating for long periods of time.

C8 Personal constructs

Personal constructs depend upon the idea that we all classify objects within the world according to our own personal scheme. The method works like this. People are presented with three things and asked how two of them are alike and different from the third. For instance, people might be presented with a picture of their mother, their teacher, and their father. They might respond by saying that their mother and their teacher were similar because both were female. Or they might respond by saying that their mother and their father were similar because they were members of their family. Or they might say that their father and the teacher were similar because they were both strict. In this instance the three classifying constructs are gender, family and strictness.

The method continues to present people with groups of threes and it turns out that most people have about thirty main classifying constructs by which they interpret the world.

The advantage of this method is that it collects all the information from the people being interviewed. The classifications do not come from the researcher but from the subjects. The disadvantage of this method is that it is very difficult to make comparisons between people, schools or teachers. What are we to do if we find that certain teachers have certain constructs in common and other teachers have other constructs in common? Can we really turn this information into anything useful with regard to education and training? No consensus exists on this matter.

C9 Action research

Action research is used to confront particular educational problems, where the word 'problem' is widely defined. Since educational problems crop up in particular situations, the problem and the situation are connected. To change the situation is to change the problem; problem and situation affect each other. Moreover, the problem situation impinges on other situations. The classroom impinges on the staffroom, the staffroom on the relationship between teachers and parents, the relationship between teachers and parents on the relationship between the governing body and the local community. This knock-on effect between one situation and another often results in action research programmes which are collaborative. Participants in the various interlocking situations can become involved.

Action research therefore is often carried out by teachers working together, sometimes in conjunction with researchers called in from outside the school. A partnership between teachers and researchers can then be created. Alternatively, some teachers can function as teacher-researchers, performing a dual role. Yet, when this sort of large-scale work is not possible, it is still open to the individual teacher to work alone and to operate at the classroom level, though obviously the kinds of changes which he or she might envisage, and the kinds of problems which he or she might solve, are smaller and more confined than those accessible to a team.

What sort of problems might action research tackle? To answer this question, we need to examine the goals and methods of action research more closely.

The goals of action research are essentially related to perceived problems. Someone, somewhere must perceive an educational problem which is unresolved. Very often these problems are unresolved because it is difficult to separate the problem from the situation in which it is embedded. Thus the phenomenon (or variable) which is at the heart of the problem is difficult to separate from its context. Two examples should make this clearer.

Where a particular teaching method is used (perhaps using formal instruction to the whole class), there is the likelihood that the context for this teaching method will be a particular seating arrangement for pupils. All the pupils will need to see the teacher and the blackboard. The teaching method and the classroom context in which it is used are connected. To change the teaching method is to change the classroom context. Or, to take another example, if a school evaluates its pupils by continuous assessment, then any major change in the sort of academic work pupils are required to do will also necessarily change the evaluation process.

The methods of action research are taken from other sorts of research. In essence, we may say that action research adopts a holistic approach and so does not fasten onto a single facet of a situation. It attempts to deal with the situation as a whole. For this reason, action research feels free to use whatever methods seem relevant to an enquiry. The use of interviews allows personal perceptions about a situation to be probed, case study information provides details of institutional realities, observation schedules allow behaviour to be charted, measures of learning outcomes show how pupils respond to teaching methods and assessments of teaching techniques permit evaluations of professional performance.

Before we look in detail at the stages an action research project undergoes, we will consider the whole process in a simplified form. This is to enable you to gain a general overview. Suppose that there is a problem with the way children fail to learn from their classroom computers. An action research project is set up to find out how best the timetable should be altered and how best the children should be regrouped. New procedures are introduced to the classroom. The children's timetable is restructured and this has an implication for the groups in which they are generally taught. Perhaps the children now work in pairs rather than in age groups. These changes in their learning pattern may cause the children to move around the classroom in a different way. Perhaps they go to the library more often or consult the computer for a range of different tasks. So, one change leads to another and the second change leads to a third. Action research monitors the whole process as it happens. It is sometimes seen in terms of a feedback loop or a self-adjusting system.

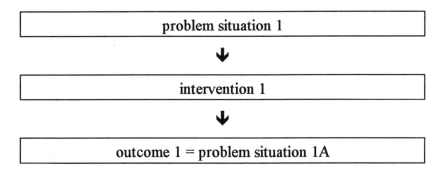

The problem situation 1 exists. Intervention 1 is made. Outcome 1 occurs. Situation 1A now exists. So, intervention 1A is made and this leads to outcome 1A. Whereupon intervention 1B is made, and so on. The research is linked with the action. The research is intended to show which actions are most suited to bring about which outcomes.

Activity C3

Draw up a list of five ways action research differs from other types of research. Take time over this task. Think especially of the aims of action research as compared with other types of research.

Comment on activity C3

Here are some of the things you might have listed. Action research:

- attempts to solve particular problems;

- attempts to bring about change;
- usually initiates experimental innovation;
- requires a system for monitoring the changes it brings about;
- is not characterised by one particular method;
- is often carried out by people who are participants in the research situation;
- is often carried out in situations where the problem and its context are difficult to disentangle;
- action research does not easily distinguish between subjective and objective methods because it uses both.

The methods of action research are usually applied in several substages which are divided into two main stages. The first stage is diagnostic and intended to bring the problem into sharper focus. The second stage is intended to solve the problem. The seven substages are as follows.

- In the *first* substage the problem is identified.
- In the *second* substage a discussion takes place between those who are going to be carrying out the research. There may be teachers, advisors, researchers present at this point and their work will often result in a written plan. The aims and objectives of the research need to be clearly noted and broad strategies agreed.
- In the *third* substage a search of relevant research literature may be made to see what light it throws on the problem and what lines of enquiry it suggests.
- In the *fourth* substage the problem may, following this examination of previous research, require redefinition. Certainly a clarification of underlying assumptions may take place at this point and the aims and objectives of the project may also need to be reassessed.
- In the *fifth* substage research procedures need to be decided upon and tasks allocated to those concerned in the work; the research procedures will concern the kind of data which is to be collected and the way it is to be evaluated.
- In the *sixth* substage data are collected and innovations and interventions are made.
- In the *seventh* substage the interpretation of the data is required both against the evaluative criteria and in view of the aims and objectives of the project.

Thus substages 1, 2, 3 and 4 are diagnostic and substages 6 and 7 are intended to solve the problem. Substage 5 is really intermediate.

Substage 6 needs to be considered more carefully. This is the heart of the project. The data will often be of many different kinds and of uneven complexity. There may be interview data, field notes, self-evaluation journals, observation schedules, and so on. The data will need to be shared by the members of the group, and a note of meetings kept. Group evaluation of the data is likely to be made and work-in-progress reports compiled.

The interventions and innovations which are made in the problem situation will often be piecemeal. They will be adjustments rather than radical changes. By this means it will be possible to solve the problem without risking unforeseen consequences. The data which are collected will be linked to the interventions and innovations. It will be data which monitors change. One of the main limiting factors to the kinds of interventions and innovations you may introduce (apart from the legal framework of education in Britain) is that of time. Your project cannot run indefinitely and must be expected to reach a conclusion within a specified period.

The problems appropriate to action research are wide-ranging and are only limited by the sorts of problems which cannot be adjusted by change. Since the kinds of problems facing education may touch on administration, attitudes, morale, teaching styles, the management of change, policy making, evaluation, in-service teacher development, the behavioural difficulties of pupils, as well as a host of others, action research is versatile and popular.

Activity C4

The school where you work has a problem with its religious education programme. Its pupils are drawn from three main religious traditions, Christian, Hindu and Muslim. You risk community displeasure and widespread withdrawals from religious education lessons if you misrepresent any of the religions.

Nevertheless, if you offer a participatory form of religious education (where pupils are encouraged to respond to Hindu festivals) all your Muslim and some of your Christian pupils will be withdrawn. You can decide whether the school where you work is voluntary aided or controlled or an ordinary state maintained one. Your problem arises from the apathy and hostility shown by pupils to religious education.

How would you apply action research to introduce a curriculum satisfactory to all the religious (and non-religious) groups? The curriculum should remove apathy and hostility as far as possible and allow all pupils to attend religious education lessons. Draw up a plan to show how you would proceed and how you hope the project would develop. You have the support of the headteacher, county advisory staff and the local university.

Comment on activity C4

The first stage is the analysis of the problem. Although we have stated that there is apathy and hostility towards religious education, we need to look more closely at this. Is there apathy and hostility towards education as a whole, to a particular teacher, to faith issues being taught by unbelievers, or what? Do the feelings of pupils arise from factors outside the school? For instance, do pupils receive so much religious teaching in the home, the mosque, the church and the gurdwara, that they feel there is no need for any more of it at school? Are there ethnic tensions between the Hindus and the Muslims within the school, or are there tensions between the Christians and the other two groups? Or, again, is the content of the religious education programme at fault, or does the real problem lie with the methods that are used, the timetabling of the subject and its lack of prestige in the eyes of pupils? Clearly, then, the problem may lie in more than one place.

The action research may be carried out by you as an individual or by a team. Since you have considerable support for your project, you would probably be wise to make maximum use of it. The first four substages of the process of action research ought to sharpen your analysis of the problem. But the number of people involved in the project will mean that you have to ensure that there are team meetings which are minuted, full discussions from the viewpoints of each participant and a search for consensus about the overall strategy you are going to adopt.

The collection of data will include, presumably, a close look at existing religious education lessons, the kinds of activities children are required to carry out, the content of the syllabus, the grouping of pupils, the linkage between religious education and assembly, the quality of teaching which is offered to pupils, the attitudes shown by pupils, the support or otherwise given by parents and religious and community leaders, the resources available within the community and, at the same time, the main taboos within the community. For example, can Muslim children feel comfortable in the presence of a Hindu shrine?

The interventions and innovations will be based on the conclusions of the data and the re-examination of the nature of the problem. It is impossible to say how each project will proceed. There may be a need to change the content of religious education, the kinds of activities children are required to carry out, the grouping of pupils, or any other factors on which data have been collected.

If hostility and apathy decline measurably, the project may be said to have succeeded. But there is one important caution which you need to bear in mind. The high profile which religious education will receive during the course of the project will get in the way of a proper reading of the situation. Once the high profile is lost during the next year or two after the project is finished, apathy and hostility may return again. What were thought to be changes brought about by action research innovations may turn out to be changes brought about by the spotlight of teacher and researcher attention.

This leads us to consider the weaknesses of action research. The strengths of action research are considerable, but the weaknesses cannot be ignored. The strengths lie with its comprehensiveness, versatility and flexibility and with its connection to action. For managing and monitoring change in a complicated system, action research is the best method available. The weaknesses lie with the subjectivity and cumbersomeness of the approach.

The subjectivity arises partly from the concentration on situational variables. What works in one situation may not work in another. Other approaches (for example, the correlational approach) attempt to produce information which is valid across a huge number of situations and which, in some instances, may claim some form of universal validity. The findings and recommendations of action research are therefore restricted and, as we have said, may be confounded by the interpolation of the researchers into the situation in which they are working.

The subjectivity also arises from the methods of data collection which are used. Much is impressionistic (though it need not be) and personal. The group dynamics of the action research group may sway the conclusions based on such data in one way or another. Strong personalities with vested interests may wish to innovate in a particular way, for instance. Such problems, of course, can exist in other forms of research, but action research is especially vulnerable to them.

Action research, when carried out by a team, is cumbersome. It requires meetings and discussions to negotiate where boundaries ought to be drawn and how topics ought to be approached. There is no standard procedure and so procedures have to be adapted to each situation as it arises. The time and energy spent on sorting out the dynamics of the team may detract from the collection and analysis of data. And, where time and people are involved, costs begin to crop up and play a part in decision-making.

Readers

Chapter 10 in L.J. Francis and D.W. Lankshear (eds) (1993), *Christian Perspectives on Church Schools*, Leominster, Gracewing, is devoted to empirical perspectives on the distinctiveness of church schools. This gives you examples of the application of educational research methods to specific issues.

Bibliography

Anderson, G. (1990), *Fundamentals of Educational Research*, London, Taylor and Francis.

Bell, J. (1987), *Doing Your Research Project: a guide for first time researchers in education and social science*, Milton Keynes, Open University Press.

Borg, W.R. and Gall, M.D. (1989), *Educational Research: an introduction* (fifth edition), London, Longman.

Burgess, R.G. (1993), *Educational Research and Evaluation: for policy and practice?* London, Falmer Press.

Cohen, L. and Manion, L. (1994), *Research Methods in Education* (fourth edition), London, Routledge.

Cohen, L. (1976), *Educational Research in Classrooms and Schools: a manual of materials and methods*, London, Harper and Row.

Edwards, A. and Talbert, R., (1994), *The Hard-Pressed Researcher: a handbook for research in the caring professions*, London, Longman.

Entwistle, N.J. and Nisbet, J.D. (1970), *Educational Research Methods*, London, University of London Press.

Francis, L.J., Kay, W.K. and Campbell, W.S. (eds) (1996), *Research in Religious Education*, Leominster, Gracewing.

Keeves, J.P. (ed.) (1988), *Educational Research, Methodology and Measurement: an international handbook*, Oxford, Pergamon Press.

Preece, R. (1994), *Starting Research: an introduction to academic research and dissertation writing*, London, Pinter Publishers.

Shipman, M.D. (1985), *Educational Research: principles, policies and practices*, London, Falmer.

Walford, G. (ed.) (1991), *Doing Educational Research*, London, Routledge.

Index of names

Index of subjects